Advance Praise for

LAW & CUSTOM

"*Law and Custom: The Thought of Thomas Aquinas and the Future of the Common Law* stands a good chance of being one of the most important books written on jurisprudence, legal history, and theology in the twenty-first century. The American legal academy and courts are slowly realizing that the twentieth century's dominant school of jurisprudence—legal realism—is deeply flawed, and that its triumph in the law schools, courts, and legislatures led to an era in which the law was sadly out of step with the community, and in which its implementation often resulted in exacerbating rather than solving social problems. David VanDrunen, in this meticulously researched and boldly argued book, offers us a different vision, one based on the natural law of Thomas Aquinas and the Anglo-American tradition of common law decision-making. Our framers believed that there could be no order without law, no law without morality, and no morality without religion. This was the belief of Aquinas as well, and if VanDrunen's fine book helps lead to a renewal of this belief among lawyers and legal philosophers in our time, he will have rendered a service that only someone superbly competent in theology and law could have performed. This is a book we've been waiting for, and it will be of profound and equal interest to lawyers, legislators, and philosophers."

—Stephen B. Presser, Raoul Berger Professor of Legal History, Northwestern University School of Law

"Thomas Aquinas's rich theology of law has been pored over by innumerable scholars over the years, but his insights into the role custom plays in the praxis of law abiding have been largely unnoticed. This serious lacuna has been now filled in by this competent, welcome book by David VanDrunen. Law that is out of touch with the moral intuitions of the populace, as expressed by their customs, becomes formal and alienating to a people. Happily, this book also connects this issue of custom to the Anglo-American common law tradition."

—John C. Haughey, S.J., Professor of Christian Ethics, Loyola University Chicago

LAW & CUSTOM

PETER LANG
New York • Washington, D.C./Baltimore • Bern
Frankfurt am Main • Berlin • Brussels • Vienna • Oxford

David VanDrunen

LAW & CUSTOM

The Thought of Thomas Aquinas and the Future of the Common Law

PETER LANG
New York • Washington, D.C./Baltimore • Bern
Frankfurt am Main • Berlin • Brussels • Vienna • Oxford

Library of Congress Cataloging-in-Publication Data

VanDrunen, David.
Law and custom: the thought of Thomas Aquinas and
the future of the common law / David VanDrunen.
p. cm.
Includes bibliographical references and index.
1. Common law—Philosophy. 2. Customary law—Philosophy. 3. Thomas,
Aquinas, Saint, 1225?–1274—Contributions in customary law. I. Title.
K588.V36 340'.1—dc21 2003006817
ISBN 0-8204-6820-7

Bibliographic information published by **Die Deutsche Bibliothek**.
Die Deutsche Bibliothek lists this publication in the "Deutsche
Nationalbibliografie"; detailed bibliographic data is available
on the Internet at http://dnb.ddb.de/.

Cover design by Lisa Barfield

275 Seventh Avenue, 28th Floor, New York, NY 10001
www.peterlangusa.com

Table of Contents

Acknowledgments

I am very grateful to the Graduate School of Loyola University Chicago, whose Crown Fellowship provided financial support for most of my research for this project. Thanks are due especially to Prof. John Haughey, S.J., of Loyola, whose encouragement and wisdom enabled and enhanced my work.

I am deeply thankful for my wife and her constant support for my labors on this book.

Part of Chapter 1 was originally published as part of a longer essay that appeared in the *Journal of Markets and Morality* 5 (Fall 2002): 315–338. My thanks to the editors for permission to reprint.

Introduction

The past century has witnessed many important changes in our law and in our legal systems. Surely one of the most striking, even revolutionary, developments is the decline of the "common law." Due in large part to the proliferation of legislative statutes and administrative regulations, the common law has sunk from a place of great prominence to one of marginal relevance. This eclipse of the common law has meant the loss of an important bridge between law and the customs of the societies that law governs.

Put in historical context, this unhinging of law from custom marks not only a departure from the legal culture of a century past but also from hundreds and even thousands of years of Western legal practice. Since its origins nearly a millennium ago, the Anglo-American common law grew as an unwritten, slowly-developing, customary law. Even earlier than this, the Roman-Byzantine Emperor Justinian's *Corpus Juris Civilis*, a sixth century codification of Roman law out of which many contemporary legal codes on the European continent have originated, acknowledged a primary place for custom as a source of law. Therefore, on both the Continent and in the British Isles, and through their influence, in North America and many other places in the world, the intimate relationship of law and custom has a long history. In light of this, the attention given to the withering of the common law in the past century is surprisingly paltry. In law schools, legal literature, and social ethics, fundamental questions about the consequences of this development are seldom pondered, and the very idea of "common law" is largely unknown to broader society. And, yet, to unleash law from custom and to identify it instead almost entirely with series of legislative statutes and administrative regulations threatens to strip the legal order of a critical aspect of its moral basis.

This book addresses this issue, though through a perhaps unexpected medium: the thought of Thomas Aquinas. Thomas Aquinas explored the relationship of law and custom, and not with solely theoretical concerns. Aquinas lived in the midst of a thirteenth-century world undergoing significant social changes that called traditional sources of legal authority into question. Strong monarchs sought to consolidate power in their own hands and thereby threatened to end the hegemony of local custom as the foundation of law. Aquinas, aware of these social pressures, reflected upon the issues at stake. He not only defended the ancient Roman law understanding of custom as a source and interpreter of law, but also embedded his thought on custom within his broader ethics and even his theological system as a whole. For Thomas, preserving a role for the people of society to shape their law through the development of custom was a way of acknowledging the dignity of those created in the image of God and of insuring that law develops in a way consistent with the manner in which the moral good can be known and pursued. It is the argument of this book that Aquinas's insights on these matters remain exceedingly relevant for the present. These insights are not entirely foreign to contemporary commentary on the fall of the common law—in fact, some recent scholars who have defended the need for a vibrant common law have identified issues at stake very similar to the ones identified by Aquinas—but Aquinas's considerations add a theological, philosophical, and ethical depth that is often lacking in contemporary discussions.

A scholarly analysis of Aquinas on the relationship of law and custom is a project whose time seems ripe. The rich literature on Aquinas's moral philosophy and theology produced in recent years provides an excellent context for an exposition of his thought on custom, though this literature itself touches upon custom only occasionally and briefly. One of the characteristics of recent scholarship on Aquinas's ethics is the rejection of older readings that made natural law the centerpiece of Aquinas's ethics and treated his natural law as a series of rigid and exceptionless rules.[1] Scholars such as E. A. Goerner, Daniel Mark Nelson, and Pauline Westerman have argued emphatically that neither natural law nor rules are the driving force behind Aquinas's moral thought, but that the virtues, especially prudence, provide its real content.[2] Many of the basic arguments made by these writers are now widely accepted, though others scholars have moderated their claims and contended for a more balanced understanding of Aquinas on the relationship of the virtues, natural law, and moral rules.[3] Other significant studies have been useful in delineating the contingent nature of moral reasoning in Aquinas's ethics. According to these works, Aquinas held that the particular circumstances in which action occurs are of utmost significance and that exceptions to practical precepts are a structural element within his thinking.[4]

In short, there has been a flood of interest in non-legalistic ways of reading Aquinas's moral thought. Rather than seeing Thomistic natural law as a series of deduced rules, contemporary writers almost uniformly wish to emphasize the contingent, circumstantial elements of his ethics, and the consequent need for prudence, experience, and the like for the development of the moral life. In light of this, it is somewhat puzzling that the importance of custom in Aquinas's theology of law has been largely ignored. Since customary law depends so intimately upon the experience of a community and upon particular social circumstances, and is not a law directly deduced from higher principles, one might expect it to spark the interest of those who read Aquinas's moral theology in these new ways. Nevertheless, even many who specifically address the foundation of human law in natural law in Aquinas's thought do not deal with it.[5] A few scholars glance ever so briefly at the significance of custom, though their understandings of it veer in somewhat different directions.[6] Alisdair MacIntyre has insightfully called attention to the issue in the context of Aquinas's legal and political world, but even he gives it just one paragraph.[7]

Thus, despite the deluge of literature on Aquinas generally and his moral thought more particularly, the role of custom as a source of law has been long overlooked—and unjustly overlooked, given the critical role that custom plays in the "Treatise on Law" in the *Summa Theologiae.* Perhaps the contemporary failure to appreciate the importance of custom for the law of our own day has obscured the importance that Aquinas assigned to it in his. However, conversely, perhaps bringing to attention the details and depths of Aquinas's understanding of custom will renew contemporary interest in the decline of the common law and, with it, appreciation for the role that custom can and ought to play in a legal system.

The following chapters seek to attain these two goals, the exploration of Thomas Aquinas's treatment of custom and law and its appropriation for the contemporary legal scene. Chapter One gives some historical perspective to the questions at issue. It investigates the importance of custom in the Roman law tradition in which Aquinas worked and narrates the rise and fall of the common law in Anglo-American legal history. Chapter Two describes Aquinas's view of custom in the context both of his broader theology of law and of the legal developments of his day. Chapters Three and Four unpack the intellectual foundations—theological, philosophical, and ethical—of his view of law and custom. First, in Chapter Three, I set Aquinas's remarks on custom within the context of his understanding of human reason. Aquinas attributed great dignity to the human race because of its rationality and he coupled humanity's rational nature with its free and social nature. He believed that custom was an expression of reason, and he often grounded the legal functions of custom in the rational, free, social nature of humanity. Second, in Chapter Four, I place Aquinas's view of law and custom within the context of the distinctively Aristotelian aspects of his moral thought. With Aristotle, Aquinas held that ethics is an inexact science, and therefore that moral understanding advances only gradually and always non-comprehensively, depending on one's own and others' experience more than upon abstract reason. I argue that Aquinas's attribution of legal authority to custom often rests upon his Aristotelian convictions about the inexact character of moral reasoning. Finally, in Chapter Five, I describe the present relevance of Aquinas's thought on law and custom. I conclude that Aquinas's beliefs about the moral necessity of a legally authoritative custom are still compelling, and indeed suggest the great benefit—and even need—of the rejuvenation of the common law in order to strengthen the moral basis of civil law.

Chapter 1

Law and Custom in the Western Legal Traditions

Some historical perspective is helpful before entering upon the principal arguments of this work. In both the Roman law world in which Aquinas lived and the common law system that grew in English-speaking lands, custom has played a prominent role in the historical development of legal life and practice. Therefore, in order to set the context for my argument, I briefly sketch in this chapter the importance of custom in the Anglo-American common law tradition and in the Roman law world of ancient and medieval times. Through this investigation, the nature of the present crisis of the common law can be better perceived and the relevance of Aquinas's thought on custom more readily appreciated for its contemporary relevance.

The Nature of the Anglo-American Common Law

The issue in the contemporary legal scene that provides the occasion for this book, the decline of the common law, provokes the important question: what is the common law? Since the common law is in many ways a complex phenomenon, with ancient origins, a description of its nature can only be quite general. Nevertheless, the fact that many people have only the vaguest idea of what the common law is makes such a discussion necessary at the outset.

Scholars have offered different suggestions as to the origin of the name "common law," but classic treatments of the English common law, such as those of Sir Matthew Hale and Sir William Blackstone, seem to settle on a very basic explanation: it is called "common" law because it prescribes a rule of justice that is common to the entire realm.[1] This means, explains legal historian Arthur Hogue, that the common law is neither a written code nor local custom. Positively, it is "a body of general rules prescribing social conduct" that "develops its principles from the grounds of decisions in actual legal controversies." Among the distinctives of the common law that Hogue highlights are its extensive use of the jury to provide courts with the facts necessary for judging cases and its emphasis upon the supremacy of law, which Hogue understands to be the principle that all agencies of government must act according to established rules.[2]

However, what is perhaps most distinctive about the common law to contemporary eyes is its unwritten character. This is not to deny that there was written, statutory law in England as far back as anyone can trace. Blackstone uses the traditional categorization when he asserts that the municipal law of England is divided into two parts, the unwritten and the written, the first which he calls "common law" and the second which he calls "statute law." This unwritten common law includes, according to Blackstone, general customs, particular customs (of certain parts of the kingdom), and particular laws observed by custom only in certain courts and jurisdictions. The first of these, general customs, are called common law "properly so called" because they, unlike the last two, are indeed common to all people on all English soil. Blackstone goes on to explain that the unwritten, common law derives its authority not from Parliament, but from immemorial usage and universal reception.[3] Indeed, there are and were written laws, but Blackstone concludes that common law, which he terms "general immemorial custom," is "the first ground and chief cornerstone of the laws of England."[4]

One thing evident in the preceding paragraph, but deserving more attention for the present study, is that the common law has generally been viewed as *customary* law.[5] Hale, speaking similarly to Blackstone, writes that the unwritten laws have gained their binding power by long and immemorial usage and by the strength of custom.[6] More recent writers agree about the customary nature of the older common law. John Hudson, for example, speaks about law and custom as "intimately related" in the post-Conquest development of English legal life. He explains that customs "are not simply neutral statements of what usually happens; rather they are prescriptions of established and proper action, prescriptions which carry authority."[7] He suggests the following definition of "custom:" "a norm, questioning of which might draw the answer 'well, that's how we do things here.'"[8] A century ago, Frederic William Maitland asserted that the custom of the king's court was what became the common law.[9] Reflecting on both ancient and more recent

English history, Maitland noted that much was left to social custom that by his own day had become regulated by legislation and controlled by courts of justice.[10] Even in the present day, however, custom is still often acknowledged as central for what remains of the common law. For example, M. Stuart Madden points out that both societal and professional customs play a recognizable role in the development of common law doctrines.[11] Similarly, scholars such as A. W. B. Simpson and Melvin Aron Eisenberg are critical of positivist understandings of the common law, which tend to view it as simply a series of rules "legislated" by judges. Both writers point to the customary nature of the common law as more effectively explaining its distinctive dynamic.[12]

However, simply saying that the common law was customary does not explain how customs came to be applied by courts and enforced as law, nor why some customs gained legal status and others did not. Hogue and Mary Ann Glendon have offered a number of answers to such questions.[13] Both Hogue and Glendon, however, the former with citation and the latter without, rely heavily on the systematic, classic presentation of Blackstone. Blackstone writes that it is judges who determine the validity of customs. They base their judgments on their experience and study, and especially on their familiarity with precedents, that is, prior judicial judgments on analogous cases. Precedent is the chief and most authoritative evidence that a custom is part of the common law. According to Blackstone, judges are not to break with precedent unless it is most evidently contrary to reason or to the divine law—in such cases, he explains, the precedent is not to be viewed as bad law, but as no law at all, and not part of the custom of the realm.[14] The seven criteria that Blackstone proposes for determining the validity of "particular" customs (i.e., those that affect people only in certain geographic regions) highlight the importance of reason for determining what is truly a part of English custom and part of the common law: valid customs are to be ancient, continuous, peaceable, reasonable, certain, compulsory, and consistent.[15]

Blackstone concludes, therefore, that precedent is the principal evidence that a custom is part of the common law. That is, if a previous court ruling has determined that a particular custom is part of the common law, it most likely is. But precedent can be clarified, and sometimes even corrected, by extra-judicial evidence weighed by judges. Some of this extra-judicial evidence is factual, such as the questions about a custom's age and continuous existence, though judges are also called to make judgments of value concerning reasonableness and consistency. This distinction between questions of fact and value is my own, not Blackstone's, and Blackstone sometimes confidently conflates them. For example, he says that the requisite goodness of a custom depends upon its being used time out of mind.[16] In other words, a custom's age is an aspect of its goodness. Blackstone's conclusion seems to be, in short, that customs that meet certain objective requirements and satisfy judges' senses of what is reasonable, clear, and consonant with the common law as a whole, especially if they have been confirmed by previous court decision, ought to be applied and enforced as law.

The impression may be given that the common law has been static and unchanging through nearly a millennium of history. This is certainly not the case, and what can be said of the common law in one era is not necessarily what can be said of it in another, whether as to its general features or as to its particular substantive rules. In fact, the organic development of the common law has been one of its most marked features. How change occurs in the common law is a difficult question to answer. Of course, legislation has affected the course of the common law.[17] However, the development of the common law over centuries cannot be attributed wholly, or perhaps even largely (until more recently), to legislation. And, for a legal system that relies so heavily on the authority of precedent, the subject of change in law becomes a pressing issue. Maitland presented a standard picture of common law change, one that in fact stresses development rather than alteration. Maitland says that precedents are honored, but he also speaks of common law customs as being "extended by analogical reasoning." In other words, a judge may seek guidance on a present case from analogous cases decided previously—that is, cases that are similar without being exactly the same.[18] A development in one line of cases may affect the development in another, and on the process goes. As new situations for judicial decision arise, the more analogical reasoning is required, and the opportunity for development grows.

The eminent legal historian S. F. C. Milsom has conducted extensive research on the development of the common law. He emphasizes that the largest changes in the law—even those that have occurred via legislation—have not been deliberate. He claims that, until the nineteenth century, change in law and in legal institutions was almost wholly the result of expediency rather than of grand planning. In essence, change occurred as legal actors sought immediate solutions to immediate problems.[19] In several places, Milsom has reflected on just how this expedient, non-deliberate change happens. He observes that "Change becomes possible when two lines of reasoning which have developed, as it were, in different compartments, happen to have come sufficiently close for a situation which has traditionally fallen under the one to be represented as within the other."[20] In other words, precedent can be overcome when lawyers and judges find new ways to categorize certain sorts of legal actions and, consequently, apply old rules to new kinds of cases. Milsom expounds upon these ideas in another essay, in which he emphasizes the conservative nature of common law judging even when it is effecting a change. According to Milsom, common law judges have not created new rules wholesale so much as maneuvered their way through existing rules and attempted to bring intellectual coherence to resolution of evolving issues. Even when substantive law has changed, says Milsom, the judges bringing about the change have ordinarily been thinking in procedural rather than substantive terms.[21] Milsom has also made the suggestive argument that progress in the common law (and here he means not simply change, but change for the better) has happened by giving increased attention to the facts of cases.[22] This idea, of course, fits with Milsom's other ideas discussed above: the more facts that are brought to light in a case, the greater the likelihood that the case as a whole can be characterized and settled in innovative ways.

The Rise and Fall of the Anglo-American Common Law

The common law originated and began its history of change and development nearly a thousand years ago. When the Normans crossed the English Channel under King William in 1066, they had little written law and jurisprudence to bring with them. William decreed that old English law was to govern the realm and he engaged in little legislative activity himself.[23] The common law system began to develop into recognizable form during the reign of Henry II, who was crowned in 1154. His achievements were probably more administrative than substantive, and he too was not an active legislator.[24] In the twelfth and thirteenth centuries, custom was regarded as the principal source of law,[25] a point recognized, even with pride, by legal scholars of the day such as Glanville and Bracton.[26] By the time that Magna Carta was signed in 1215, Hudson notes, key elements of the later common law had been established, including a system of royal courts, consistent forms of litigation and classifications of offences in certain areas, and the availability of the jury in criminal cases. He concludes that a common law had been formed both in terms of being common throughout the realm and in terms of its continuity with the development of the common law in the years to come.[27] Edward I, who reigned in the late thirteenth century, was a relatively active legislator.[28] Nevertheless, despite the increase in legislative volume under Edward I and the growing distinction made between the unwritten common law and written statutes, Milsom observes that in the fourteenth century statutes were by no means seen as existing external to the common law as a whole. To lawyers of this time, statutes were viewed as internal alterations to the great fabric of the law, alterations that lived in this context and hence were granted neither mechanical nor unalterable application.[29] In other words, statutes were interpreted in terms of the common law that surrounded them.

In the seventeenth century, the great judge Sir Edward Coke advocated this same relationship between common law and statutes, albeit in a controversial way:

> And it appears in our books, that in many cases, the Common Law will controul Acts of Parliament, and sometimes adjudge them to be utterly void; for when an Act of Parliament is against common right and reason, or repugnant, or impossible to be performed, the Common Law will controul it, and adjudge such Act to be void.[30]

The most important scholar of law in this century was Sir Matthew Hale, whose *The History of the Common Law of England* was the first book of its kind. Hale made the familiar distinction between the two kinds of laws that govern England, the written and unwritten. He equated the common law with the "general custom of the realm" and with "customary law."[31] General customs, according to Hale, constituted the common law "properly so called," and he claimed that the unwritten laws were of a "vast extent."[32] Hale also commented that customs obtain the force of law by their general reception in the country. Hale's description of what things give authority to the common law provides evidence of the continuing centrality of custom at this time. The first was the common usage, practice, or custom of the kingdom. The second was enactments of Parliament; not, however, enactments that one could find on the books, but enactments that had been lost but preserved by immemorial custom. Finally, Hale included judicial decisions that had been consistent with each other over the succession of time. These last, however, were not strictly laws, but very important evidence of what the law is.[33] According to Hale, then, custom of one sort or another underlay every source of common law authority.

In the eighteenth century lived Sir William Blackstone, whose *Commentaries on the Laws of England* became both legendary and practically normative for generations of lawyers on both sides of the Atlantic. Blackstone's division of English law into written and unwritten[34] resembles that of Hale, and some of Blackstone's claims about the customary nature of the common law have already been described earlier in this chapter. Though Blackstone acknowledged Parliament as a legitimate source of law, he also confidently asserted that the common law, or what he calls "general immemorial custom," was "the first ground and chief corner stone of the laws of England."[35] And far from seeing this customary foundation of law as a source of embarrassment or primitiveness, Blackstone called the common law "the perfection of reason,"[36] a statement that was later to be mocked by his critics. For Blackstone, what was not reasonable was quite simply not part of the common law.

However, this era also saw some of the first sustained criticism of the common law order. In England, utilitarian philosopher Jeremy Bentham's sustained and biting critique of the idea as well as the practice of the common law is widely acknowledged as a landmark in English legal thought, and even as a crucial turning point in the history of legal philosophy.[37] Milsom muses that it is remarkable that no one was so provoked by the common law before Bentham.[38] It is noteworthy that Bentham, even as a critic of the common law, spoke of the common law as unwritten and customary. The common law's general identity and prominence were not in dispute. One basic and important aspect of Bentham's legal philosophy was his positivist definition of law, which in itself made the common law really something other than law. His definition begins: "A law may be defined as an assemblage of signs declarative of a volition conceived or adopted by the *sovereign* in a state...." For Bentham, customary laws were nothing less than primitive, in contrast to the maturity of statutory laws. In essence, customary law was a fiction, something which was not law because it could not be clearly known before or after the rendering of judicial decisions. Common law judicial decisions were legislation by subterfuge. Bentham called for a comprehensive statutory code of law: all English law, he said, must be written.[39]

In America, where the common law of England had been transplanted to the Colonies and was later adopted and received by the independent states, forceful voices of critique emerged in the nineteenth century. One particularly colorful example of American resistance to the common law is found in the oratory of Robert Rantoul. In one address, Rantoul compared the common law, a thing created in time, to everlasting and glorious Justice, an expression of the Divine wisdom. He excoriated the common law, which he called "judge-made law," for its many failings. For Rantoul, common law is created *ex post facto* and is therefore unjust, it constitutes special legislation (i.e., an unconstitutional law-making aiming at particular parties rather than being generally applicable), its content can never be known for certain, it is created when judges extort from precedents what they do not contain, and its content cannot be known even after judicial decisions because the latter are so narrowly constricted. Rantoul believed that it was legislators, not judges, who spoke the public voice and were therefore competent to be law-makers. The common law was for a barbarous age, best-suited for a country in which everything is stationary. Since America was an advanced and quickly-developing nation, he called for all of its law to be statutory.[40] Rantoul's orientation was not far removed from Bentham's. Rantoul believed that there was an objective standard of justice capable of being known and immediately applied by a sophisticated legislature into a comprehensive statutory code that could be and should be comprehensive.

If Rantoul's tirade demonstrates anything, it is that the customary common law was still alive and well in the nineteenth century, still a force worth the effort to combat. Maitland's concerns were primarily historical, but it is interesting to note his off-handed remark late in the century that even contemporary legislation was like a superstructure regulating and amending a larger base consisting of the indefinite mass of the common law.[41] Maitland, as noted above, preferred written law to unwritten, but he spoke matter-of-factly about contemporary statutes as living in what was still a predominantly common law world. The great nineteenth century English constitutional law scholar A. V. Dicey also confirmed the continuing power of unwritten law.[42] This reality, however, was poised to end soon.

Using the word "revolution" to describe what became of the common law in the twentieth century is perhaps too radical, but it makes a point: the common law has moved from a position of prominence in the legal landscape to one of marginality. Conversely, statutes have moved from being exceptions to being the rule. This is not to say that the principles of the common law have been overturned wholesale, for in many cases legislation has preserved and codified common law rules. But the common law as such, the unwritten, customary, slowly-developing staple of Anglo-American legal life has been eclipsed as the center of its judicial systems. The comments of

Connecticut Supreme Court Justice Ellen Ash Peters are instructive on this issue. At the beginning of the twentieth century, she writes, the views of Harvard law professor Christopher Columbus Langdell prevailed: common law cases were the principal, if not the exclusive, source of law in the United States. There were statutes, she says, but only "here and there."[43] Peters traces the decline of the common law over the next decades to two primary causes:

> On the one hand, the school of jurisprudence called legal realism challenged the methodological authority of the rule of law as elicited from a particular line of cases by demonstrating the ease with which a competing rule of law could be derived from a competing line of cases depending upon one's selection of a relevant fact pattern. Secondly, the New Deal, by accelerating the rate of change in the law, essentially by the use of legislation set the stage for statutory patterns in the law that I believe to be irreversible in form....[44]

Guido Calabresi adds a few related explanations, including increased demand for immediate change in law, the rise of the welfare state, and the perceived need to respond to economic crises.[45]

By mid-century, Winston Churchill could still speak of unwritten law as constituting "much" of the English law in his day, but this is in obvious contrast to his description of unwritten law as constituting "most" of English law in the age of the common law's origin.[46] In the America of 1982, however, Peters observed that a "scant" ten percent of the cases coming before her court in the previous term had been pure common law cases. She saw no end in sight for this trend, and predicted that by the end of the century the legal landscape would be all the more thoroughly dominated by statutes. There is no reason to think that her prediction has turned out to be incorrect, and indeed others have subsequently confirmed it. Peters reasoned that even where common law seemingly still prevails, the specter of an omnipresent legislature casts a considerable shadow on innovation in its growth and development. Her verdict was that the twentieth century had seen a nearly 180 degree turn in the relationship between common law and statutes.[47]

Others have commented on the decline of the common law in the Anglo-American legal world. Two examples are F. A. Hayek and Bruno Leoni, who make their observations not as purportedly objective historians, but as lawyers writing a brief for the continuing need for customary law. I interact with their arguments in the final chapter. Leoni and Hayek both speak of the common law tradition and characterize it in ways consistent with what has been written above. Most of all, they see it as unwritten and customary law.[48] Neither scholar could miss the obvious fact that this tradition was being decimated in his day. Leoni, for example, speaks of the eclipse of the English common law at the hands of statutory law as probably the most striking characteristic of the age. Though writing in 1961, Leoni already uses the term suggested above, "revolution," to describe the gradual overturning of the common law in England by the hand of statutes.[49]

One of the most important categories of law, contracts, provides a specific example of these trends away from common law and toward statutes. As legal scholar John Edward Murray notes, the fundamental principles of contract law developed slowly, over the centuries, through the countless disputes and judicial decisions of the English common law processes. Contract law was a predominantly common law subject, with statutes modifying the basic principles here and there. However, as Murray notes, this is not the case anymore, due to the enactment of the Uniform Commercial Code (henceforth, UCC), more or less as a whole, in all fifty states and the District of Columbia. The UCC is a body of legal rules encompassing much of the landscape of the traditional common law of contracts, and even in areas of contracts that it does not address it has a considerable influence, insofar as judges tend to apply it analogously.[50] The product of the labors of a number of prominent American jurists, the UCC was first adopted by a state (Pennsylvania) in 1953, and subsequently by every state over the next decades. A permanent revision committee was established in 1961, and state legislatures sporadically adopt its revisions and expansions of the UCC. Though it derives many of its rules from the common law, and though it still assumes the existence and legal relevance of non-Code contract law, the UCC provides a clear example of how statutory law has been brought to the forefront of American law and common law pushed into the background.[51]

In light of the concerns of this work, Robert S. Summers' comments on the prevailing attitude of legal scholars toward the UCC in its early days are illuminating. Summers recounts a spirit of "romanticism" toward the UCC, imbued with a conviction that a comprehensive code of commercial law is possible, that such a code would increase certainty and predictability in the law, that it would produce uniform law across state lines, and that it would make change in law smooth and only infrequently necessary. The passage of time has proven each of these convictions fanciful or even false, concludes Summers.[52] The failure of the codification of law to produce all of the expected results provokes important ethical and legal questions that may otherwise have escaped notice.

Before turning to such questions more directly, it is helpful to remember that the historic preeminence of custom in Anglo-American law in many ways mirrors the important role accorded to custom in the development of the Roman law. Even more, this important role of custom in the Roman law went through a period of serious challenge in the thirteenth century—the time of Aquinas—albeit not as dramatic as the story of the common law in the twentieth. To reflect upon this history of the Roman law of custom and the context of its own crisis evokes greater appreciation for why Thomas Aquinas's response to this crisis provides insight for contemporary questions.

Custom and the History of the Roman Law

Perhaps the most enduring document and classic statement of Roman law is the Emperor Justinian's *Corpus Juris Civilis* (hereafter, *CJC*). The *CJC* consisted in large part of collections of legal rules and opinions culled from past centuries of Roman law, thereby preserving the legal developments of previous ages rather than introducing a brand new body of law. Though drawn from the past, the *CJC* shaped the future of European law profoundly. Long before serving as the basis for many codes of law in recent times, the rediscovery of the *CJC* in the late eleventh century sparked a renewal in legal studies and culture in the century and a half before Aquinas. Aquinas himself showed significant knowledge of and dependence upon the *CJC* in his treatment of law in the *Summa Theologiae*.[53]

The precise role of custom through the centuries of development of the Roman law before the promulgation of the *CJC* is difficult to determine, and there is understandable discrepancy among legal historians on this matter. Those historians bold enough to comment on the law of Rome's earliest days substantially agree that custom was a chief source of law.[54] However, little concrete knowledge is available about Roman law before the appearance of the Twelve Tables in the middle of the fifth century, B.C. It is thought that these Twelve Tables codified the prevailing law of the day.[55] Hence, presumably, the first written law of Rome represented a description of contemporary customary rules.

Historians offer rather widely different conclusions in regard to the role of custom in the law of the early Roman Republic.[56] Scholars also dispute the place of custom in the later Republic and early Empire. It was fashionable a century ago to describe a prominent role for custom in the law of this period.[57] But historians writing more recently seem agreed that custom was, at best, a relatively minor source of law.[58] Recent scholarly opinion is again considerably more sanguine than earlier scholarship about the importance of custom in the days of the Empire's flourishing.[59]

A lack of a clear scholarly consensus is still evident concerning the later Empire, known as the Dominate or, from a legal perspective, as the Bureaucratic or Post-Classical period. The ambiguities, however, may be in large part due to ambiguities inherent in this era's jurisprudence itself. Many scholars agree that statutes emerging from imperial legislation were a key, if not exclusive, means of law-making.[60] Nevertheless, the legal doctrine of the age did not ignore custom. For example, Peter Stein notes that the central government was relaxing control of the provinces in this period, and that provincial variants of Roman law were categorized as local custom.[61] In addition, Fritz Schulz writes that jurisprudence was heavily reliant on the prior, classical period for its substance, and hence was quite non-revolutionary despite its increasing turn to statutes for expression of laws.[62] He also claims that it was exactly in this legislating era that legal doctrine began to articulate the idea that customary law was on the same footing as statutory law.[63] Likewise, one noteworthy legislative monument of this period, the Theodosian Code (promulgated in 438 A.D.), acknowledged custom to be a source of law when consistent with statutory provisions.[64]

To draw general conclusions about the place of custom in pre-Justinian Roman law is certainly fraught with difficulties. J. M. Kelly's cautious conclusion, that custom held a "very modest position" among the forms of Roman law through the history just surveyed, is prudently guarded, and is perhaps the best that can be said.[65] But, whether or not it had an explicitly preeminent place in the actual law applied by Roman courts and enforced by emperors or others in authority, there were certain factors at work that may have contributed to the eventual emergence of custom to a more central position in the legal canopy. First, important intellectual figures, such as Cicero, himself an eminent lawyer, accorded a place to custom in the fabric of the civil law.[66] Second, jurists and their opinions played an essential role in the development of Roman law.[67] The always-growing edifice of extant lawyerly judgments on particular issues, upon which contemporary lawyers were compelled to rely, was clearly a particular form of customary law and a real alternative to the imperial will as a source of legal authority. Third, a number of scholars, in their own ways, describe the character of Roman law as conservative, a-theoretical, and traditional, and its historic development as smooth, spontaneous, and organic.[68] Finally, many Roman jurists expressed the idea that though the emperor's will was law, his authority and that of the state in general arose only from below, that is, from the people themselves.[69] In other words, the emperor enjoyed no inherent power, but rather the power that the people as a whole had ceded to him at some point in the past. Each of these four factors provided the soil out of which a vibrant body of customary law could blossom.

What is now known as the *Corpus Juris Civilis* was the product of the ambitions of the Roman-Byzantine emperor Justinian. Justinian set to work a group of jurists known to history as "compilers," so-called because of their harvesting of older legal rules, opinions, and customs. With impressive energy and output, these compilers produced the three documents that constitute the *CJC*. The first, called the Digest, was a collection of classical law. It was promulgated on December 16, 533. The second, called the Institutes, was issued just two weeks later, and was intended to serve as an introductory textbook for law. The third document is known as the Code. A first Code was produced, but it has been lost to history. The second was produced in 534 in order to acknowledge changes to the first made necessary by the promulgation of the Digest and Institutes. Over the next several years, Justinian added to his collections many new laws, generally know as Novels. Historical knowledge of the Novels is indirect.[70]

Justinian's legal minions were not called "compilers" without reason. They compiled, or, perhaps better, plundered legal material of the classical era and inserted it into their codification,[71] making the Digest and Code essentially a series of quotations. Certainly the codifiers wished their product to be non-contradictory. Though efforts were made to eliminate contradictory material, it is recognized that they fell far short of complete success. The material on custom to be surveyed below is in large part a collection of quotations from older jurists. Thus, though I describe the ideas that the *CJC* propounds, I make no claim that it is a wholly coherent, self-contained system.[72]

The texts of the *CJC* acknowledge a role for custom in the body of civil law. Early on, the *Institutes* refers to "Every community governed by laws and customs,"[73] clearly implying that laws and custom indeed governed the community addressed by the *CJC*. Of the three documents comprising the

CJC, the *Institutes* is the most amenable to the hermeneutical practice of one section interpreting another, since it is an original composition, and not a compilation of previously written texts. With this in mind, internal evidence suggests that the phrase "laws and custom" (*legibus et moribus*) should be understood as *written* laws and customs. Two sections later, the *Institutes* notes that law (*jus*) is divided into written (*scripto*) and unwritten (*non scripto*) law, and that there are three kinds of written law, one of which is simply called *lex*.[74] Reading these two sections together, therefore, the *Institutes* appears to introduce the whole landscape of Roman law under the general heading of *jus*, which is then divided into two general categories, *lex*, or written law, and *mos*, custom, which is unwritten law. This declaration of custom's importance, right alongside of written laws, is noteworthy. The *Digest* pays more explicit homage to custom. It quotes a passage from the jurist Paulus that speaks of the great authority of a law that has been approved to such an extent that it does not need to be perceived by writing.[75] The *CJC*, therefore, sets forth the principle that law can be unwritten, and this unwritten law is identified with custom.

Each of the three documents comprising the *CJC* has material specifically explaining the role of custom in the body of law, though it is a relatively small amount of material considering the size of the entire *CJC*. From these sections that describe custom, three principal legal functions of custom emerge: the creation, the abolition, and the interpretation of law. As to the creation of law, the *Institutes* explains: "The unwritten law is that which usage has established; for ancient customs, being sanctioned by the consent of those who adopt them, are like laws."[76] The *Digest* too, speaks of this ability of custom, received by the (unwritten) judgment and approval of the people, to be established as law. A quotation from the jurist Julian reads, in part:

> What ought to be held to in those cases where we have no applicable written law is the practice established by customs and usage [*moribus et consuetudine*].... Age-encrusted custom [*Inveterata consuetudo*] is not undeservedly cherished as having almost statutory force, and this is the kind of law which is said to be established by use and wont. For given that statutes themselves are binding upon us for no other reason than that they have been accepted by the judgment of the populace, certainly it is fitting that what the populace has approved without any writing shall be binding upon everyone. What does it matter whether the people declares its will by voting or by the very substance of its actions?[77]

Two other quotations from this section of the *Digest* are also especially noteworthy for their explicit identification of custom as a creator of law. In one of these, the greatest of the jurists, Ulpian, states: "Everyday usage [*Diuturna consuetudo*] ought to be observed in place of legal right and statue law in relation to those matters which do not come under the written law." In the other, Hermogenian writes: "But we also keep to those rules which have been sanctioned by long custom [*longa consuetudine*] and observed over very many years; we keep to them as being a tacit agreement of the citizen [*tacita civium conventio*], no less than we keep to written rules of law."[78] The *Digest* speaks of this law-making function of custom as having special force in circumstances where (written) laws are ambiguous. Quoting Callistratus, it reads: "In fact, our reigning Emperor Severus has issued a rescript to the effect that in cases of ambiguity arising from statute law, statutory force ought to be ascribed to custom [*consuetudinem*] or to the authority of an unbroken line of similar judicial decisions."[79]

Custom not only creates law, but also abolishes law. The *Institutes* denies that natural law, which all nations observe and which divine providence establishes, can be changed, but states that "the laws which every state has enacted, undergo frequent changes, either by the tacit consent of the people, or by a new law being subsequently passed."[80] The phrase *tacito consensu populi* seems to be a reference to custom. The power of the people to abrogate law is also explicitly affirmed by a quotation from Julian in the *Digest*, part of which was quoted above in regard to custom's ability to create law. The end of this passage reads: "Accordingly, it is absolutely right to accept the point that statutes may be repealed not only by vote of the legislature but also by the silent agreement of everyone expressed through desuetude [*tacito consensu omnium per desuetudinem*]."[81]

The third function of custom that emerges in the *CJC* is interpretation of the law. The *Digest* speaks of custom not only as a valid interpreter of law, but even as its *best* interpreter, quoting Paulus: "If a question should arise about the interpretation of a statute, what ought to be looked into first is the law that the *civitas* had previously applied in cases of the same kind. For custom is the best interpreter of statutes [*optima enim est legum interpres consuetudo*]."[82] The *Code* is not as explicit on this role of custom. But its reference to custom as an imitator and maintainer of law suggests some interpretative function: "Also, custom, long ago approving laws themselves and firmly preserving them, is imitated and maintained."[83]

Two items in the *CJC* seemingly in tension with the teaching about custom found in the previous quotations should be noted. Whether they really give evidence of contradictory streams of thought within the *CJC* is not terribly important for present purposes, and may not even be an answerable question. But they are worth mentioning because they become relevant issues in forthcoming discussions of Aquinas's writings on law. The two claims in view are that the ruler's pleasure is a source of law and that the people have given up their law-making powers. Both matters emerge in this passage from the *Institutes*:

> That which seems good to the emperor has also the force of law [*legis*[84]]; for the people, by the *lex regia*, which is passed to confer on him his power, make over to him their whole power and authority. Therefore, whatever the emperor ordains...is unquestionably law [*legem*]....[85]

The years following the promulgation of the *CJC* were rather barren from a legal perspective, though there was some important work in jurisprudence done in Western Europe in the early Middle Ages. Perhaps the foremost figure was Isidore of Seville, whose influence on jurists long after his time, as well as on Aquinas, would be weighty.[86] Isidore, who drew considerable inspiration from the *CJC*, was also an original legal thinker.[87] Among his ideas about law was the conviction that human law had been established by custom, and even that law itself *becomes* custom.[88] As discussed below, this concept also appears in Aquinas's jurisprudence, and it may well have directly derived from Isidore.

However, no one would identify the early medieval period as a fruitful time for jurisprudence, theoretically or practically. Though Justinian promulgated the *CJC* in certain regions of Italy that he won back for the empire, even in Italy there is no evidence of knowledge of the *CJC* from the seventh century to the eleventh.[89] Before the eleventh century it appears that there were no schools of Roman law in Italy, even while Lombardic law was taught in some places.[90] Elsewhere in Western Europe the situation was apparently no different.

Though virtually no legal theory of lasting value had been produced for several centuries, the eleventh century marks a great milestone in the history of Western law. At this time, there sprouted a sudden revival in the study of Roman law whose impact on legal practice would be immense. The leading figure of this revival was a teacher at the University of Bologna named Irnerius. Irnerius began to lecture on the *Digest* in 1088.[91] The interest he inspired was quick and intense, and during the great awakening of classical studies and the flourishing of the University of Bologna in the century to come it was the *CJC* that provoked perhaps the most attention and scholarship.[92] Breen claims that whereas the thirteenth century was the great century for theological studies, the twelfth was the great century for jurisprudence.[93]

Students streamed to Bologna from many parts of Europe. Scholars have speculated about why the reaction was so spirited. Wolfgang Kunkel thinks that the broader intellectual climate of the day provided the skills needed for the undertaking.[94] Quirinus Breen points to the attractions of Roman law for the many new city-dwellers, who found the traditional agrarian/feudal law of little relevance to them.[95] Whatever the reasons, and they were surely complex, Irnerius's re-introduction of the *CJC* into the mind of Western Europe was a momentous event.[96] It was not long before the interest in the *CJC* became more than just academic, and began also to pervade practical legal life.[97] Even beyond the field of law, Irnerius's interest in pagan sources was a sort of firstfruits of much greater interest in such sources, in many different fields, in the near future.[98]

Of obvious interest for the present project is Irnerius's impact on Thomas Aquinas and his view of custom. Breen argues that Irnerius had significant effect on contemporary theological and philosophical studies. Irnerius approached his subject matter in an objective, scientific fashion, concentrating on the available data rather than on the consolatory and inspirational. Breen concludes that Aquinas "succeeded best in doing for theology what the masters of Bologna had done for the law."[99] R. W. and A. J. Carlyle transmit Irnerius's sentiments on the importance of custom for law:

> Irnerius, in a gloss, speaks of the threefold nature of *jus*—that which is established by law (*lex*), by custom, and by the necessity of nature.... In his 'Summa Codicis' he deals with the matter very fully, and brings out very clearly the important pointthat it is not only the custom of the Roman people, but that of any city which has the force of law—subject, of course, to the written law of the Empire; and he urges that as the principles of the written law are to be drawn out to meet similar cases which may not be directly provided for, the same is to be done with the unwritten law of custom. Only in regard to unwritten as well as the written laws we must consider the principles of justice and equity on which alone they can be founded. Custom is the best interpreter of laws, for by custom also laws themselves are abrogated.[100]

The father of medieval jurisprudence, therefore, propounded the three functions of custom specified in the *CJC*: the creation, abrogation, and interpretation of law.

The relationship of custom and law was an active font of discussion among the jurists following Irnerius, up to the time of Aquinas. The Carlyles describe a good deal of consensus among these medieval jurists on the idea that in older days custom had the force of law and that the Roman emperor derived his authority from the people.[101] What was not unanimous was opinion on the force of custom in contemporary times and whether the people had retained their law-making powers.[102] One very influential legal figure, the twelfth century scholar Gratian, author of the famous *Dectretum*, defended an important role for custom in both civil and canon law.[103] However, the Carlyles observe increasing sentiments in this era that law could be created by those holding appropriate authority, and they specifically identify the thirteenth century as a time of a growing conception that the prince was the sole source of law.[104] Aquinas lived, therefore, at a time when various issues regarding custom and law were in some flux. His own teacher, Albert the Great, weighed in on the subject, in a manner not dissimilar from the judgments Aquinas himself would express.[105]

Even while custom was a fertile source of theoretical reflection in the early and high Middle Ages, it also had a prominent role in the practical legal life of these eras. Whereas the role of custom in the ancient legal systems remains in many ways a mystery to modern historians, the great practical significance of custom as a source of law in the Middle Ages is a certainty. Susan Reynolds makes an impressive argument that custom was indeed a central facet of medieval legal life. She argues that collective activity drew cohesion from deep-rooted ideas and values in medieval Europe, in ways similar throughout the different European communities.[106] Commenting on the generations before 1140, she speaks of custom as the bedrock of law throughout Western Europe, even arguing that there was no real distinction between law and custom until the twelfth century or later.[107] Of course, particular customs differed from place to place, but everywhere custom served as an intelligent and effective source of collective activity and social harmony.[108] It even checked the power of medieval kings.[109]

Reynolds also describes some important legal changes in the years 1140–1300—within which time Aquinas lived. The place of custom in this era was somewhat weakened, as governments and kings became more powerful, courts became more formal, and more legal rules and practices were put into writing.[110] Customs in different places became more diversified, but custom continued to be of great importance. It remained a mark of a community's political autonomy, continued to check the actions of princes, and still provided the only matrix within which new laws could be created.[111] Reynolds concludes that despite many intellectual developments in this era, Roman law was still very traditional in 1300, the terminus of her study.[112]

At this point in the development of Roman law, trouble was brewing for the centrality of custom. Two strong monarchs with dreams of centralizing power in their hands were about to inherit important thrones in Europe. But a subject of both these kings at various times in his life, a Dominican Friar named Thomas Aquinas, was also poised to engage the relationship of custom and law with his formidable intellectual powers. This crisis in the role of custom and Aquinas's answer to this crisis brings us to the theme of the next chapter.

Chapter 2

Custom and Law: The Contribution of Thomas Aquinas

Thirteenth century Europe saw significant challenges to the hegemony of the customary law of the previous centuries and, in the midst of these challenges, Thomas Aquinas presented his own treatment of the relationship of law and custom. This chapter introduces Aquinas's thought on this issue in the context of his contemporary legal world. I first describe some aspects of the legal context of Aquinas's day and then give a brief account of his broader theology of law. This sets the stage for the primary goal of this chapter, which is to provide an exposition of the role of custom in Aquinas's understanding of natural and human law.

The Age of Aquinas

Thomas Aquinas was born in 1224 or 1225 in the county of Aquino, between Naples and Rome. He received his early education at the nearby monastery of Monte Cassino and later at the *studium generale* in Naples. Here, in 1244, he joined the Dominican order. The Dominicans sent Thomas to Paris in 1245, where he continued his philosophical studies and perhaps began his study of theology. It was in Paris that he first came into contact with the eminent and controversial Dominican thinker, Albert the Great, whom he followed to Cologne in 1248. In Cologne, he instructed students in the Bible and served as a "bachelor" under Albert's tutelage. Thomas moved back to Paris in 1252 to teach the *Sentences* of Peter Lombard, and after completing this work over four years was awarded the *licentia docendi*. After three more years teaching in Paris, Thomas returned to Italy, where he lived and worked for nearly ten years. In 1268 or 1269, he was sent back to Paris again, where he addressed controversies over the teaching of Aristotle and the place of the mendicant orders. In the spring of 1272, Aquinas went to Naples to found a new *studium generale*. He continued his active teaching through 1273 and died on March 7, 1274.[1]

These years in which Aquinas lived were times of significant social, cultural, and intellectual development in Western Europe. Thomas O'Meara describes the "cultural moment" in which Aquinas was born:

> Pope Honorius III was continuing the renewal and prestige of Innocent IV.... the Muslims continued to expand in parts of Spain, while the Latin kingdom of Jerusalem established by the Crusaders became increasingly fragile. Western Crusader lords occupied parts of the eastern Mediterranean, and far to the north and east the Mongol invasions disclosed something of Asian peoples. Thomas's life more or less corresponds to the time of the High Middle Ages with its study and integration of the new sciences recently received from the ancient Greek works, and with its new arts of building and decorating churches.[2]

O'Meara adds that this was a time of "economic growth and social evolution," with populations increasing, building and agriculture improving, feudalism declining, and commercial cities growing. "The West was moving from one cultural milieu to another."[3]

Though Thomas spent most of his days in the relative isolation of the monastery and university, he often showed a surprising familiarity with this evolving social world and its practical problems. In part, this may have been the result of Aquinas's generosity in responding to practical queries posed to him by various people active in the life of the world. Commenting on his time in Orvieto from 1261–1265, Torrell finds Aquinas to be "a theologian at work in the world of his own time, attentive to problems that are posed to him, and trying to respond as best he can. The solitude of his priory had nothing of the isolation of an ivory tower."[4] One illustrative example supplied by Torrell is Aquinas's writing of *De emptione et venditione* in 1262. Someone in Florence, a major commercial center, proposed the subject of the work to him. In this treatise, Aquinas discussed ethical questions about buying and selling on credit, usury, and speculation, and he even consulted two experts before putting pen to paper.

The Status of Custom in the Age of Aquinas

Thomas's cognizance of such matters is an important point for the present study, for one of the areas of contemporary social flux was the role of custom in legal life. The last chapter documented the predominance of custom in the law of Western Europe in the time leading up to Aquinas's life. But several events, particularly the ascension of two powerful monarchs to important thrones, brought this state of affairs into question.

Two of the realms in which Aquinas spent much of his life, the Kingdom of the Two Sicilies and France, were ruled by these remarkable monarchs whose reigns exemplified emerging tensions between the centralization of governmental power and the continuing claims of local authorities and local customs. The two monarchs were Emperor Frederick II (1194–1250)[5] and King Louis IX (1214–1270).[6] Frederick, a man of wide-ranging talents who descended from the Hohenstaufen line, ruled large parts of both Italy and Germany and was also a crusader who was crowned King of Jerusalem at one point. Yet he regarded the Sicilian territories as the heart of his possessions and took special interest in their welfare. Aquinas was born under the auspices of his rule. Louis, also a crusader, became King of France as a youth and enjoyed a long reign over his lands. Though a successful head of government, Louis was best remembered for his sincere piety, a trait that led to his canonization just 27 years after his death. Aquinas's many years in Paris were spent during Louis's reign. Aquinas dined with Louis at least once, though Aquinas is reported to have spent the evening in intense theological introspection, mostly oblivious to his surroundings! Alistair MacIntyre has suggested that the events of state under these two monarchs provide a crucial backdrop for understanding the importance of Aquinas's theology of law.[7] MacIntyre even identifies the issue of custom as a key illustration of how Aquinas responded to the actions of Frederick and Louis, though he does not develop this point at much length.[8] Given Aquinas's cognizance of and even personal involvement with practical social matters of his day, and given the history of the legal reforms introduced by Frederick and Louis, MacIntyre is certainly on firm ground.

Frederick's attitude toward Sicily's customs was ambivalent. A considerable part of his legislative agenda consisted of imposing upon Sicily many old Norman customs that had prevailed under past kings. However, this entailed doing away with a number of customs currently prevailing in his territories.[9] As David Abulafia notes, Frederick by no means despised customary practices, but he refused to bless customs and laws simply because they were old, seeing himself instead as one appointed by God to guard the laws and to make and unmake them as was fitting.[10] Though scholarly opinion differs about just how radical and unique were Frederick's law-making enterprises, historians agree that Frederick saw himself as the sole-lawgiver in his realm. Sicilian laws were to be promulgated by Frederick alone, without the need for their harmony with custom or the consent of the princes.[11] Thomas Van Cleve states:

> But, if the laws of Fredrick appeared to have their origin in precedent, they became, when embodied in his *Constitutiones*, royal laws, subject to change only by the will of the sovereign. Fredrick did not share the medieval opinion that law is a permanent structure or that immemorial custom is capable of embodying all questions of human relationships....He was the creator, not the 'finder of law' in the accepted medieval sense—he was the maker or creator of new law.[12]

Along with this concern to center all legislative power in his own hands, Frederick was also attentive about keeping control of the judicial powers. He required that his subjects seek justice only in the royal courts and prohibited anyone from serving in judicial functions apart from his appointment.[13] These centralizing moves by Frederick meant, of course, a corresponding decrease in authority for other secular and ecclesiastical officers. The barons of Sicily were stripped of many of their castles and lands, and fiefs were granted only in return for service to the state.[14] Frederick was also adamant that his legislative activity was independent of the Pope and the church,[15] and his assumption of legislative power provoked papal response.[16] Van Cleve, though himself occasionally hagiographic in his description of Frederick, concludes that his "concept of efficient government can best be described as Caesarism or enlightened despotism."[17]

Louis IX, though certainly more devout and less dictatorial than Frederick, was no less an interesting figure, and his reforms in France moved in many of the same directions as Frederick's. When Louis returned to his kingdom from the crusades, he began a serious program of reform that, according to Jean Richard, affected not only institutions but also the ethos in which they operated.[18] In line with his reputation as a pious Christian, Louis is uniformly described as a just man with a great concern for rectitude in his legal duties. In spite of this character—or, perhaps, because of it—Louis assumed for himself a great degree of social power that most fellow medieval kings could envy but not match.[19] Influenced by some of the Roman law doctrines that were being actively studied in his realm, particularly at the University of Orleans, Louis made himself the supreme judicial figure in the land. Contrary to previous custom, Louis insisted that the barons' judicial authority was derived only from him.[20] Louis's perspective on the legislative task was similar. Margaret Labarge observes that the power to make law was not generally recognized in the medieval world up to this date. Instead, law essentially consisted of customs, which might be altered in implementation but not in substance. Labarge says that this began to change with Louis, who was not afraid to introduce new principles of law, though not without the approval of his barons and counselors.[21] Richard writes:

> This adage [that the king of France recognizes no superiors in temporal matters] enabled the legists to conclude that the king they served had, like the [Roman] emperor, the capacity to make laws....The king possessed, he [Peter of Fontaines] concluded, the power to make *etablissements*, and 'what pleases the prince has the force of law.' The *Livre de justice et de plaid* [of Louis] says just this.... There can be little doubt that Louis IX implicitly adopted this doctrine, without consciously attacking any particular custom....[22]

Louis apparently had a substantial knowledge of the contemporary customary laws of France.[23] Such knowledge would have been crucial for the just administration of his realm, given the judicial dichotomy of France at this time. The southern regions of the country had been heavily influenced by Roman law, following the rediscovery of the *CJC* in the late eleventh century. The northern regions, however, remained firmly under the unwritten laws of older French custom.[24] Like Frederick, Louis displayed an ambivalent attitude toward older customary law. Richard observes that Louis respected custom but did not hesitate to overturn it when he believed it to be unjust.[25] Inevitably, this attitude brought Louis into tension with those whose sentiments or interests rested in the customary practices.[26] One commonly cited example of Louis's abrogation of old custom was his prohibition of the judicial duel, including trials by ordeal. However reasonable such reforms may sound, it drew resistance from many of the barons, both by protest and by disobedience.[27] The struggle between Louis and the barons was real, though it should not be exaggerated. Louis was considerably more concerned with the rights of his vassals than were his immediate predecessors, though certainly in the interest of gaining their necessary loyalty.[28] Richard also points out that the barons' motives for defending the old and customary were in the interests of retaining their own power. Nevertheless, the great barons, who themselves benefited considerably from many of Louis' policies, tended to be close relatives of Louis, and the lesser barons lost substantial authority under these same policies.[29] In the end, local custom "was that to which the enemies of royal centralization characteristically appealed," as MacIntyre comments on the era of Louis IX. In addition, he adds, the fact that the barons and others would themselves challenge custom in the interests of their own authority meant that the "appeal to custom was therefore one that placed its proponents in opposition to all the great wielders of power—royal, baronial, and even, we need to add, ecclesiastical."[30] Aquinas wrote about custom against this backdrop.

Aquinas's Theology of Law

An understanding of Aquinas's view of custom presupposes knowledge of the general structure of his theology of law. Therefore, though many useful treatments of Aquinas's theology of law have been written, a brief outline of its structure is presented here for readers unfamiliar with it. The exposition that follows is taken primarily from his comprehensive treatment of law, the so-called "Treatise on Law" of the *Summa Theologiae.* After setting forth these foundational matters, I turn specifically to his treatment of custom.

The Nature of Law

The Treatise on Law begins with a question concerning the essence of law. Despite Aquinas's interest in concrete issues of law, he initiates his study by examining the concept of law in the abstract. The four articles which comprise this question provide Aquinas with a suitable definition for law of every sort: "an ordinance of reason for the common good, made by him who has care of the community, and promulgated [*rationis ordinatio ad bonum commune, ab eo qui curam communitatis habet, promulgata*]."[31] In order to get to this point, Aquinas examines questions about reason, common good, competent authority, and promulgation as they bear upon law.

Aquinas first addresses the reasonable nature of law, a crucial aspect of his thought. He bases his belief that law pertains to reason upon a rather simple formula. First, he claims that "Law is a rule or measure of acts whereby man is induced to act or is restrained from acting." He then asserts: "Now the rule and measure of human acts is the reason, which is the first principle of human acts...."[32] By simple deduction, then, he concludes that law is an ordinance of reason. Though Aquinas at times also speaks of law as an expression of will, he denies the status of law to anything not derived from reason. For Aquinas, law is never an expression of will alone, but of will as governed by reason. Following this discussion, Aquinas immediately broadens his perspective. Law not only pertains to reason, but also aims at the common good. Having already established that reason is a principle of human acts, Aquinas observes that there must be something in the reason that serves as the principle of all the rest, a principle with which law is chiefly concerned. Aquinas identifies this principle as happiness, the last end of human life. He then concludes: "Moreover, since every part is ordained to the whole, as imperfect to perfect; and since one man is a part of the universal community, the law must needs regard properly the relationship to universal happiness." This universal happiness is what Aquinas understands as the common good. Anything that does not aim at this goal lacks the nature of law.[33]

The other two elements that comprise the general essence of law are concerned with the more practical issues of how law is made and comes into force. The first item concerns *who* may establish law. No individual person is competent for this task merely by possessing rationality. Instead, the authority of law-making may belong either to "the whole people or to a public personage who has care of the whole people."[34] This two-fold option for law-making power is of particular importance in the discussion of custom below. The second item concerns *how* a law is put into force, the matter of promulgation. Aquinas teaches that a rule or measure (which is what law is) "is imposed by being applied to those who are to be ruled and measured by it." Such application, which is required for law to be binding, occurs when notice is given, and this is what is meant by promulgation.[35]

After setting forth this general framework for law, Aquinas fills in the picture by identifying four different types of law: eternal law, natural law, human law, and divine law.[36] A description of the first three types follows. The fourth, divine law, is divided into two kinds, old and new, corresponding to the standard division of the Christian Scriptures. It concerns the orientation of human beings to the end of eternal happiness, beyond the end proportionate to their natural faculties.[37] Though I do not specifically examine divine law in this section, elements of Aquinas's discussions of divine law do appear in the chapters to come.

The Eternal Law

The eternal law is the starting point for Aquinas's exposition of the different kinds of law. All other laws derive from the eternal law in one way or another. Aquinas initially notes that divine providence rules the whole world, and from this premise he concludes that "the whole community of the universe is governed by Divine Reason. Wherefore the very Idea of the government of things in God the Ruler of the universe, has the nature of a law [*legis habet rationem*]."[38] In this short statement, Aquinas identifies three of the four elements of his definition of law: the eternal law is rational, focuses upon the good of the whole (i.e., the universe), and comes from a competent authority (God). In the immediate context, Aquinas also affirms that the eternal law is promulgated.[39] Aquinas develops the connection of eternal law with divine providence by speaking of the eternal law as "the type of Divine Wisdom, as directing all actions and movements."[40] He analogizes God's governing of the whole world by means of eternal law to the work of an artist. There pre-exists in the mind of each artist a type (that is, a model or exemplar) of whatever is to be created. The eternal law is such a type or exemplar, and by this pre-existing model God governs all the acts of each of the creatures that he has made.[41]

Remarkably, Aquinas claims that human beings have knowledge of this eternal law. Aquinas concedes that the eternal law is known "as it is in itself" only by the blessed who see God's essence in heaven. But a thing may also be known "in its effects" (as the sun is seen not in itself but by its rays), and in this way human beings know the eternal law here and now. In fact, every rational creature knows the eternal law to some extent, "in its reflection." However, this merely partial knowledge of the eternal law actually constitutes the sum of our understanding of the truth: "For every knowledge of truth is a kind of reflection and participation of the eternal law [*irradiatio et participatio legis aeternae*], which is unchangeable truth."[42]

In light of its epistemological preeminence, Aquinas subjects all things to the eternal law, including all plans, laws, actions, and movements. For example, he writes: "Since then the eternal law is the plan of government in the Chief Governor, all the plans of government in the inferior governors must be derived from the eternal law."[43] Likewise, he adds that God "imprints on the whole of nature the principles of its proper actions." This imprinting takes place in different ways. Irrational creatures are moved by providence, but in a manner different from that of rational creatures, who are moved through their ability to understand God's commandments.[44] Aquinas explains that the rational nature is subject to eternal law in two ways, by means of knowledge and by means of inclination. Though both ways are imperfect and partially destroyed in the wicked, and more perfect in the good, neither is completely destroyed in any person.[45]

The Natural Law

The second kind of law that Aquinas identifies is the natural law. As he has explained elsewhere, all things partake of the eternal law to some degree, and from it derive their proper inclinations to acts and ends. But rational creatures have a special share in the eternal law, by which they share in the Eternal Reason. He defines the natural law as "the rational creature's participation of the eternal law [*participatio legis aeternae in rationali creatura*]." The function of the natural law, then, is to discern what is good and evil by the light of natural reason, which is "an imprint [*impressio*] on us of the Divine light."[46]

Aquinas expands his discussion by first introducing the notion of "synderesis." Synderesis is the "law of our mind," or "a habit containing the precepts of the natural law, which are the first principles of human actions."[47] Properly speaking, therefore, natural law itself is not a habit, though people hold the general principles of the natural law by this habit of synderesis.[48] Through synderesis, all people know infallibly the basic requirements of the natural law. Proceeding logically, Aquinas then asserts that the natural law consists of several self-evident precepts, not just one. He identifies a first precept of the natural law, that "good is to be done and pursued, and evil is to be avoided." All the other precepts—even the whole of morality—are based upon this: "whatever the practical reason naturally apprehends as man's good (or evil) belongs to the precepts of the natural law as something to be done or avoided." Aquinas teaches that human beings share certain natural inclinations with all of creation and, more specifically, with all animals. Yet people also have inclinations to good that are unique to their rational capacities (such as knowing the truth about God and living in society), and "whatever pertains to this inclination belongs to the natural law."[49] Similarly, Aquinas concludes that the natural law prescribes all virtuous acts. This does not mean that human beings are equally inclined by nature to all acts of virtue. But, since the natural law is about the right use of reason, and since we discover what acts are useful through reasonable inquiry, the natural law does prescribe every virtuous act, at least indirectly.[50]

Aquinas attributes a certain constancy to the natural law. First, the natural law is equally known by all people, though this conclusion is qualified. As to its general principles, the natural law is the same for all people and equally known by them. However, when one descends from these general principles to matters of detail, this uniformity begins to erode. Because of differing circumstances, the requirements of the natural law are not always the same in concrete situations. Even when they are, Aquinas notes, different people do not know them equally well. The more detail into which one delves, the greater the uncertainty becomes.[51] Secondly, Aquinas ascribes to the natural law a degree of immutability. Again, the claim is qualified. Aquinas grants that the natural law may be added to, either by the revelation of divine law or by various human laws. However, he denies that the natural law, as to its first principles, can be changed by subtraction, except "in some particular cases of rare occurrence" which he does not specify. As to secondary precepts, the specific requirements of the natural law change as circumstances change.[52] Third, the natural law cannot be obliterated from the human heart. Here again, a distinction between general and secondary precepts of the natural law is necessary. Due to synderesis, the general principles can never be completely blotted out in a person. As to particular applications, however, various evil persuasions, customs, or habits may obscure the direction of the natural law.[53]

Human Law

The third kind of law identified by Aquinas, and the last to be examined here, is human law. The creation of human law according to the principles of the natural law is of central concern to this book and, as such, is considered in great detail in later chapters. This being the case, it is sufficient here merely to sketch the skeleton of Aquinas's treatment of human law.

Aquinas states the purpose of human law in various ways; for example, as the temporal tranquility of the state, or the directing of people in their relations with one another.[54] However, his initial concern is the very necessity of human law, which lies in training people in virtue. Though all people have a natural inclination to virtue and some need only parental instruction in order to advance in virtuous living, many others need an external constraint, which human laws provide.[55] At another level, perhaps, Aquinas learned from Aristotle about the necessity of human law. Aristotle believed that we want law, not a human being, to be our ruler. Since people seek their own interests, any community in which rulers govern by decree really has no government at all.[56] Commenting on this analysis, Aquinas asserts that a good government does not allow people to rule according to whim and passion, but instead entrusts authority to the law, which is a dictate of reason, or to people who act according to reason.[57]

Several different sorts of human laws may be distinguished in various ways: first, as the law of nations and civil law; second, according to the different kinds of work that people do; third, according to the different forms of governmental polity; and, fourth, according to the matters with which they deal.[58] Aquinas makes these distinctions in part to take account of the different ways in which human law is derived from the natural law. Aquinas defines human laws as "particular determinations, devised by human reason" as it proceeds to more concrete matters from the "indemonstrable principles" of the natural law.[59] But he explains that human laws derive from the natural law in different ways. Laws may be derived from the natural law as "conclusions from premises," in which case they have precisely the same force as the natural law. Laws may also be derived by making determinations from certain generalities. Such laws are more remotely related to the natural law, and have only the force of human law. Nevertheless, no human law can be rightly disconnected from the natural law, for "if at any point it deflects from the law of nature, it is no longer a law but a perversion of law."[60]

Since legitimate human laws are derived from the natural law, Aquinas ascribes authority to them. Aquinas dwells on this subject at considerable length. First, he requires that human laws be framed not for private benefit, but for the common good, and thus must be general propositions applicable to many people.[61] Such human laws ought to forbid vices. Since laws are general propositions applicable to many people, and since people are of various characters and conditions, it is not possible that all vices be prohibited. Nevertheless, human law ought to forbid the worst vices, particularly those that hurt others and make social life impossible.[62] Similarly, since human laws are meant for all sorts of people, many of whom are not particularly virtuous, requiring the exercise of all the virtues would not be expedient. Nevertheless, human law, on principle, is able to prescribe all the virtues, and ought to prescribe as many as is beneficial to the common good.[63] Aquinas also explains that properly established human laws have the power to bind the conscience. Though laws not framed according to the required standard perhaps may, and in some cases must, be disobeyed, even many deficient laws have the power to bind the conscience when spurning them would cause scandal or disturbance.[64] Even the sovereign is subject to the *directive* force of human law (though no sovereign can be *coerced* by it).[65] However, human laws are not absolutely binding in all cases. Legislators cannot foresee every situation, and one ought not follow their laws when doing so causes injustice to be done in particular circumstances.[66]

An important issue related to this last point is the concept of *aequitas* (Latin) or *epieikeia* (Greek), i.e., equity, that by which one sets aside the letter of the law when higher dictates of justice and the common good demand.[67] Many scholars have pointed to Aquinas's discussions of equity as an essential aspect of his legal and moral thought.[68] Aquinas asserts that equity is necessary for the judicial process, due to the contingent nature of human action in general and of human law in particular. Since legislators do not have the comprehensive knowledge needed to make rules for every possible situation, they must legislate for the majority of cases.[69] Inevitably, circumstances arise in which strict application of the law produces an injustice. Aquinas is adamant, however, that equity is not to be seen as a disparagement of law or as an indictment of a legislator's competence. Laws *must* be framed generally and with a view to what ordinarily happens. Exceptional cases are to be expected, and the need to apply equity to such cases does not compromise the value of law, whose purpose is never to provide infallible answers to every question. As Aquinas says, equity does not pass judgment on a law, but deals with particular contingencies and simply moderates the observance of the letter of the law.[70] Similarly, Aristotle described equity as a method of restoring the balance of justice when the law tilts it. Like Aquinas, Aristotle stressed that the application of equity does not make a law bad. In fact, the practice of equity is in keeping with the intention of the legislators, who do not want their generally-applicable laws to be applied in unjust ways.[71]

Along similar lines, Aquinas claims that human laws can be changed. Reason may discover a better rule over the course of time, or different circumstances may arise that compel new laws to be established.[72] Though either occurrence might legitimate a change in law, Aquinas urges caution. The mere act of changing law is itself prejudicial to the common good, and no law should be changed unless the good to be attained by the new law surpasses the inevitable harm done by the alteration.[73] One important means by which law can be changed is custom. Custom can declare law—that is, express a command of human reason—just as legislation can, and thus changes, expounds, and interprets law.[74] This leads to the principal concern of this chapter.

The Legal Functions of Custom

Within this general framework of eternal, natural, and human law, Aquinas attributes a special importance to custom. The remainder of this chapter describes custom's particular legal functions, leaving to future chapters reflection on why Aquinas came to such conclusions. The material in this chapter is drawn primarily from his "Treatise on Law" of the *Summa Theologiae*, and secondarily from other sources, particularly *De Regno*, his treatise to the king of Crete.

Creates, Abolishes, and Interprets

As discussed in the previous chapter, Justinian's *Corpus Juris Civilis* set out a threefold legal function for custom: the creation, abolition, and interpretation of law. Irnerius, the father of medieval jurisprudence and the inspiration behind the renaissance of Roman Law, also identified these three crucial roles for custom. Thomas Aquinas followed his predecessors in this matter. In perhaps his most clear and detailed description of the relationship of custom and law, Aquinas writes:

> Now all law proceeds from the reason and will of the lawgiver.... Now just as human reason and will, in practical matters, may be made manifest by speech, so may

> they be made known by deeds: since seemingly a man chooses as good that which he carries into execution. But it is evident that by human speech, law can be both changed and expounded, in so far as it manifests the interior movement and thought of human reason. Wherefore by actions also, especially if they be repeated, so as to make a custom, law can be changed and expounded; and also something can be established which obtains force of law [*qui consuetudinem efficient, mutari potest lex, et exponi, et etiam aliquid causari quod legis virtutem obtineat*], in so far as by repeated external actions, the inward movement of the will, and concepts of reason are most effectually declared; for when a thing is done again and again, it seems to proceed from a deliberate judgment of reason. Accordingly, custom has the force of law, abolishes law, and is the interpreter of law [*consuetudo et habet vim legis, et legem abolet, et est legum interpretatix*].[75]

Such a description grants a crucial role to custom within a legal system.

One remarkable aspect of this three-fold function attributed to custom is its similarity to the roles that Aquinas assigns to legislated, positive law. He reminds his readers that law proceeds from the reason and will of a lawgiver. In regard to practical matters, reason and will can be expressed by speech, which manifests interior movements and thoughts. By such speech—which today is called "legislation"—law is changed and expounded. However, Aquinas also attributes to custom this power to change and expound the law. He not only says explicitly that custom can change and expound the law, but also adds that custom can establish something that has the force of law. In other words, custom can create law *de novo* in addition to modifying and explaining the law already in place.

Aquinas's rationale for this conclusion is examined at length below, though it must be noted now at least in passing. Custom is able to shape civil law just as legislation shapes it because custom derives from reason and will just as legislation does. A crucial aspect of Aquinas's definition of law is that law be an expression of reason, and custom-that-becomes-law satisfies this requirement. Reason and will are not only expressed by words, but also by repeated actions. In fact, inward will and reason are "most effectually declared [*efficacissime declaratur*]" by these repeated actions, that is, by customs. There is something about repeatedly acting in a certain way that displays what people are thinking even better than words do.

The first legal function of custom is that it may attain the force of law.[76] Aquinas shows little interest in describing detailed legal or political mechanisms for the recognition and implementation of custom as law. Nevertheless, Aquinas provides a few indications of how he sees custom donning legal force as a practical matter. Two sorts of people may develop custom, according to Aquinas. The first is a free people who make their own laws and whose ruler has lawmaking power only to the extent that he represents them. The second sort of people are not free to exercise this supreme lawmaking authority. For the first people, Aquinas specifically points to custom as the means by which they make their own law: "For if they are free, and able to make their own laws, the consent of the whole people expressed by a custom [*consensus totius multitudinis...quem consuetude manifestat*] counts far more in favor of a particular observance, than does the authority of the sovereign...."[77] However, even the second people, though not free in their lawmaking authority, wield significant power for the shaping of society through their development of customs. Aquinas explains that "a prevailing custom obtains force of law, in so far as it is tolerated by those to whom it belongs to make laws for that people." Such toleration implies approval.[78] Therefore, even among a non-free people, social custom has a sort of *a priori* force: valid until the sovereign says otherwise.

Elsewhere in the *Summa Theologiae*, Aquinas offers two somewhat helpful concrete examples of this ability of custom to take the force of law. The first concerns the propriety of lawyers taking fees. Aquinas says that this practice may be permissible, but that particular decisions must be made with consideration for the client, for the matter at hand, for the labor entailed, and for the custom of the country.[79] The second example arises as he explains that the measure of salable commodities is different in different places due to variations in supply. He writes that governors in each locale are to determine the proper measure, taking consideration of the conditions of time and place. But he adds that it is unlawful to disregard the measures established either by public authority or by custom.[80] In both of these examples, custom takes on law-like authority in matters of social relations.

Abolition of law is the second legal function of custom. Again, though Aquinas does not describe institutional mechanisms to illustrate this work of custom, he does provide an interesting explanation of the general process that he envisions. After noting that particular human laws can fail in some circumstances, he writes:

> Wherefore it is possible sometimes to act beside the law; namely, in a case where the law fails; yet the act will not be evil. And when such cases are multiplied, by reason of some change in man, then custom shows that the law is no longer useful: just as it might be declared by the verbal promulgation of a law to the contrary [*manifestatur per consuetudinem quod lex ulterius utilis non est: sicut etiam manifestaretur si lex contraria verbo promulgaretur*].[81]

Presumed in this statement is that different circumstances require different laws, and that human laws need to be adjusted as society develops. One way to know that the social context has changed so as to require new law is through custom. Aquinas has already argued that an individual may act against a law that fails in a particular circumstance. If circumstances arise that cause a law to fail repeatedly, people may act contrary to the law often enough that this contrary behavior becomes customary. In such a case, the very formation of the custom manifests that the law is no longer fitting. In effect, then, custom supercedes and thereby abolishes a formerly valid law. Here again, custom's role in the determination of civil law is described as paralleling that of legislated, positive law. Custom shows that a law is no longer useful, explains Aquinas, just as verbal proclamation of new legislation does.

The third legal function of custom is the interpretation of law. Aquinas says little about how law, once rightly established, is to be interpreted in its application to specific situations. Generally speaking, it seems that Aquinas wishes to minimize the role of interpretation in the judicial process. In the face of a perennial debate in jurisprudence, Aquinas obviously favored a position that maximized legislative clarity and minimized judicial discretion. In considerable detail, he listed reasons why a group of legislators, dealing with problems in the abstract and before they occur, are able to make better decisions than judges, who decide concrete cases as they arise.[82] Likewise, he adopted Isidore of Seville's requirements for positive law, among which was the demand that it be clearly expressed. The purpose of this requirement, he explained, was to prevent any harm that might ensue from the law itself.[83] Nevertheless, Aquinas did not pretend that clearly-worded laws make interpretation of their provisions wholly unnecessary. For example, Aquinas, again delving into a perennial jurisprudential controversy, claims that the lawgivers' motives, as well as their words, should be taken into account when applying law.[84] Since lawgivers cannot anticipate everything, their rules sometimes fail. Yet law is meant for the common good, and there is therefore no justification for applying it to the harm of those whom it governs.[85] One consequence is the need for the dispensing power, that is, the authority to declare a law of no force in a particular circumstance.[86] To make such determinations about the good or harm to be produced by the application of a law demands attention to the exigencies of custom. Those who wish to understand social circumstances and the consequences of particular laws must take the time to reflect carefully upon the customs of society.[87]

A Constitutional Check on the Validity of Law

In addition to the legal functions of custom just discussed, namely, the creation, abolition, and interpretation of law, Aquinas also attributes to custom a quasi-constitutional role within a legal system: law can be considered valid only within the boundaries established by custom. He develops these matters in his consideration of Isidore of Seville's description of positive law, which Aquinas deems authoritative:

> Law shall be virtuous, just, possible to nature, according to the custom of the country [*secundum consuetudinem patriae*], suitable to place, necessary, useful; clearly expressed, lest by its obscurity it lead to misunderstanding; framed for no private benefit, but for the common good.[88]

Of particular concern here is the statement that law shall be according to the custom of the country. Aquinas does not identify custom with law, as if it were the case that there is no distinction between them, but the force of Isidore's claim demands that law at least be consistent with the prevailing custom of society. I call this a "constitutional" idea because of its similarities to the American system of constitutional judicial review. The United States Constitution and state constitutions do not prescribe in detail what laws the American Congress and state legislatures are to make; but they do set boundaries within which legislation must fall if it is to be legally enforceable. Similarly, Aquinas's adoption of Isidore's claim implies that custom, while it need not dictate every detail of civil law, does indeed set boundaries within which all law must tend.

In his defense of Isidore, Aquinas moves through each of the criteria for law and comments upon its appropriateness. He grounds the criterion under consideration here in the social nature of humanity: law "should be according to human customs [*secundum humanam consuetudinem*]; since man cannot live alone in society, paying no heed to others...."[89] Therefore, Aquinas not only defends custom's threefold function of creating, abolishing, and interpreting law by noting that custom is an expression of reason (a key element of the nature of law), but he also defends the idea that law must be according to custom by speaking of custom as an expression of our common, social nature (another key element of the nature of law). This latter idea, like the former, is explored in more depth below.

Aquinas does not make this claim about custom naively, but considers the obvious concern that he links custom and law too tightly. In an objection that he poses to Isidore's criteria, Aquinas presents another claim of Isidore: "written law is condivided with custom [*lex scripta...contra consuetudinem dividitur*]."[90] Rather than carefully analyzing this claim, he simply states, at the conclusion of the *Respondeo* of 1a2ae 97.3, that he has sufficiently answered this objection (and three others). He takes no more space to reply specifically, contrary to his ordinary practice throughout the *Summa Theologiae*. Evidently, Aquinas deemed his original explanation of why law is to be according to custom to say all that is necessary. Because he accepts the distinction between law and custom, Isidore's comment about their distinction is unobjectionable. However, despite their distinction, the importance of custom for understanding human social nature means that law and custom are inextricably linked.

Human Law as Custom

A final aspect of the relationship of law and custom in Aquinas's thought is that he speaks of human law as if it is itself one aspect of the larger phenomenon of social custom. To my knowledge, Aquinas never claims that what is customary is also necessarily law (except to the extent that custom serves as a sort of basic, or constitutional, law, as considered above). But he does speak as though what is human law is also a part of custom. Again, Aquinas does not make law and custom identical. He specifically distinguishes the two at one point in his "Treatise on Law," where the particular mark of distinction seems to be that force lies behind law, but not behind custom.[91] However, while custom is not identical to law, nor is everything that is custom also law, Aquinas does imply that everything that is law is also custom.

The context from which this implication can be drawn is Aquinas's discussion of whether human laws should always be changed when better alternatives arise:

> Human law is rightly changed, in so far as such change is conducive to the common weal. But, to a certain extent, the mere change of law is of itself prejudicial to the common good: because custom avails much for the observance of laws, seeing that what is done contrary to general custom, even in slight matters, is looked upon as grave [*Quia ad observantiam legum plurimum valet consuetudo: intantum quod ea quae contra communem consuetudinem fiunt, etiam si sint leviora de se, graviora videantur*]. Consequently, when a law is changed, the binding power of the law is diminished, in so far as custom is abolished [*inquantum tollitur consuetudo*]. Wherefore human law should never be changed, unless, in some way or other, the common weal be compensated according to the extent of the harm done in this respect.[92]

Despite the temptation on the part of legislators to change the law every time some flaw in a legal provision is identified, Aquinas warns that the presumption ought to be *against* changing the law. The reason is plain: every time the law is changed, harm is caused to the common good, the very thing that law ought to promote. Any new law must be so much better than the old law that the benefits of the new law more than compensate for the harm that is done by the mere fact that the law is changed. Aquinas leaves the impression that this is a difficult burden of proof to bear.[93]

Aquinas's explanation for this presumption against change in law is grounded in the fact that prevailing law *is* custom. A change of law in itself is prejudicial to the common good because "custom avails much for the observance of laws, seeing that what is done contrary to general custom, even in slight matters, is looked upon as grave." To change a law is to act contrary to general custom, and to honor custom is to promote law-keeping. The claim that changing a law constitutes a rupture of general custom is only explicable if the law itself is an element of this general custom that is violated. A similar implication must be drawn from what he states shortly afterwards: "when a law is changed, the binding power of the law is diminished, in so far as custom is abolished." The respect due to law and its authority in society are damaged when law is changed, and this precisely because a change in law constitutes an abolition of custom.

The reason for Aquinas's linking law and custom in this way is easily surmised: since an established law is ordinarily obeyed, the conduct it prescribes becomes a part of the prevailing practice of the community. The way in which Aquinas deals with this issue is remarkable in how it brings the relationship of law and custom full circle. Custom determines law, and law determines custom. On the one hand, custom creates, abolishes, interprets, and sets constitutional boundaries for law. On the other hand, law becomes custom. This reciprocal interaction highlights how vital custom is as an aspect of Aquinas's understanding of law.

The Coherence of Aquinas on Custom

The preceding section sets forth the contours of the legal functions that Aquinas assigns to custom. However, Aquinas also says a number of things that seem rather inconsistent with the important role of custom just observed. He speaks, for example, of the possibility of customs being evil, of law as something written, and of law as the product of will. This section attempts to harmonize these seemingly discordant claims and argues that Aquinas's understanding of custom is not contradicted by these other elements of his thought.

Evil Customs

First, Aquinas's view of the legal functions of custom might strike the reader as shockingly naïve, resting upon an overly-optimistic opinion of the inherent goodness of custom. His confidence in custom appears sharply opposed to our frequent observation of customs that are evil and harmful rather than good and beneficial. While it is true that Aquinas *did* have a high view of the moral worth of custom and of its importance for civil law, it must be noted that he also recognized that customs can be bad as well as good.

Several times in the "Treatise on Law," Aquinas frankly acknowledges that some customs are evil. One example appears in his defense of the idea that the natural law is the same in all people. In a carefully nuanced answer, Aquinas distinguishes between the general principles of the natural law and its more specific conclusions. While the general principles are the same in all people, the truth in regard to specific conclusions is not always the same for everyone nor is equally known by everyone. The truth is not always the same for all people because some things that are morally upright most of the time (for example, that one ought to return good held in trust) are injurious on certain occasions (when goods held in trust are reclaimed in order to fight against one's country). But why is moral rectitude not always equally known to all people even when the truth is the same for them? Aquinas explains:

> In some the reason is perverted by passion, or evil habit [*ex mala consuetudine*], or an evil disposition of nature; thus formerly, theft, although it is expressly contrary to the natural law, was not considered wrong among the Germans, as Julius Caesar relates.[94]

According to Aquinas, therefore, custom can be evil and can even pervert one's use of reason so as to hinder knowledge of the truth. Rather than viewing custom as an infallible moral pedagogue, then, Aquinas recognizes the potential dangers of immoral custom. This passage reinforces the conclusion that Aquinas considers custom to be potent, but also asserts that its potency may not always be directed along a morally acceptable course.

A second example of Aquinas's recognition that custom may be evil occurs in a context substantially similar to the preceding. In the midst of arguing that the natural law cannot be abolished from the human heart, Aquinas distinguishes once again between the general principles of the natural law and their particular applications. He denies that the natural law can be abolished, but applies this only to the general principles. In regard to the particular applications, Aquinas writes:

> The natural law can be blotted out from the human heart, either by evil persuasions...; or by vicious customs and corrupt habits [*pravas consuetudines et habitus corruptos*], as among some men, theft, and even unnatural vices, as the Apostle states (Rom. i), were not esteemed sinful.[95]

Again, he acknowledges not only the reality of wicked customs, but also imputes to them the power of blotting out the natural law from human hearts. Such statements prohibit accusations of an unreflective naivete in Aquinas's exposition of the legal functions of custom.

In light of this, some qualifications must be made to Aquinas's assigning to custom the roles of creating, abolishing, interpreting, and the constitutional bounding of civil law. Whatever authority it enjoys, custom is unquestionably subservient to natural law and divine law. Aquinas writes:

> The natural and Divine laws proceed from the Divine will, as stated above. Wherefore they cannot be changed by a custom [*per consuetudinem*] proceeding from the will of man, but only by Divine authority. Hence it is that no custom [*nulla consuetudo*] can prevail over the Divine or natural laws: for Isidore says...: *Let custom yield to authority: evil customs should be eradicated by law and reason* [*Usus auctoritati cedat: pravum usum lex et ratio vincat*].[96]

As discussed in detail in a subsequent chapter, custom's moral and legal authority derives from its effective concretization of the principles of the natural law. For Aquinas, the natural law must always take priority over custom.

The relationship between evil custom and human law is more complex. According to Aquinas, both custom and law derive their force from the natural law, and both at times fail to reflect the natural law properly. Aquinas's most relevant words on the proper view of human law toward evil custom have already been considered above, though in a different context. He claims that when human law "fails," people may act against it with impunity. If a given human law fails repeatedly, acting against it may become customary. In this circumstance, such a custom both shows that the law is no longer useful and supercedes it as to legal force. However, Aquinas makes exceptions to this process. When the reason for which the law was first established remains valid, the law is still to be enforced and the contrary custom rejected. In other words, customs do not always develop for good reasons and wholesome purposes. Though a custom that develops contrary to an established law ordinarily supercedes that law, under these circumstances the pre-existing law must be retained.[97]

However, the final resolution to this issue is slightly more complicated. For one thing, after clearly stating that a law ought to supercede a contrary custom if the original rationale for the law remains sound, Aquinas immediately qualifies his conclusion. He recalls Isidore's requirement that law ought to be according to the custom of the country. This is such a compelling principle for Aquinas that even when the original rationale for the law still holds, a contrary custom might nevertheless be preferred. It is difficult, he says, to set aside a custom of the whole people.[98] Therefore, an evil custom, or at least one that involves rules of conduct inferior to a well-established law, might still prevail simply because it is a custom. In the end, Aquinas seems intent on leaving room for discretion to those in authority. The general rules about the relationship of custom and law are (generally!) to be followed. But pursuing the common good is preeminent. Observing custom offers excellent guidance for those seeking to discern the common good, but it offers no absolute guarantees.[99] Aquinas gives few absolutes about social organization, a point explored in greater detail below, and few absolutes appear in his discussions of custom. Nevertheless, his strong presumption in favor of observing custom is remarkable, and this presumption is evident even in the passage just discussed.

Law as Written

Another issue that raises questions about the consistency of Aquinas's view of custom is less substantial, but still deserves brief consideration. At one point in the "Treatise on Law," Aquinas speaks of (human) law as something written.[100] The context of this statement indicates its harmony with the legal functions that Aquinas imputes to custom, whose existence does not depend on any writing. In the midst of the discussion, in which Aquinas defends the proposition that law should be promulgated, he ponders a rather obscure objection. This objection states that promulgation is not essential to law, because law's binding force extends even to the future, while promulgation concerns only those who are present. Put in another way, those living in the future are bound by laws that are promulgated only in the present, which indicates that laws need not always be promulgated to be valid.

Aquinas's reply to this objection is simple: "The promulgation that takes place now, extends to future time by reason of the durability of written characters, by which means it is continually promulgated." He then notes a statement from Isidore to the effect that *lex* is derived from *legere*, implying that law is written.[101] Thus, Aquinas, speaking about human law, identifies its *written* character as that which ensures that it is properly promulgated to future generations who will be bound by it.

There is no explicit answer as to how this is harmonized with the fact that Aquinas attributes legal force to custom, but an answer can be surmised. Aquinas asserts that promulgation is necessary for law because law, in order to be properly binding, must be applied to those governed by it. Such application requires that the people receive some sort of notice.[102] But Aquinas does not think, by any means, that such notice always has to be in writing. If it does, then eternal law and natural law are not promulgated, and are therefore not properly called law. Yet Aquinas explicitly defends the promulgated character of both eternal law and natural law. Of the latter he writes: "The natural law is promulgated by the very fact that God instilled it into man's mind so as to be known by him naturally."[103] And of the former he explains: "Promulgation is made by word of mouth or in writing; and in both ways the eternal law is promulgated: because both the Divine Word and the writing of the Book of Life are eternal."[104] Therefore, Aquinas views promulgation as possible in multiple ways. The central element is whether notice has been given.[105] For Aquinas, the very nature of custom, as a practice of the "whole people,"[106] carries with it the assumption of being known by all the members of a society, and thus qualifies as "promulgated." On the other hand, this issue does raise questions about how and whether customary law ought to be enforced against visitors in a community.[107] With the ease and frequency of travel in our own day, this may be a much more acute issue than in Aquinas's, though the increase of commercial activity in the thirteenth century suggests that it was not an irrelevant matter in Aquinas's time either.

Voluntarist Descriptions of Law and Sovereignty

The final, but perhaps most important, point at which the consistency of Aquinas's thought on custom needs to be addressed concerns the matters of legal positivism or voluntarism. By "positivist" or "voluntarist" I refer to the conviction that law is law because it has been willed and decreed as such by someone with authority. A legal system that appeals to the customs of the many members of the community as a primary source of law would seem to have little place for a conception of law that is defined nearly entirely by the will of a sovereign ruler. Therefore, there may be few things that would jeopardize the internal consistency of Aquinas's theology of law more seriously than strains of voluntarism. However, such strains do seem to appear in his writings and thus need to be addressed.

Aquinas's treatise on kingship and government, *De Regno* (also known as *De Regime Principum*), contains some of the assertions that are most difficult to reconcile with his claims about the preeminence of custom.[108] This treatise, which was written for the king of Cyprus, opens with a rousing defense of kingship as the best form of government, a position certainly attractive to his audience. Aquinas begins by explaining that the rule of one king over many people is analogous to the rule of the head over many members of the body.[109] Likewise, he claims that a government is all the more useful the more it keeps the unity of peace. Such unity is best effected by one person, thus making the rule of one more useful than the rule of many. This is in accord with natural things, such as the rule of one God over the universe.[110] Later in this treatise, Aquinas recaps these claims by encouraging the king to be in his kingdom what the soul is in the body and what God is in the world.[111]

This description of the solitary rule of a king over his kingdom may sit uneasily with a high view of custom as a legal authority. Even more puzzling, however, are Aquinas's claims about the king's responsibility to establish (or at least to know how to establish) a kingdom. As noted above, Aquinas analogizes a king's rule over his kingdom to God's rule over the universe, and here he parses the analogy. Two of God's works in relation to the universe are creating it and, subsequently, governing it. Hence, kings are to have a double role over their kingdoms: to establish them initially and to govern them thereafter. Both roles must be learned from God's actions toward the world. Aquinas's claims about establishing a kingdom are especially pertinent. He admits that governing a kingdom is more properly the duty of a king than is establishing it; nevertheless, the latter is essential too. Aquinas even asserts that kings who inherit their kingdoms, and hence never actually have the responsibility to found one initially, still have the duty to learn how a kingdom is properly established. One cannot understand how to govern a city if one is ignorant about its establishment.[112]

Aquinas provides an impressive list of what a king must do in order to found a kingdom properly. First, kings must choose a location in a temperate climate.[113] Next, the precise site must be selected, considering factors such as altitude, the direction of the sun, the nature of the indigenous crops, the quality of the water, and even the complexion and build of the inhabitants (the more ruddy and sturdy they are, the healthier the place is).[114] Other requirements that Aquinas mentions are that the king find a place fertile enough to provide food for the city and a location that will charm the inhabitants by its beauty.[115] All of this seems to offer a substantially different picture of the structuring of society from that offered in the descriptions of custom introduced above. Whereas Aquinas's elevation of custom suggests a society whose character and history is largely shaped from the bottom up (that is, from the mutual interaction of the whole people in daily life), his instructions to a king seeking to found a kingdom suggest a society whose inspiration and plan derive from the top down (that is, from a single monarch animating the community).

Several matters in the "Treatise on Law" also create similar difficulties in harmonizing Aquinas's theology of law. One matter arises from his explanation of why making people good is an effect of law. Aquinas points first to Aristotle's claim that the "intention of every lawgiver is to make good citizens."[116] Then he adds his own comments:

> [A] law is nothing else than a dictate of reason in the ruler by whom his subjects are governed. Now the virtue of any subordinate thing consists in its being well subordinated to that by which it is regulated: thus we see that the virtue of the irascible

> and concupiscible faculties consists in their being obedient to reason: and accordingly *the virtue of every subject consists in his being well subjected to his ruler*, as the Philosopher says (*Polit.* i). But every law aims at being obeyed by those who are subject to it. Consequently it is evident that the proper effect of law is to lead its subjects to their proper virtue.[117]

Aquinas analogizes the relationship of ruler to people to that of reason to irascible and concupiscible faculties. In both cases, the former rules and the latter are ruled. Law is conceived as a *dictate of reason in the ruler* by whom *his subjects are governed*. This idea is similar to the material considered above in *De Regno*, where social organization was envisioned as flowing down from a lone monarch to a people waiting to be commanded. Not only does law emerge here from a dictate of the ruler's reason, but it also has the specific purpose of making the people more virtuous. Rather than the people's character shaping the laws through their customs, Aquinas here seems to advocate a single ruler's judgment shaping the character of the people through his dictates called "law." It is not immediately clear how to reconcile the idea that a people's virtue consists in being well-subjected to their rulers with the conviction that a people's customs may take on legal authority.

Other matters in the "Treatise on Law" also probe Aquinas's attribution of legal functions to custom. One example is his discussion of legislation and ongoing judicial discretion. Aquinas ponders the usefulness of what might be called the rule of law itself: should legislators make laws to govern conduct ahead of time, or should individual judges use their discretion to decide cases one-by-one, as they are presented to them? Though Aquinas stresses the flexibility of general rules of conduct and the importance of prudence, he does not attempt to take responsibility away from legislators and place it solely upon prudent judges. He offers three reasons why legislation is to be preferred to ongoing judicial discretion: first, it is easier to find a few wise people to be legislators than many to be judges; second, it is easier to perceive the right course of action when taking into account many considerations ahead of time than when pronouncing judgment on each particular case as it arises; and third, legislators judge in the abstract, of future events, whereas judges consider present things in which various emotions and sentiments may cloud their reason. Therefore, as few matters as possible should be left to the discretion of judges.[118] One can appreciate Aquinas's challenge on this point, as he weighed the benefits of a well-defined rule of law against the inevitable failure of human laws in particular circumstances. What is perhaps most curious about his resolution of this problem is its failure to utilize his ideas about custom. He considers but two options: legislation or judicial discretion. However, Aquinas's view of custom seems to present a most relevant third option. On the one hand, law formed by custom, as described by Aquinas, has a certain advantage over legislation, in that its formation is neither so abstract nor limited to the judgment of just a few people. On the other hand, customary law also seems to have an advantage over judicial discretion, in that custom is an objective standard that can be known to disputants ahead of time. Law formed by custom would seem to provide Aquinas with the best of both worlds: it preserves the rule of law, with all of its benefits that are lost if everything is left to judges' discretion, and yet it is tied to the concrete and particular in a way in which legislation cannot be. Aquinas does not say anything in this context that directly contradicts his assertions about law and custom, but it is curious that he does not appeal to these ideas at what appears to be an opportune time.

Therefore, the challenge is to reconcile and harmonize Aquinas's teaching about the legal functions of custom with these statements presenting or suggesting a seemingly contrary view of sovereignty and social ordering. One easy answer is simply that Aquinas was inconsistent. However, a comprehensive and systematic thinker like Aquinas deserves the benefit of the doubt, especially considering that many of the passages that are apparently in tension sit practically side-by-side in the "Treatise on Law." In fact, a few considerations do explain how Aquinas could say these different things and yet retain an overall consistent theology of law.

First, despite certain passages that lend themselves to voluntarist or absolutist interpretations, Aquinas makes clear in other places that no ruler has absolute power to frame laws. This applies even to God in his rule of the world, though on a different plane of reality. One example concerns a question that is central to Aquinas's theology of law: is law something pertaining to reason?[119] This question, the first one asked in the "Treatise on Law," is answered with a ringing affirmative. One objection that Aquinas faces in this article comes from an old Roman law legal principle: "Whatsoever pleaseth the sovereign, has the force of law."[120] Aquinas acknowledges "the Jurist" as an authority, and he does not deny the truth of this statement. But he does sharply qualify it. After noting that reason's power of moving comes from the will, he explains:

> But in order that the volition of what is commanded may have the nature of law, it needs to be in accord with some rule of reason. And in this sense is to be understood

> the saying that the will of the sovereign has the force of law; otherwise the sovereign's will would savor of lawlessness rather than of law.[121]

For Aquinas, law is by definition reasonable. Whatever authority a civil ruler might enjoy, it does not and cannot include making unreasonable laws. At this point, it is helpful to recall that custom plays a central role in determining when a "law" is unreasonable and, therefore, not truly law. No difficulty exists in the fact that Aquinas refers law to will, for reason can only act through the exercise of will. But if will is not moved by reason in the establishment of law, there is not really law at all.

Along the same lines, Aquinas explores the limits of ruling authority in asserting that all are subject to the law.[122] In order to clarify his position, he again answers an objection derived from a claim in Roman law: "the sovereign is exempt from the laws."[123] Aquinas grants the exemption in one sense, namely, that sovereigns are not under the *coercive* force of laws. The simple reason is that sovereigns are the ones who exercise coercion, and one cannot exercise coercion on oneself. But Aquinas rejects this claim of exemption from law in another, and very important, sense. The sovereign is morally obligated to follow a law's *directive* force: "Hence, in the judgment of God, the sovereign is not exempt from the law, as to its directive force; but he should fulfil it of his own free-will and not of constraint."[124] As a practical matter, Aquinas recognizes that there may be no human way of curbing a ruler who does not follow the law of the community. But as a moral matter, according to the "judgment of God," as he puts it, sovereigns are obliged to obey the law just as their subjects are.

A second consideration that bolsters this harmonization of the seemingly discordant strains in Aquinas's theology of law builds upon the first: monarchs are not the only ones who may hold the highest authority in society. Aquinas teaches that the civil coercive power and the supreme law-making authority can rest in one of two places. They may be held by a sovereign, a person vested with power over the entire community, or by the people as a whole.[125] Aquinas's occasionally strong statements about the authority of a single ruler over a kingdom must be read in light of this fact. Where the supreme authority rests makes a difference, among other things, for the legal role of custom in a community. When the people have supreme law-making power, custom is, at least, an important mechanism for the exercise of this power. (Though, even where a monarch holds this supreme authority, custom still plays a significant role in the development of a society, as seen above.)[126] The upshot is that Aquinas's statements about the power of a monarch do not refer to the only morally legitimate state of affairs. However, one might object to this last conclusion by pointing out that Aquinas sometimes grounds the sovereign authority of a monarch in nature and in the very character of God.

An answer to this objection emerges from the third and final consideration countering the idea that Aquinas was inconsistent in granting central legal importance to custom. While it is true that Aquinas, at times, grounds his descriptions of the superiority of monarchy in God and nature themselves, the context even of some of Aquinas's boldest statements discourages a literal reading of them. For example, though English translations of the "Treatise on Law" often use the word "sovereign," Aquinas's understanding of this term is not as severe as that often adopted in contemporary discussions, and is certainly not of the character of the concept excoriated by Jacques Maritain.[127] To revisit a passage already considered in some detail, Aquinas distinguishes between societies in which people are free to make their own laws and those in which they are not. In regard to the former, he writes:

> For if they are free, and able to make their own laws, the consent of the whole people expressed by a custom counts far more in favor of a particular observance, than does the authority of the sovereign, who has not the power to frame laws, except as representing the people.[128]

What is most interesting here for the present context is that Aquinas uses the word "sovereign," *princeps*, to describe a ruler who does not hold supreme law-making power, and, indeed, is able to make law only insofar as he represents the people (who are the supreme law-makers). Aquinas uses other words besides *princeps* in the "Treatise on Law" to refer to the civil ruler, such as *gubernator*. The point, however, is that Aquinas's use of a word like *princeps*, often translated "sovereign" and usually applied to a ruler with great authority, does not demonstrate that he has voluntarist or absolutist tendencies. Not only here, but also elsewhere in the "Treatise on Law," it is precisely the *princeps* who is constrained by reason, obliged to obey his own laws, and may even be subordinated to the higher civil authority of the people.[129]

A similar qualification of Aquinas's understanding of sovereignty is found in *De Regno*. As seen above, *De Regno* contains some of Aquinas's strongest statements about the supreme power of a monarch when it grounds supreme monarchical power in nature and compares it even to God's rule of the universe. But other considerations from this work itself clearly hint that such statements are not to be taken absolutely. For example, in the midst of his explanation and defense of monarchy as the best form of government, Aquinas speaks about the right and authority of deposing a tyrannical monarch:

> Furthermore it rather seems, that to proceed against the cruelty of tyrants is an action to be undertaken, not through the private presumption of a few, but by public authority. First of all, if to provide itself with a king belongs to the right of any multitude, it is not unjust that the king set up by that multitude be destroyed or his power restricted, if he tyrannically abuse the royal power. It must not be thought that such a multitude is acting unfaithfully in deposing the tyrant, even though it had previously subjected itself to him in perpetuity; because he himself has deserved that the covenant with his subjects should not be kept, since, in ruling the multitude, he did not act faithfully as the office of a king demands.[130]

Shortly thereafter, he adds: "If, however, it pertains to the right of some higher authority to provide a king for a certain multitude, a remedy against the wickedness of a tyrant is to be looked for from him."[131] One way or another, this most impressive figure of the sole monarch, the analogue of God in his rule over creation, is also subject to removal by the authority of the multitude or by another civil ruler with higher authority. Though Aquinas viewed the figure of the king over society as the reflection of God over the world, this analogy, like all analogies, is imperfect, and a vibrant and authoritative social custom is quite compatible with the always-less-than-absolute authority of a monarch.

In short, Aquinas's various statements, some exalting the place of the sovereign monarch, others exalting the role of a people's customs, must be read together and be mutually qualifying.[132] Aquinas believed that the kingly figure at the head of society served an important function, but he also indicated the need for ongoing input from the rest of society's members as they interact with each other in the concrete tasks of life. Good government and good law take both into account. The distinction that Aquinas makes between despotic supremacy (which is like the absolute authority of a master over a slave) and political/royal supremacy (in which the free are governed but not wholly subject to command) must be remembered.[133] These two strands of Aquinas's thought—the kingly figure and a free people—converge in this passage:

Two points are to be observed concerning the right ordering of rulers in a state or nation. One is that all should take some share in the government: for this form of constitution ensures peace among the people, commends itself to all, and is most enduring, as stated in *Polit.* ii. 6. The other point is to be observed in respect of the kinds of government, or the different ways in which the constitutions are established.... Accordingly, the best form of government is in a state or kingdom, wherein one is given the power to preside over all; while under him are others having governing powers: and yet a government of this kind is shared by all, both because all are eligible to govern, and because the rulers are chosen by all. For this is the best form of polity, being partly kingdom, since there is one at the head of all; partly aristocracy, in so far as a number of people are set in authority; partly democracy, i.e., government by the people, in so far as the rulers can be chosen from the people, and the people have the right to choose their rulers.[134]

Chapter 3

Anthropological Foundations of the Legal Authority of Custom

The previous chapter explored the role of custom in Thomas Aquinas's theology of law. Aquinas granted to custom a central and vital function within the human legal enterprise, describing its power to create, abolish, and interpret law, as well as to form a quasi-constitutional boundary outside of which no new law may be established. The next two chapters investigate the ideas underlying and grounding Aquinas's views on the relationship of custom and law. Chapter Three has a specifically anthropological focus. Though Aquinas believed that the whole of creation reflects God's perfections, he pointed to human beings alone in the corporeal universe as the image of God. Human beings enjoy this unique status particularly because they possess reason, and because of reason, also freedom and sociality. For Aquinas, the creation of human law is an expression of the dignity that accompanies divine image-bearing, and thus is to be accomplished by a rational, free, and social process. This chapter concludes that establishing human law through the development of custom is a means of law-creation that accounts for the reasonable, free, social nature of each human being in a preeminent manner, according to Aquinas. In the face of the reforms of powerful monarchs who wished to centralize law-making power largely in their own hands, Aquinas defended the right of the people as a whole to create their own law, and he thereby upheld their dignity as bearers of the image of God.

The Concept of Reason in Aquinas's Thought

Reason is a central theme in Aquinas's thought, a thread that weaves its way through many aspects of his theology and philosophy. Aquinas understands human reason to be the power of the intellect. In particular, it refers to the human person's intellect advancing from one thing to another, by means of inquiry and discovery, so as to come to *understanding* of intelligible truth—"reasoning" is the movement toward the truth and "understanding" is the rest in that truth.[1] For Aquinas, the human soul is called "intellectual" because of its participation in intellectual power, which he identifies as God himself.[2] Aquinas also speaks of different aspects of intellect and reason, without assigning them to distinct powers of the soul. Of particular importance for present purposes, Aquinas distinguishes the speculative and practical intellects. The speculative intellect is theoretical in character, directing the things that it apprehends to consideration of truth; the practical intellect, on the other hand, directs what it apprehends to action.[3] It is the practical intellect that is of special relevance to Aquinas's moral thought.

Nowhere, perhaps, is the concept of reason so central as in Aquinas's treatment of the moral life. To say that reason defines what is good and evil for human conduct is no overstatement.[4] Reason enables people to act for an end, which is itself the essence of moral action.[5] The goodness or evil of both the human will and human action is determined by the order of reason,[6] and living according to the activity of reason is deemed the proper role of the human being.[7] In light of this, Aquinas treats the all-important moral concept of virtue in terms of its correspondence with rationality. Various statements from his writings illustrate this. He identifies the nature of virtue as the task of directing a person to good according to the rule of reason, and portrays justice as the chief of the moral virtues precisely because it is most akin to reason.[8] Furthermore, Aquinas identifies the "mean" of moral virtue as the rational mean[9] and equates the life of reason and the life of virtue.[10] Conversely, sin is considered in terms of its variance with the order of reason. Aquinas explains that sin lacks conformity with the *proximate* rule of action, which is human reason, and with the *first* rule, which is the Eternal Law, or God's reason.[11]

Both aspects of the preceding sentence are important. Aquinas, indeed, teaches that the whole of human moral conduct is defined by its relationship to human reason. But Aquinas also traces human reason back to its origin, which is the divine reason possessed by God alone, and sometimes spoken of by Aquinas in terms of "Eternal Law." The power and dignity of human reason does not lie merely, or perhaps even at all, in its own remarkable abilities. It possesses its remarkable abilities only because it participates or shares, in a finite way, in the infinite and ultimately incomprehensible intellect of God. The very structure of the *Summa Theologiae*, as interpreted by Aquinas himself, reflects this. In the prologue to the *Prima Secundae*, Aquinas explains to his readers that the just-completed *Prima Pars* speaks about God the exemplar and about things coming forth from him. Further, he says that the forthcoming *Prima Secundae* is about man, God's image, as he (man) is the principle of his own actions, having free will and control over his actions. That Aquinas is willing to treat the moral life (the general topic of the *Prima Secundae*) in terms of human beings as the principle of their own actions is surely significant. This displays a strong sense of human autonomy that itself magnifies the inherent dignity of the human rational nature. Yet, in the final analysis, Aquinas's thought cannot be understood without reading the *Prima Secundae* in light of the *Prima Pars*. There would be no human rational autonomy apart from human rational participation in God's intellect.[12] I now turn, therefore, to consider the foundation of the dignity of human rational nature—God and his reason—and how human beings have come to participate in the divine mind.

The Theme of Participation

The idea that human reason "participates" in divine reason is one that is commonly attributed to the neo-Platonic strains in Aquinas's thought.[13] Though Aquinas's teacher, Albert the Great, is primarily known to history as a pioneer in the rediscovery of Aristotelian thought in Western Europe, Albert also instilled in his students a knowledge of and appreciation for the important streams of theological reflection manifesting a neo-Platonic orientation. Among the representative thinkers were Augustine and Pseudo-Dionysius. While studying in Cologne, Aquinas heard Albert's lectures on Pseudo-Dionysius's *De Divinis Nominibus*, and may even have heard Albert lecture through the entire Dionysian corpus over the stretch of his first stay in Paris and subsequent work in Cologne.[14]

Many aspects of Aquinas's early and mature writing display this neo-Platonic influence. One example is his utilization of the *exitus/reditus* scheme in his first major work, a commentary on the *Sentences* of Peter

Lombard composed during his second period in Paris,[15] and later in his *Summa Theologiae*.[16] According to this scheme, notes Aersten, "things are to be considered according to their pattern of their proceeding from God as their source...and insofar as they return to him as their end."[17] In addition, though Aquinas's moral thought was so significantly shaped by Aristotle, Hall identifies his foundational moral idea of synderesis, the infallible moral sonar possessed by all people, as a neo-Platonic element within his largely Aristotelian epistemology.[18] Paul E. Sigmund also writes that Aquinas's thought reflects something of the neo-Platonic view of the hierarchical character of the universe and of society, an idea briefly explored in the last chapter.[19]

The theme of "participation" in Aquinas's metaphysics was surely also inspired by the neo-Platonic heritage, and it proved a significant idea in his writings.[20] A recent commentator has reminded readers of Aquinas of the great difficulty in establishing a satisfactory definition or description of the idea of participation. Nevertheless, he explains Aquinas's position: "when we find a quality or perfection possessed by a given subject in only partial rather than in total fashion, such a subject is said to participate in that perfection."[21] For the present study, this very brief description should at least justify an exploration of the idea of divine reason for the purpose of shedding light on the character and importance of human reason, which "participates" in it.

The Divine Intellect

Aquinas teaches that God is perfect. All the perfections that human beings know or understand from their experience find their source and fullness in the divine nature. Aquinas says, for example, that God's goodness contains the goodness of all things.[22] Whatever finite perfections there may be in the created world exist in an infinite sense in God. However, Aquinas is quick to qualify this teaching with the classical Christian doctrine of the divine simplicity: God is one, and is not comprised of parts. God possesses a plenitude of being, but only in a unity.[23] In human speech about God, God is accorded diverse names and perfections, yet Aquinas warns that this speech is to be interpreted in a way consistent with his simplicity.[24] The infinite divine perfection (singular) is reflected in God's creation, but, as considered below, finite creatures can only reflect the divine perfection in partial and diverse ways. In their finite thinking about God, human beings cannot help but speak of divine perfections in the plural, even while recognizing that in reality these perfections are one and simple.

One of God's perfections, so to speak, is his knowledge. God's knowledge extends to all things,[25] and is in fact the cause of all things.[26] One of the distinguishing characteristics of God's knowledge, as infinite, is that it knows all things at once. There is great contrast with human reason at this point. Human knowledge, always partial as it is, is learned in parts, progressively over time. Similarly, human beings come to many particular conclusions only by thinking through things, that is, by beginning with premises and reasoning logically toward conclusions. Aquinas characterizes such knowledge as habitual, discursive, and ratiocinative. God's knowledge, on the other hand, is "intellectual." God knows nothing simply by habit or by a process of reasoning, but knows everything eternally and all at once.[27] This characteristic of the infinite divine mind cannot be replicated in the finite human mind. Though the divine reason is vast and incomprehensible, God does not will that it should exist by itself or for itself only. Aquinas teaches that God created a world in which his reason is both reflected and shared.

The Order of the Universe and Divine Providence

As a Christian theologian, Aquinas believed that God created the world out of nothing, contrary to Aristotle's view that the world is eternal.[28] God's creative activity extends to all matters, even to the distinction, multitude, and inequality of things that are seen in the universe.[29] Two features that particularly characterize the world that God has made are its order and its perfection.[30] For Aquinas, order permeates the entire universe and holds it together. The order of the universe is teleological, that is, it is an order towards an end, which is none other than God and his goodness.[31] The universe consists of many different parts, and none is ordered to God independently or autonomously, but only together with every other part. There is order among the parts and the whole is sound in its parts, or integrated, so that a true continuity exists between the different levels of being. According to Aquinas, this order among the parts of the universe is the greatest created good,[32] and the form that God chiefly intends in created things is the good of the order of the entire universe.[33] The variety of created beings is one of the things in which the order of the universe consists, though in this variety is unity, for it is precisely the order of the universe that proves the unity of the world. The world is called one, says Aquinas, by the unity of order.[34]

Closely related to this idea of the order of the universe is its perfection. Oliva Blanchette claims that the notion of perfection is a pervasive theme in Aquinas's thought, in many respects tying all of the realms of his thought together. The perfection of the universe is the "synthesizing element" in Aquinas's conception of the universe, such that "the totality that characterizes what is meant by 'universe' is in many respects another terms for 'perfection.'"[35] Aquinas identifies a number of matters required for the perfection of the universe. Among them are all grades of things, of goodness, and of being, as well as diversity and plurality.[36]

God brought the universe into being through creation and continues to sustain and govern it by providence. Aquinas defines providence as the type of the order of things towards their end, preexisting in the divine mind.[37] All things are subject to divine providence, not merely in a general way, but even in their individual beings.[38] Nevertheless, and this important point is considered in more detail below, providence utilizes intermediaries in the execution of its order and imposes no necessity upon things so as to destroy the contingency proper to them.[39] Aquinas refutes the philosophical opinion that all things happen by chance and argues instead that all things without exception are subject to God's government.[40]

Central to the idea of divine providence, and to the ideas of the order and perfection of the universe governed by providence, is the grandeur of the divine mind. As James Oscar Brown discusses, the concepts of providence and the Eternal Law, which is the Divine Reason, are co-extensive in Aquinas's thought.[41] For Aquinas, the whole of nature is like an artifact in the divine artistic mind that unfolds into being.[42] He describes the distinction and order of the parts of the universe as rooted in the intellect of the first cause, who is God.[43] The comprehensive order of providence is explained by God's perfect foresight.[44] Since the providential order of all things is traced back to the divine mind, Aquinas states that everything disposed by divine providence follows a rational plan.[45]

The mind that governs the universe by providence, therefore, is the perfectly rational mind of God. Thus, the world that is governed unfolds according to a perfect, orderly, rational plan. Such a world reflects the very attributes of the one who created it and sustains it, including, especially, rationality. In fact, Aquinas asserts that rational creatures are necessary for the perfection of the universe.[46] This calls for consideration of how creatures, and particularly rational creatures, reflect the character of God, even by participating in his being and perfections.

Creaturely Reflection of God

In the entire created universe there is likeness to God. According to Aquinas, ideas exist in the divine mind that are forms to which the created world is the likeness. These ideas are identical to God's essence.[47] Thus, the likeness borne in the world extends even to the very being, perfections, and attributes of God. Though the universe has the distinct privilege of participating in this perfection of the divine being, nothing in the world, nor even the world taken as a whole, can reflect God's perfection fully. Hence, there is need for a diversity of creaturely perfections. What no one part of creation can reflect completely, a vast multiplicity of creatures, at every level of being and possessing all sorts of different functions, can reflect much more fully.[48] In other words, the infinite one is communicated more fully to the finite many than to the finite one.

Aquinas describes this creaturely participation in the divine perfections and being in a variety of ways and in a variety of places in his writings. At times he explains it in terms of causation: the form of an effect is found in its cause, in some similar yet not identical way, and therefore creatures are like God as to their perfections, even as they remain also unlike him.[49] Aquinas also speaks of creaturely participation in the divine being and perfections as occurring as creatures carry out the order of divine providence.[50] Furthermore, by the mere possession of certain attributes this participation takes place. For instance, creatures participate in the divine perfection insofar as they have goodness,[51] or, what is practically equivalent, insofar as they have being itself.[52] From this arises the idea of the "analogy of being" in Aquinas's thought. As Heinrich A. Rommen defines it: "All created being, though of an altogether different kind from the divine Being, is an image of the latter and a participation in it—from merely inanimate being of inorganic nature up to man, whom God created after His own image."[53]

This idea of image is an important one to Aquinas. In numerous places in his writings, he uses the ideas of image and likeness to describe the relationship of every created thing to God.[54] For Aquinas, however, the human being especially is the image and likeness of God, as pronounced in Genesis 1. Indeed, the image of God remains imperfect in human beings, and is enjoyed by angels to an even greater degree than by them, yet only rational creatures, properly speaking, are made in God's image.[55] Hence, in the visible world, human beings alone are God's image in the precise sense of the term. The fact that rationality characterizes the highest creaturely enjoyment of God's being and perfections must now be explored.

Human Reason and the Image of God

N. Max Wildiers explains that the predominant medieval cosmology held to a perfect, hierarchical world order that was at heart anthropocentric.[56] For Aquinas, the anthropocentric character of the universe was, without doubt, explained by the rationality of the human being. The attribute of reason is not one human attribute among many, but that which constitutes humanity's highest dignity and most clearly distinguishes it from the rest of creation. Though every aspect of creation both imitates and shows forth the divine goodness, this is especially true of rational creatures.[57] As discussed above, the image of God is found primarily and properly only in rational nature, that is, in angels and in humanity.[58] In fact, the image of God is more perfect in angels than in human beings precisely because angelic intellectual nature is more perfect.[59] Aquinas explains the distinction between the reflection of God in rational and non-rational creatures—and even between the rational and non-rational parts of the rational creature itself—in this way:

> While in all creatures there is some kind of likeness to God, in the rational creature alone we find a likeness of *image*...; whereas in other creatures we find a likeness by way of a *trace*. Now the intellect or mind is that whereby the rational creature excels other creatures; wherefore this image of God is not found even in the rational creature except in the mind; while in the other parts, which the rational creature may happen to possess, we find the likeness of a *trace*....[60]

Aquinas uses various language to describe the consequences of rational, intellectual creatures possessing this unique image of God. Intellectual creatures, he says, exist after the mode of God's own nature.[61] Likewise, God's act of intellect is the measure and cause of every other intellect[62] and the human intellectual power is a participated likeness of God's intellect.[63] Westerman describes this phenomenon in terms of a "divine style," similar to an artist's style, that intellectual creatures alone can recognize existing in themselves and hence can imitate.[64] Aquinas says that the intellectual soul, though one in operation, is manifold in power and in operations because of its perfection, which requires various dispositions in the parts of the body.[65] He goes so far as to say that only rational creatures know God as he is in himself.[66]

According to Blanchette, Aquinas believes that the purpose of the whole natural order is to bring a certain number of rational individuals to completion, and that the rational, human creature is the summit of the order of generation.[67] Human reason is connected with the perfection of the universe. The intelligent soul is able to have the perfection of all things in itself, on which basis it is superior to everything else in nature, and the presence of intelligent creatures in the world is necessary for the universe's perfection.[68] Human beings contribute to the perfection of the universe by engaging in activities common to all rational creatures, such as understanding the truth, desiring the good, and doing justice, so that all lower beings attain their perfection as parts of the universe only through their being ordered to the human being.[69] In fact, Blanchette explains, Aquinas views the rational human soul as a sort of hinge that links the material and immaterial parts of the universe.[70] Though human beings belong among the corruptible beings in the lowest part of the universe, they also rise above the heavens because of their soul, which, through its rationality, has power to communicate directly with the good of the universe.[71]

Clearly, the rationality of human beings sets them apart from the rest of the visible creation and causes them, to a special degree, to reflect God's image and to participate in his being and perfections. The majesty of the divine reason, which spills over into the rational plan of the whole universe, finds its particular expression in rational creatures. The infinite greatness of the divine reason is mirrored in a finite manner in the human reason and, as explained below, key aspects of this power and dignity of the human reason are free will and free action.

Human Freedom

The concept of human freedom is of great importance to Aquinas's thought in general, particularly in regard to the present discussion. Human freedom is a noble thing that is displayed in communicating goodness in a way similar to God's communication of goodness.[72] Aquinas begins his so-called "Treatise on Human Acts," in the *Prima Secundae* of the *Summa Theologiae* with a lengthy question (of eight articles) on the voluntary character of human action. In the first article, he reasons that human acts must be voluntary, since people know the end of their work and move themselves.[73] This means that the will does not act out of necessity, from force of any extrinsic principle, whether of violence or compulsion.[74] Human beings are true actors, authors of their own operations in the face of multiple alternatives.[75]

To Aquinas, the existence of human freedom follows necessarily from human rationality. He explains: "Man has free-will: otherwise counsels, exhortations, commands, prohibitions, rewards and punishments would be in vain." Moreover,

> man acts from judgment, because by his apprehensive power he judges that something should be avoided or sought. But because this judgment, in the case of some particular act, is not from a natural instinct, but from some act of comparison in the reason, therefore he acts from free judgment and retains the power of being inclined to various things. For reason in contingent matters may follow opposite courses, as we see in dialectic syllogisms and rhetorical arguments. Now particular operations are contingent, and therefore in such matters the judgment of reason may follow opposite courses, and is not determinate to one. And forasmuch as man is rational is it necessary that man have a free-will.[76]

As something so closely wedded to reason, human freedom constitutes an essential aspect of the image of God. Citing John of Damascus, Aquinas writes in the Prologue to the *Prima Secundae* that human beings are in God's image "in so far as the image implies *an intelligent being endowed with free-will and self-movement*." Appropriately, then, Aquinas accords the status of "proper" human action only to those acts that proceed from a deliberate will.[77] Furthermore, he states that the mere act of possessing good is proper only to rational creatures, since they are those who have power to dispose of their good through free will.[78]

The existence of rational creatures with free-will even has cosmic implications. Many of the cosmological themes in Aquinas's thought that were treated above emerge as relevant for the present discussion. For example, Aquinas explains that the order of the universe, which constitutes the chief good of the creation, would be destroyed if there were not creatures that have power to act and to order.[79] Similarly, the diversity of the universe, upon which the perfection and beauty of the universe depend, requires that humans be the cause of other things.[80] Not only the beauty of the order in creation, but also the immensity of God's goodness, is evident precisely in God's creating some things to be the cause of others.[81]

Such a defense of the existence of human freedom is difficult to harmonize with Aquinas's equally strong exposition of the all-comprehensive character of divine providence as ordering and governing even the most minute, particular things. This is, of course, an issue of perennial challenge for Christian theology, but Aquinas displays little fear of accounting for both doctrines. God is indeed the cause of operation of all operating things,[82] but creatures have an active role in the production of natural effects.[83] Divine providence, though all-comprehensive, does not exclude contingency, free-will, fortune, or chance, nor does it impose necessity.[84] Nor are these things excluded by God's will or by predestination.[85] Rather, Aquinas is adamant that providence is accomplished by secondary causation.[86] In fact, he claims that God's government is the *better* as it makes created things the cause of other things.[87]

Human free action is important, therefore, at every level of existence that has been examined thus far in this chapter. Not only is it an essential feature of the rational human being created in God's image, but it is also necessary for the order and perfection of the universe, and even for the manifestation of the perfect goodness of God. For Aquinas, human beings are free as well as rational at the center of their nature.[88] And, as free, rational beings, their action imitates both the created order and the divine action itself.

Free, Rational Action in Imitation of the Created Order and of the Divine Action

Thus far, this chapter has traced a certain line of development that is found in the thought of Thomas Aquinas. The line begins in the very nature of God, who possesses the full measure of all perfection, including that of mind or intellect. God is supremely rational. The line continues into the world that God made. The universe is one of perfect order and beauty, reflecting the rational plan of the one who created it and containing all sorts of finite perfections. Then the line extends to one particular part of the universe, its summit and greatest part, the human being. Human beings are the greatest part of the visible creation because they are rational, and thus they participate in the highest degree in the divine perfections. As rational creatures they are also free creatures, authors of their own actions in ways mirroring the infinitely free action of God. The creator and the creation exist in a beautiful structure and unity in which the concept of reason and its correlative concept of freedom are central.

A few effects of this structure may be observed as rational, free beings are considered a sort of *microcosmos*, a microcosm or world-in-miniature. First, Aquinas perceives in the structure of human life a miniature picture of the world at large. He observes the multiple orders of society and compares them to the multiple orders that interrelate in nature. Even above the visible world, Aquinas sees the angelic hierarchy as analogous to the order and government of human hierarchies.[89] This order among groups of people is also reflected in the soul of the individual rational being. Aquinas explains that the interrelation of intellect, sense, and bodily power is in a mutual order that reflects in turn the mutual order among people and that of the universe as a whole.[90] Significantly, Aquinas does not see this reflection of the order of the universe in the order among and within human beings as a morally-neutral phenomenon. The rationality of the human order implies an order of morality, and hence the moral life of humanity is also to reflect the larger order of the universe. Aquinas expects benevolent results when people voluntarily adhere to the divine order as natural things adhere to their own due order.[91] Likewise, he compares the way in which the actions of the wise proceed in an orderly way toward an end to the way in which the workings of nature proceed toward an end in their own manner.[92] In Aquinas's mind, virtue itself imitates the order of nature.[93]

Even more significant is the number of ways in which Aquinas perceives human free, rational action as imitating God's own action. For Aquinas, nothing is more essential to a free, rational being than the ability to order and govern oneself and other things, and on numerous occasions he points to the human acts of ordering and governing as modeled after God's ordering and governing the universe.[94] It is reason that knows mutual relations and proportions for the sake of ordering things.[95] Hence, Aquinas also sees rational legal activities as imitating the divine. The establishing, interpreting, and dispensing from law is human action in reflection of God's, as is the rewarding and punishing of people by those entrusted with the imposition of law.[96] In addition, human virtues are mirrors of the divine, as well as imitators of the order of nature, as seen above. Aquinas states that God has virtues—for example, prudence and justice[97]—and these divine virtues are exemplars of human virtues.[98] In fact, for Aquinas, the ultimate end of creaturely action is the divine likeness.[99]

The Social Nature of Human Reason and Morality

Aristotle taught that the human being is by nature a social animal,[100] a judgment followed by Aquinas in no uncertain terms.[101] This idea entails that individual human beings need all sorts of things that one person alone cannot provide, including even the necessities of life.[102] However, at a much deeper level than the acquisition of material possessions, the social nature of humanity entails something important about the rational, moral life of human beings. For Aquinas, human beings reason and execute moral actions precisely as social creatures.

This truth comes to bear in each individual's reasoning. No single person can reason about everything, since there is far more to reason about than there is rational power in any given person. If persons were isolated and solitary, grave problems would result. But humanity's social nature makes the narrow, particular focus of each individual's reason not only compatible with the continuation of life, but even conducive to it. Rather than each person vainly attempting to be competent at everything, each may attempt to achieve mastery in a given area:

> But it is not possible for one man to arrive at a knowledge of all these things by his own individual reason. It is, therefore, necessary for man to live in a group so that each one may assist his fellows, and different men may be occupied in seeking by their reason to make different discoveries, one, for example, in medicine, one in this and another in that.[103]

Therefore, the social nature of the human person fosters the kind of specialization and focused persistence that is necessary for the rational cultural progress of the human race.

However, the human being's social nature does more than simply provide a context within which each individual's reason can pursue its own particular task. Every reasoning person also needs the assistance of others in making concrete decisions. Aquinas addresses this matter in his discussion of "counsel," an inquiry of the human mind that precedes the choice of a course of action. He notes that taking counsel involves several people rather than one alone, and then writes these illuminating words on the social nature of human *moral* reasoning:

> Now we must take note that in contingent particular cases, in order that anything be known for certain, it is necessary to take several conditions or circumstances into consideration, which it is not easy for one to consider, but are considered by several with greater certainty, since what one takes note of, escapes the notice of another; whereas in necessary and universal things, our view is brought to bear on matters much more absolute and simple, so that one man by himself may be sufficient to consider these things.[104]

The relation between the social and the rational natures of the human being in Aquinas's thought is manifested in at least one other way: humanity's social nature sets the parameters for what the rational nature must take as its concerns. Their social nature determines that people must always hold the community of which they are a part as a concern concurrent with their concern about themselves. Each person is inevitably a part of society, and thus to be concerned about oneself is to be concerned necessarily about the particular society to which one belongs. The life of reason is a life lived in community, and thus to be fully reasonable creatures is to reason about the life shared with others. For Aquinas, as Porter explains, the natural law

> is not just a source of private morality, but the basis of a rational public order. To put it another way, the natural law is to the community what humanity is to a human being. That is, it represents the rational character of the community, according to our best understanding of it.... To violate the rational character of the community, as expressed in the prohibitions of natural law, is therefore to undermine it. Moreover, because the good of the individual consists in part in her harmonious relationship with a well-ordered community (and therefore with her actual community, insofar as it is well-ordered), her violation of the ideal norms of such a community, that is, the norms of the natural law, will be harmful to her as well, by putting her at variance with her community as it should be.[105]

In addition, human sociality not only demands that moral reason take concern for the community of which one is a part, but also dictates which part of the community ought to be of special concern. People cannot love all others equally, but naturally—and rightly—love more those who are more closely related to them either by birth or by way of life.[106]

Rational and free moral lives are also social.[107] Nothing could be more highly valued or bring to human beings greater dignity than these facts: we are created to participate in God's perfections and to imitate his very action through our moral existence as rational, free, and social creatures. Notably, it is for all rational creatures, and not just some, to bear the great privilege of showing forth the divine. Even slaves and subjects exercise reason, and thus must share, in some way, in the tasks of ruling and governing.[108] The implication of Thomas Aquinas's thought on these matters is clear: human moral tasks must take account of humanity's rational, free, social nature. Anything less would be to make people less than human and strip them of their great dignity as those bearing the image of God.

The Rational, Free, Social Nature of Law

For Thomas Aquinas, the development of human law is a preeminently moral task. This being the case, Aquinas's theology of law reflects the same characteristics that mark his broader moral thought. Thus far, this chapter has examined the importance of the rational, free, and social aspects of moral thinking for Aquinas. This next section explores how these ideas of rationality, freedom, and sociality are worked out in Aquinas's theology of law, and particularly in his thought on human law. This can be done rather briefly, since many of these ideas were introduced in the previous chapter. Here, however, it remains to consider them specifically, in order to set the stage for the final section of this chapter, in which the role of custom in the development of the rational, free, social nature of law is set forth.

The Reasonable Nature of Law

As seen in the previous chapter, Aquinas includes the concept of reason in his short definition of law: "an ordinance of reason for the common good, made by him who has care of the community, and promulgated."[109] Of the various aspects of this definition, there is a certain primacy to the statement about law's reasonableness. In the first article of the first question in his "Treatise on Law" in the *Summa Theologiae*, Aquinas introduces the reader to his theology of law by inquiring whether "law is something pertaining to reason." The *Respondeo* reads:

> Law is a rule and measure of acts, whereby man is induced to act or is restrained from acting: for *lex* (law) is derived from *ligare* (to bind), because it binds one to act. Now the rule and measure of human acts is the reason, which is the first principle of human acts, as is evident from what has been stated above (Q.1, A.1 *ad* 3); since it belongs to the reason to direct to the end, which is the first principle in all matters of action, according to the Philosopher (*Phys.* ii). Now that which is the principle in any genus, is the rule and measure of that genus: for instance, unity in

> the genus of numbers, and the first movement in the genus of movements. Consequently it follows that law is something pertaining to reason.[110]

Aquinas's logic is transparent: law is a coercive sort of rule or measure of human acts; reason is *the* rule and measure of human acts; and thus law must be something pertaining to reason. Law is nothing if not reasonable. Reason is the great, overarching rule of human action, while law is a sub-rule of human action, with the purpose of inducing or restraining one to act. For Aquinas, law abides in a world where reason must be all-pervasive. Aquinas speaks of law in similar ways in the *Summa Contra Gentiles*: law is a rational plan (in a governing capacity) and a rule of operation.[111]

Aquinas understands each kind of law in terms of its rationality. Of the Eternal Law, Aquinas writes: "Now it is evident, granted that the world is ruled by Divine Providence, as was stated in the First Part (Q. 22, AA. 1, 2), that the whole community of the universe is governed by Divine Reason. Wherefore the very Idea of the government of things in God the Ruler of the universe, has the nature of a law."[112] The Divine Reason, then, is the law-like governing of the entire universe, and this Divine Reason is the font of all other types of law. For example, Aquinas writes of the natural law:

> Now among all others, the rational creature is subject to Divine providence in the most excellent way, in so far as it partakes of a share of providence, by being provident for itself and for others. Wherefore it has a share of the Eternal Reason, whereby it has a natural inclination to its proper act and end: and this participation of the eternal law in the rational creature is called the natural law.[113]

Only rational beings can be concerned with the natural law, and the natural law itself is wholly defined in terms of participation in the divine reason. At another level removed from the eternal law, but really no less rooted in it, is human law. Aquinas writes: "it is from the precepts of the natural law, as from general and indemonstrable principles, that the human reason needs to proceed to the more particular determination of certain matters. These particular determinations, devised by human reason, are called human laws...."[114] The eternal law is about God's reason, the natural law is about human reason participating in God's reason, and human law is about human reason proceeding to more particular conclusions. Law, more than anything else for Aquinas, concerns reason.

Human Freedom and the Law

As discussed earlier in the chapter, Aquinas believed that the rational nature of human beings also implies the voluntary nature of their actions: to be rational is to be free, necessarily. This truth applies in the realm of law as well. In light of the rational nature of law explored above, Aquinas also attributes freedom to human beings in exercising their rational task of establishing and implementing human law. The structure of Aquinas's theology of law, that of human law in some sense derived from natural law, which in turn is derived from the eternal law, might seem to present a great constraint upon the freedom of human legal activity. However, from the opposite perspective, God grants remarkable freedom to humanity in the task of human law. In the non-Mosaic era, virtually the entire range of civil law is the creation of human beings. The previous discussion of human free action remarked that God displays his own greatness by creating creatures to be the cause of other things in the world. And to be a cause of other things is a source of dignity for the created cause.

The formation of human law is a grand example of God's utilization of secondary causation. Aquinas defends the necessity of human law for the human community,[115] yet places the task of creating and executing such a law entirely in human hands. The natural law's participation in eternal law as to general principles is not in itself sufficient for this task, for human reason proceeds from the general principles down to particulars.[116] The conclusions of such proceedings of human reason are not all equally evident. Some conclusions are obvious; Aquinas calls these "demonstrated conclusions...drawn from the principles."[117] A second method of proceeding from the general principles involves conclusions that are not so obvious: "the second mode is likened to that whereby, in the arts, general forms are particularized as to details: thus the craftsman needs to determine the general form of a house to some particular shape." The first sort, the conclusions, have the force of the natural law itself, but Aquinas explains that these second sort "have no other force than that of human law."[118] Therefore, human beings not only have the privilege of forming human law themselves, but also are given wide areas to work in which solutions to problems are neither obvious nor inevitable, but demand the wise, creative, artistic discretion of a craftsman in order to put the world of human law into proper shape. To Aquinas, God has bestowed freedom on rational beings in the task of human law.

One aspect of this freedom envisioned by Aquinas is an ongoing role for the people as a whole in the law-making process. Though he lived most of his life under strong monarchs, as discussed in the previous chapter, Aquinas places the people on par with the prince as potential sources of supreme legal authority. He writes:

> Now to order anything to the common good, belongs either to the whole people, or to someone who is the viceregent of the whole people. And therefore the making of a law belongs either to the whole people or to a public personage who has care of the whole people.[119]

For Aquinas, therefore, human freedom in the establishment of human law was such as could extend broadly to every member of the community.

The Social Nature of Law

Another matter of great concern to Aquinas is that law be understood as something pertaining to a community rather than to an individual. After defending the reasonable nature of law at the opening of the "Treatise on Law," Aquinas immediately proceeds to speak of law as something directed to the common good. Aquinas's explanation of this attribute of law is lengthier than that of any of the other attributes of law elsewhere in Question 90 of the *Prima Secundae*. He begins by developing the idea that happiness is the last end of human life, and that law must therefore concern the achievement of happiness. Then he states: "Moreover, since every part is ordained to the whole, as imperfect to perfect; and since one man is a part of the perfect community, the law must needs regard properly the relationship to universal happiness." This regard for universal happiness, or the common good, is meant to apply to every law, even those with seemingly non-social purposes. Aquinas adds: "Consequently, since the law is chiefly ordained to the common good, any other precept in regard to some individual work, must needs be devoid of the nature of a law, save in so far as it regards the common good. Therefore every law is ordained to the common good."[120] This social nature of law applies even to the eternal law, the divine reason, which is said to concern the "whole community of the universe."[121] Likewise, Aquinas describes the natural law in social terms when he states that "the rational creature is subject to Divine providence in the most excellent way, in so far as it partakes of a share of providence, by being provident both for itself and for others."[122]

The social character of human law, which is of particular concern for the present study, is observed in numerous places. Aquinas claims that the purpose of human law is chiefly to direct people in relation to each other (whereas Divine Law is chiefly to direct people to God).[123] A nation, according to Aquinas, is a body of people united by consent to the law and the community of utility. From this, he derives the need for mutual relations between people to be ordered by just law.[124] This social nature of human law means that human law is not to concern itself with every matter. It is not to forbid everything that is contrary to virtue, but only that which is destructive of human intercourse.[125] Likewise, because the end of human law is the temporal tranquility of the state, it ought to direct actions only in regard to what disturbs the peaceful condition of the community.[126] Furthermore, Aquinas appeals to the social nature of law to explain why the general rule that human law should be silent on matters of divine worship does not apply when such matters concern the common good or common morals.[127]

This social concern of human law shapes Aquinas's understanding of justice. Aristotle taught that laws are drawn up for the good of the community, and thus that the just is whatever creates or conserves happiness for the political association.[128] Aquinas follows Aristotle, particularly in regard to legal justice, or justice in general, which directs immediately to the common good.[129] For Aquinas, the common life of human beings pertains to justice, whose proper function is to direct the human community or, similarly, to direct people in relation to others.[130] Further, Aquinas explains that operations of justice are ordered to the preservation of peace among people, and that ordered concord is preserved precisely when each gives to others their due, which is justice itself.[131]

Law, then, and especially human law, has a distinctively social nature and function. Thus far, this chapter has argued that morality is fundamentally about reason, and that human reason, grounded in the divine reason, is free and social in its activity. Law, as one very important aspect of morality, is itself thoroughly reasonable as well as free and social in its development. It remains now to examine these themes in relation to custom.

The Rational, Free, Social Nature of Custom

The rational, free, and social character of morality and law is essential to their nature. The question arises as to how this applies to custom, which the last chapter presented as a central element in the establishment and implementation of human law. I argue here that Aquinas speaks of the development of custom as a thoroughly reasonable, free, and social activity, and that this fact provides much of the explanation for why Aquinas ascribes custom such an important role in his theology of law.

Custom and Reason

For Aquinas, the development of custom is a process of human reason. He explains the reason for this in Question 97, Article 3 of the *Prima Secundae*. After noting that law must proceed from the reason and will of the lawgiver, Aquinas claims that there are two ways by which this reason and will are made known: "Now just as human reason and will, in practical matters, may be made manifest by speech, so may they be made known by deeds: since seemingly a man chooses as good that which he carries into execution."[132] For Aquinas, these two methods of manifesting reason, speech and deeds, correspond to two methods of law-making: legislation and the development of custom. He writes:

> But it is evident that by human speech, law can be both changed and expounded, in so far as it manifests the interior movement and thought of human reason. Wherefore by actions also, especially if they be repeated, so as to make a custom, law can be changed and expounded; and also something can be established which obtains force of law, in so far as by repeated external actions, the inward movement of the will, and concepts of reason are most effectually declared; for when a thing is done again and again, it seems to proceed from a deliberate judgment of reason.

Aquinas then concludes this article by stating: "Accordingly, custom has the force of law, abolishes law, and is the interpreter of law."[133] Custom, therefore, is explicitly a product of reason. Indeed, the development of custom is a way by which the concepts of reason may be "most effectually declared."

This last claim is particularly interesting. The repetition of external actions, by which customs are established, is not simply one way by which the thoughts of human reason may be made known. Rather, Aquinas writes that the repeating of external actions is the *most effectual* way by which human reason is declared. The implication is that the formation of law is even more reasonable when accomplished through custom than when accomplished through speech, that is, by legislation. This is a remarkable claim to twenty-first century minds programmed to think of custom as quaint and perhaps even sub-rational, and to think of legislation as the necessary means of rationally organizing the vast machine of the modern state. Yet, for Aquinas, developing the law of social organization through custom was the more highly rational mode of operation.

Unfortunately, Aquinas does not explain explicitly why he reaches this conclusion. Perhaps he thinks that repeating an external action is a more serious act than simply stating a matter once. Words can be spoken carelessly and thoughtlessly, but repeated actions bring one quickly into the realm of the real world and its consequences. Therefore, perhaps Aquinas thinks that there is little to check an unreasonable word from being spoken, while there is much to check an unreasonable action from being repeated. Or, to put it another way, perhaps Aquinas thinks that repeated actions, because of their very nature as external and numerous, are much more likely to express what people are really thinking than is a spoken word, since careless words are so frequent. Whatever the explanation, Aquinas's conclusion stands as critically important for the present argument. Aquinas believed that custom was a rational—even the most highly rational—means of the legal ordering of society. Because of this character, custom was to serve as an effective and legitimate means of the establishment and implementation of human law.

Custom and Human Freedom

As seen above, human rationality implies human freedom for Aquinas. Likewise, in Aquinas's scheme, the development of human law is one of the great exercises of human freedom. God has left the vast range of rules necessary for the ordering of society in human hands, to be reasoned toward and discovered by humanity's own action. Precisely along these lines the development of custom appears as a manifestation of this freedom that God has left to the responsibility of human beings. For Aquinas, law is a part of the custom of a society.[134] This implies, however, that custom is much broader than law. It orders areas of life that law does not touch. The truth of this conclusion is seen in the fact that the minutest details of life for the individual, family, business, school, or neighborhood are governed and ordered by customs. The fact that so many customs represent only one reasonable way of doing things among many possibilities deepens the sense that this is a way for human beings to create their worlds in ways not predetermined, but according to how they see fit.

Aquinas specifically associates the thriving of custom with societies in which the people enjoy maximal political and legal freedom. As seen above, one of the ways in which human freedom is displayed in the task of human law is by the people as a whole exercising the chief law-making authority in society.[135] Later in the "Treatise on Law," Aquinas speaks about this power of the people as an exercise of their freedom and he describes the importance of custom when the people enjoy such liberty:

> The people among whom a custom is introduced may be of two conditions. For if they are free [*Si enim sit libera multitudo*], and able to make their own laws, the consent of the whole people expressed by a custom counts far more in favor of a particular observance, than does the authority of the sovereign, who has not the power to frame laws, except as representing the people.[136]

Aquinas goes on to say that the customs of a non-free people may also have legal authority, but this only insofar as the sovereign tolerates them. Therefore, it is clear that the development of custom at its most comprehensive, that is, in regard to the governing not of small parts of the community, but of the community itself in a law-like manner, is especially associated with the freedom of a people. For Aquinas, the ability of the people to order the community themselves rather than to do so primarily through a governing representative is an expression of human social freedom *par excellence*. And the instrument for exercising this freedom is none other than the development of customs. This exercise of freedom through custom is more than just one option among many. It is ultimately the ideal. As Aquinas says, "all should take some share in the government: for this form of constitution ensures peace among the people, commends itself to all, and is most enduring...."[137]

Custom and Human Social Nature

Aquinas's description of human beings as social animals was examined above. As observed, Aquinas follows Aristotle in treating the rational, free human person as a social being in all of its moral action. Consequently, Aquinas speaks of law as something concerning the multitude rather than the isolated individual. Law and justice are not concerned about the entire range of problems of morality, but only about those problems that concern the common life that people live with each other. Aquinas also treats the legal authority of custom as an issue pertaining to humanity's social character. In certain senses, the social nature of custom is overt. It takes groups of people to develop customs generally, and specifically it takes the community at large to develop a custom that calls forth the "consent of the whole people," as Aquinas puts it.[138]

However, Aquinas also speaks explicitly about the relationship of custom and human social nature. The relevant passage appears in his explanation of Isidore's description of what constitutes law. One of Isidore's criteria is that law must be according to the custom of the country. Aquinas defends this requirement by appealing to humanity's social nature. Aquinas's words at this point have been quoted above in full; the relevant section reads: "and [law] should be according to human customs; since man cannot live alone in society, paying no heed to others."[139] Aquinas arrives at this claim by fairly intricate reasoning. He interprets Isidore's list of requirements for positive law as an elaboration of three general criteria: "that it foster religion, inasmuch as it is proportionate to the Divine law; that it be helpful to discipline [*quod disciplinae conveniat*], inasmuch as it is proportionate to the natural law; and that it further the common weal, inasmuch as it is proportionate to the utility of mankind."[140] For Aquinas, the requirement that law be according to custom is a specification of the second of these criteria, helpfulness to discipline. Next, Aquinas breaks down into three more components the idea that law should be helpful to discipline: "human discipline depends first on the order of reason… – secondly, it depends on the ability of the agent… – thirdly, it depends on certain circumstances…."[141] The second of these is broken down even further. The ability of the agent demands two things: "discipline should be adapted to each one according to his ability [*secundum suam possibilitam*]…; and should be according to human customs [*secundum humanam consuetudinem*]…." The logic of Aquinas's scheme reads something like this: among other things, positive law must be proportionate to natural law; to be proportionate to natural law, law must be, among other things, helpful to discipline; to be helpful to discipline, law must be, among other things, according to the ability of the agent; to be according to the ability of the agent, law must be, among other things, according to the customs of the country. Aquinas grounds this final, sub-sub-sub-requirement in the social nature of humanity.

Though Aquinas's breakdown of the "quality of positive law" is rather difficult to interpret, his logic with respect to custom seems clear. If positive law is somehow to be derived from the natural law, then it must promote social discipline. Social discipline can only be effectively maintained if the law demands actions that people are capable of doing, for if it asks the impossible it will not be done. This elementary point shows the need for law to be according to custom: to demand that someone act against custom is to demand withdrawal from participation in social life, and this is impossible. Aquinas explains: "man cannot live alone in society, paying no heed to others." Human beings are social animals by nature, and to act against custom is to act a-socially. Therefore, adherence to custom, in the legal arena, is a necessary way to account for that essential social character of human nature.

Conclusion

This chapter has explored why Aquinas attributes important legal functions to custom. It has followed one particular line of explanation, namely, that the development of custom expresses the rational, free, social nature of the human moral creature in its law-making task. For Aquinas, as a general matter, making law through custom is to act in an even more reasonable way than making law through legislation. Likewise, for the people as a whole to make law through the development of custom is ultimately the work only of a people with the freedom to be themselves the chief law-making authority in society. Finally, to keep all of society's laws within the bounds of custom is a necessary expression of the fact that we live together as social creatures. Rationality, freedom, and sociality, three great characteristics of moral life in general and legal life in particular, are expressed in the development of custom.

This is a significant part of the explanation of why Aquinas set such store on custom in the moral outworking of the human legal enterprise. To put it simply, for a people to order society through their development of custom is to express their nature as image-bearers of God and participants in the divine perfections. The development of custom as a legal authority is an assertion of human dignity before God. Though a monarch at the head of society is a proper and even necessary part of a well-ordered society, to leave the structuring of society entirely in the monarch's hand is to strip the rest of society, composed of rational, free, social beings, of an element of their full humanity. To be human is to be rational, free, and social. To be human is to have some share in that great task of rational, human freedom, that of ordering the community in its communal life. To be only ordered passively is for the sub-human creature. To order actively is to show forth the divine glory and goodness by imitating God himself.

The beginning of Chapter Two described the political and legal reforms instituted by Fredrick II and Louis IX, powerful emperors under whose authority Aquinas lived much of his life. Both rulers were reformers, unafraid to seize authority from local custom when it interfered with the more efficient operation of their realms. Some contemporary historians are tempted to see such figures as men born too soon, precursors of a better and advanced age in which the primitive is set aside and the sophisticated introduced.[142] To defend custom in the face of the reforming genius of such larger-than-life men may seem quaint and reactionary. Yet Aquinas was such a defender of custom. To dismiss him as simply a reactionary conservative is hardly an appropriate verdict to render toward one who sat on the cutting edge of the reintroduction of Aristotle to the Western intellectual world. The explanation for his view of custom is much more profound. Part of the explanation, as unfolded in this chapter, is that Aquinas saw the protection of the rights of custom as the protection of the human dignity of those created to imitate, in a social way, God's rational, free work of ordering and governing. Another aspect of the explanation for Aquinas's view of custom is the subject of the next chapter.

Chapter 4

Ethical Foundations of the Legal Authority of Custom

Aquinas's views on the legal authority of custom are grounded in his anthropology, as seen in the last chapter. For Aquinas, respect for the rational, free, and social nature of humanity compels a view of law that incorporates the rational, free, and social character of the formation of custom. This chapter continues the investigation of the moral and theological context of Aquinas's thought on the relationship of custom and law. Of significance here is his interest in Aristotle and his Aristotelian conviction that ethics is an inexact science. For Aquinas, following Aristotle, the great dignity of humanity that derives from its rational nature does not nullify the important limits of human reason. Unable to grasp all of the truth all at once, human reason must search, learn, and approximate in its quest to understand the moral path. Human beings must be satisfied with a partial, incomplete grasp of practical truth. In his discussions of law and custom, Aquinas applies his view of ethics as an inexact science, and the rationale behind the legal authority that he attributes to custom is often rooted in a concern to account for the limitations of moral reasoning. Therefore, this chapter first explores the limitations of human reason and the consequences for ethics. Then, it describes how Aquinas applies this in his theology of law and how custom plays an important role in the development of human law precisely because of law's inability to encompass all of the truth at once.

The Limitations of Human Reason

Though Aquinas believed that rationality is the greatest source of human dignity, to emphasize only the power and glory of human rationality misrepresents his thought. Aquinas also recognizes significant limitations of human reason's ability to comprehend the truth, especially practical truth concerning moral conduct. He is cognizant of the human propensity to act irrationally and of the inevitability that even well-functioning human reason fails to grasp the truth as a whole.

Aquinas calls ignorance of the intellect one of the unavoidable evils of the present life.[1] This characterizes human knowledge of high and lofty matters, such as knowledge of God and the divine nature.[2] Ignorance of the intellect also applies to human knowledge more generally. For example, the very weakness and failure of our memories means that we sometimes become certain of things that are in fact untrue.[3] Aquinas analyzes the limitations of human reason historically. Even before the Fall into sin, sinless humanity possessed no perfect knowledge, but had to learn gradually, through discovery or instruction.[4] After the Fall, the limitations of reason were exacerbated. In the time between the Fall and the giving of the old law to Israel, human beings were left to the devices of their own reason in order to learn by experience that reason is deficient.[5] The divine law was introduced, explains Aquinas, in order to assist reason both as to its inherent insufficiencies and as to the many errors to which it is subject.[6] The feebleness of human intellect also means that people require help from angels to attain perfect knowledge.[7] Reason is limited especially in regard to knowledge of God and must render service to faith, the greater attribute.[8] To understand better these limitations of human reason, it is helpful to consider the threefold quality of human understanding that Aquinas identifies: multiplicity, mutability, and defectibility.[9]

The Finiteness of Human Reason

The human intellect's "multiplicity" is grounded in its finitude. Though the splendor of human reason is its reflection of the divine reason, as seen in the previous chapter, the wide discontinuity between human and divine reason must be recognized alongside the continuity. While God's reason is vast and infinite, able to grasp all of the truth at once, human reason is finite, able to comprehend the truth only gradually and incompletely. Because of its finite nature, human rationality reflects the necessary qualities of multiplicity and diversity. The human soul itself requires various operations and powers in order to attain its goodness.[10] Unlike the divine intellect, which knows all things at once, the human intellect knows through composition and division,[11] and knows God through the diverse perfections of creatures.[12] The name of God, which is in fact undivided, is known by the human intellect divided, that is, as God's *names*.[13] Aquinas emphasizes that the natural light of human understanding is a finite power that reaches only a certain fixed point and manifests only certain general principles. However, there is distinction of various principles within human knowledge.[14] The intellect is less prone to err on first principles, and more prone to err on the concrete conclusions drawn from them.[15] This important point deserves further attention below.

Aquinas explains that a peculiar characteristic of reason is to grasp truth gradually, so that a human person can be perfected in knowledge only little by little.[16] Along the same lines, Aquinas asserts that we gain our understanding of the singular and the individual prior to gaining knowledge of universals.[17] This plays out in the various processes of human reason. For example, in order to function properly as a rational power, prudence must obtain its knowledge of the future by a process of comparison of things that have occurred in the past.[18] Likewise, the rational power of "counsel" proceeds only as experience reduces the infinite number of singular phenomena to a finite number that occur as a general rule. Consequently, counsel always retains a degree of uncertainty.[19] These inevitable limitations of human reason entail an inability to think out all the particulars in the order of providence ahead of time.[20] Reason only gradually bridges the enormous gaps in human knowledge.

A World of Infinite Particulars and Contingencies

The second quality of human understanding identified by Aquinas is "mutability." The limitations in human reason that result from its finitude are closely related to, and greatly enhanced by, the fact that human reason operates upon a world of practically infinite particulars. This is an especially important issue for Aquinas in the realm of human moral action. Aquinas writes that there is an infinite variety of matters of action,[21] as well as of the evils that human action may produce.[22] Finite minds see many circumstances that arise by luck or by chance, though in fact this is true only in regard to inferior causes and not in regard to the higher cause.[23] In other words, human intellect cannot tie together all the occurrences in the world and understand their harmonious purpose, though in fact such a purpose exists.

In analyzing the response of human moral conduct to this complex world of infinite possibilities, Aquinas identifies three grades of moral precepts. First, very general principles are evident and certain to the reason, such as the command to love God. Second, some precepts are more detailed, yet easily grasped, such as the commands of the Decalogue. Finally, yet more detailed precepts are evident only to the wise. The bulk of the Old Testament laws exemplify this last category. The more detailed one gets—and detail is necessary in the realm of concrete human action—the less evident and certain the moral answers become.[24]

In light of this, Aquinas teaches that human knowledge often fails in regard to contingent singular matters like human acts.[25] Their contingent nature produces great uncertainty in moral reasoning, which is precisely why reason must take counsel before making decisions.[26] Aquinas emphasizes the difference between speculative and practical reason. Reason is not obscured in the abstract, as to universal natural law principles, but it is obscured as to particular actions.[27] Quite simply, human reason cannot fully grasp singular and contingent things.[28] Instead, moral reasoning proceeds only by pretending, as it were, that the infinite number of singulars is really a finite number that experience sees occurring as a general rule.[29]

Human Sin and Divine Grace

The third quality of human understanding is "defectibility." Aquinas clearly asserts that the limitations of human reason and the corresponding inexactness of ethics would be present even in a sinless world, though finitude does not necessitate sin. Nevertheless, Aquinas also teaches that the fall into sin exacerbates the limitations of human reason. Though his thought undoubtedly reflects a more optimistic anthropology than that of other prominent Christian theologians like Augustine, Martin Luther, and John Calvin, Aquinas had a genuine sense of human sinfulness, perhaps more comprehensive than that of the mainstream of medieval theology.[30] Aquinas defined sin as any thought, word, or desire contrary to the eternal law, or, more specifically, as something lacking conformity with both the proximate rule of action (human reason) and with the first rule (the eternal law).[31] This last distinction corresponds to the different perspectives of the philosopher and theologian: the philosopher considers sin as it is contrary to reason, the theologian as it is an offence against God.[32] Aquinas carefully explains that human sinfulness does not make people irrational. In fact, those who are irrational are incapable of sin, since sin is defined in terms of reason.[33] Aquinas defends the ability of sinful creatures to do particular good in their corrupted nature, though he affirms that they can do nothing perfectly.[34] All sorts of things conspire to hinder our use of reason and lead us into sin, such as pleasure, pain, anger, passion in general, the lower powers of the human person, and even the devil.[35]

All of these factors highlight the need for grace in addition to the natural powers of reason.[36] Aquinas holds that human beings stand in need of grace apart from sin, due to their inherent finite nature.[37] But human sinfulness magnifies the need for grace. Aquinas speaks of the necessity of grace in terms of sin's darkening of the intellect and reason.[38] Reason is not a fully sufficient guide for human life, because the lapse of reason into many errors calls forth the need for faith.[39]

The Ethical Consequences of Reason's Limitations

These limitations of human reason have distinctly ethical consequences. As seen in the previous chapter, Aquinas holds together inseparably the rational and the moral natures of the human being: to act morally is to act rationally. Inevitably, Aquinas's descriptions of finite reason's inability to grasp everything at once shape his exposition of the moral life and, more specifically, ground his view of ethics as an inexact science, a perspective that drew inspiration from Aristotle.

Aquinas and Aristotle

The discussion that follows depends significantly upon seeing Aquinas as an "Aristotelian," a label that is not uncontroversial. This calls for a brief respite from the present argument in order to consider the relationship of Aquinas to Aristotle. Aquinas lived in a time of great controversy in the European intellectual world over the use of Aristotle. Some of Aristotle's works had been known to previous generations of scholars, but the thirteenth-century reception and Latin translation of the Aristotelian corpus provided a substantially new way of looking at the world.[40]

Aquinas's exposure to these new philosophical winds came early in his education. He probably learned some Aristotelian philosophy from the pioneering figure, Peter of Ireland, during his studies at the University of Naples.[41] When Aquinas moved from Naples to Paris, he found a turbulent theological world, and teaching Aristotle was central among the controversies.[42] Surely the most important Aristotelian influence on Aquinas was his mentor, Albert the Great, whom he first met in Paris. Though Albert taught the standard Platonic works, as discussed above, his teaching of Aristotle drew him into special prominence and placed him at the center of the disputes in Europe on the issue of Aristotle.[43] Weisheipl concludes that despite some minor disagreements, the basic Aristotelian sympathies of Albert and Aquinas put the thought of the two men in great harmony.[44] Aquinas's love of Aristotle began early: his commentary on the *Sentences* quoted Aristotle more than twice as many times as the next most popular author (Augustine).[45] Aquinas also commented extensively on Aristotle's writings—a remarkable fact, given that such work was never an official part of his academic duties.[46]

The question of the extent, or even the very existence, of Aquinas's "Aristotelianism," has been hotly debated. Commentators point to many issues for which Aquinas is dependent upon Aristotle, including matters relevant for the present study such as his philosophy of nature and general view of the cosmos, his conception of natural and human law, his understanding of virtue, and his view of government as the rule over free people able to direct themselves.[47] However, other scholars have challenged standard conceptions of Aquinas's Aristotelianism.[48] Some have identified intellectual influences that shaped Aquinas's thought in its various aspects more thoroughly than did the influence of Aristotle,[49] and others consider Aquinas's use of Aristotle to consist mainly in a borrowing of technical language and of basic, common ideas—in short, as an instrument in the construction of his own Christian philosophy.[50] Significant differences between Aquinas and Aristotle on some important philosophical matters have also been noted.[51]

The present study cannot resolve these contentious and complicated matters. References to Aquinas as an "Aristotelian" here are not meant in any sense to question the fact that he was first of all a Christian theologian, steeped in the Bible and the history of the church's theological reflection.[52] Nevertheless, his view of ethics as an inexact science, which is fundamental to understanding the issues in this chapter, displays a considerable debt to Aristotle that deserves acknowledgment before proceeding.

Ethics as Inexact and Indeterminate Science

The preceding discussion of the limitations of reason noted that human knowledge often fails, especially in regard to contingent singulars like human acts.[53] For Aquinas, general matters are relatively easy to understand—precisely because they are general. When matters become more concrete, they demand more specific and pointed answers. But the more one descends into details, the more difficult it becomes to provide firm, definite, and universal descriptions of what one is dealing with.

Similarly, near the opening of his *Nicomachean Ethics*, Aristotle warns students of ethics and justice that they must be satisfied with rough outlines of the truth and broad conclusions, due to the inherent nature of the subject matter.[54] Moral decisions cannot be mapped out ahead of time, but must be made as they arise, just as medical decisions are made by physicians as they encounter problems of health.[55] Aquinas comments that the data of human behavior is not reducible to uniformity, for one cannot predicate universally of what is contingent.[56] The uniqueness of each moral situation raises acute difficulties for anyone seeking to postulate universally applicable rules beyond the most general principles. Aquinas, as Aristotle before him, considers this simply a fact that students of ethics must face, though he does treat it as something of a tragedy.[57] It does not destroy, but rather defines, the present life. Many of Aquinas's commentators recognize the centrality of this issue for understanding various aspects of his moral thought.[58] The fact that human reason does not grasp moral truth completely and immediately, but inexactly and contingently, shapes the moral theology of Aquinas in countless, critical ways.

Morality and Utility

One of the consequences of the finiteness of human reason and the corresponding inexactness of ethics is the important function of utility in Aquinas's moral thought. Since people cannot understand concrete moral truth immediately, discerning the *utilitas* of courses of action becomes a critical part of moral reasoning. The importance of utility in Aquinas's ethics emerges from the teleological nature of his ethics in general, which is not first of all rule-centered, but end-centered. The moral life is about attaining certain goals, and right and wrong is largely determined by whether particular actions are conducive to attaining the proper ends. In adopting this perspective, Aquinas closely follows Aristotle, who began his *Nicomachean Ethics* by explaining that the object of every activity is the attainment of some good, and that the good is that at which all things aim.[59] Likewise, Aquinas claims that people always act for an end and that the end is the principle in human operations.[60] He states that deeds are judged worthy of blame or praise according to the moral quality of their ends.[61] This is the context in which utility plays such an important role. For example, Aquinas writes:

> Good directed to the end is said to be useful [*utile*]; and this implies some kind of relation.... Now, in the genus *relation* a thing is denominated not only according to that which is inherent in the thing, but also according to that which is extrinsic to it.... Accordingly, since the goodness of acts consists in their utility [*utiles*] to the end, nothing hinders their being called good or bad according to their proportion to extrinsic things that are adjacent to them.[62]

Aquinas makes a distinction between the useful and the virtuous. The former is a means for tending toward something else, while the latter is tended to for its own sake. Yet the idea of utility is helpful, and even necessary, for determining what is virtuous. In the "Treatise on Law," Aquinas defends the claim that all acts of virtue are prescribed by the natural law,[63] thereby suggesting that there is something immutable about the virtues. However, in the same section, Aquinas identifies two ways to speak about virtuous acts: "first, under the aspect of virtuous; secondly, as such and such acts considered in their proper species." Looking at these acts from the first perspective, Aquinas asserts without hesitation that all virtuous acts belong to the natural law. He explains that everything to which a person is inclined by nature belongs to the natural law, and people are inclined by nature to act according to reason. Therefore, since acting according to virtue is equivalent to acting reasonably, virtuous acts are prescribed by the natural law. In short, the natural law says, in general, "be virtuous" (= "be reasonable").[64]

However, when thinking about specific acts of virtue, Aquinas considers them according to their "proper species." Here, Aquinas admits that not all specific virtuous acts are laid out in the natural law, "for many things are done virtuously, to which nature does not incline at first; but which, through the inquiry of reason, have been found by men to be conducive to well-living [*quasi utilia ad bene vivendum*]."[65] Some virtuous acts are virtuous not by necessity of nature, everywhere and at every time, but instead because particular circumstances suggest a certain course of conduct. As the quotation immediately above indicates, the idea of utility, or usefulness, is presented as the central test for determining whether such acts truly are virtuous. Reason, as it considers the circumstances, determines which specific acts are *utilia*—useful or conducive—for living well. The end of living well is central, and the acts that reason determines to be *utilia* for achieving this goal are accorded the title "virtuous." Aquinas compactly summarizes this view: "Moral duty is twofold: because reason dictates that something must be done, either as being so necessary that without it the order of virtue would be destroyed; or as being useful [*utile*] for the better maintaining of the order of virtue."[66] Human utility of every kind is ordered to happiness, the last end of each person.[67]

Morality, Habits, and Virtues

Another limitation of moral reasoning that must be accounted for in Aquinas's thought is that it never operates in a vacuum. Moral reasoning is done by a reasoner, a human person with a nature and with all sorts of distinctive characteristics. Hence, reason can never operate independently of the sort of person who utilizes it. Aquinas's moral thought recognizes that people's characters are defined in large part by their habits and personal customs, and by their virtues and vices, which themselves are habits.

Aquinas speaks often of the significance of habits and personal customs (the latter, of course, are distinct from social customs, which are the particular focus of this book). Though they are similar, custom, which does not engage all of the powers of one's mind, is weaker than habit.[68] Habits engage the whole person—body, soul, intellect, and will[69]—and are defined as dispositions by which one is disposed either well or ill.[70] They are ordered to acts.[71] Aquinas explains that people possess some habits that are partly from nature,[72] but he emphasizes that habits are chiefly formed by performing appropriate actions repeatedly.[73] Conversely, habits are diminished by acting in the wrong way or by ceasing altogether to perform the necessary acts.[74]

Customs, and especially habits, shape people's characters in ways that are almost, though ultimately not, indelible. Aquinas states that both customs exercised in childhood and habit take on the force of nature.[75] Elsewhere, he explains that custom becomes a *second* nature that produces inclinations similar to natural inclinations.[76] This allows people with the appropriate customs to recall things quickly to mind.[77] Habits, being even stronger than customs, are so difficult to change precisely because they become, practically speaking, part of one's nature.[78] It is interesting to note that Aristotle, though he defended human free agency, also stated that dispositions are voluntary only as to their beginnings, for they become involuntary once the corresponding habits are developed.[79]

For Aquinas, habits may dispose a person to either good or evil, and habit that disposes people in distinctly good directions is virtue.[80] As habits, the virtues exist in people as if they are part of their very nature, and they produce inclinations similar to natural ones.[81] In summary, Aquinas held that one must have virtue in order to act well.

Prudence

One of the "cardinal" virtues, and one to which Aquinas devotes particular attention, is prudence. Aquinas calls prudence a necessary virtue that perfects the reason,[82] whose subject is the rational power in its essence.[83] Before him, Aristotle asserted that all the other virtues work in collaboration with prudence.[84] A number of recent works on Aquinas's ethics have emphasized the importance of prudence in his moral thought.[85] One of the commentators, Daniel Westburg, calls for a full-orbed understanding of Aquinas's prudence. He states that prudence itself is "right practical reason," and not something that is just brought to bear in particular circumstances. According to Westburg, the essence of prudence is found in its effective linking of universal principles and particular situations, and not in mere knowledge of one or the other.[86]

A study of Aquinas's writings supports such claims and justifies the recent interest in a recovery of Aquinas's view of prudence, even if some of the proponents of this recovery have been too radical in de-emphasizing law in the interest of emphasizing prudence.[87] Aquinas states his understanding of prudence in various ways. For instance, he writes that prudence is right reason, or knowledge in regard to things to be done, or knowledge in regard to problems of action.[88] More concretely, Aquinas says that prudence applies universal principles to particular conclusions of practical matters. In doing so, it regulates the means to the end, but does not itself appoint the end.[89] Prudence particularly comes to bear when an end is in view that might be achieved in a variety of ways.[90] Prudence is, quite simply, the work of deliberating well.[91]

The development and exercise of prudence requires a number of actions and qualities on the part of a person, which in turn reveal additional aspects of the inexact nature of ethics for Aquinas. One example derives from the fact that prudence is about contingent, singular things,[92] yet can never take account of all relevant contingent, singular things. Prudence therefore must identify, through experience, a finite number of singulars that occur as a general rule, and then base its judgments on these.[93] Prudence also requires docility, or teachability. Again, since matters of action are of infinite variety, no one by one's own effort is able to consider them quickly or sufficiently, and hence one must learn from other people.[94] Aquinas also associates the qualities of *euboulia* and *gnome* with prudence. *Gnome*, discrimination in judgment in regard to matters not covered by common rules of action, and *euboulia*, the taking of good counsel, manifest the need for prudence to be exercised both with flexibility and with the help of others.[95]

Other qualities required of a prudent person are memory and foresight. Aquinas explains that prudence requires foresight in regard to future contingents, with a view to how they will help or hinder things to be done in the present. At the same time, one only understands how to anticipate the future by remembering the past and how things worked out.[96] Finally, a prudent person must exercise caution. Aquinas elevates caution both because of the mixture of good and evil that one finds in contingent matters of action and because of the great variety of such matters. The limitations of moral reasoning are evident here too. The potential evils in matters of action are infinite, and caution can be directed only toward those that occur more frequently.[97]

Prudence, as right reason, is present in all rational creatures. Aquinas associates the exercise of prudence particularly with the tasks of ruling and governing. Thus, he concludes that everyone who is rational has some share of ruling, and so is proportionally competent to have prudence.[98] Both the universal and the relative aspects of the last sentence are important. Everyone, from monarch to slave, ought to exercise prudence. Yet, each does so in different ways. Different sorts of prudence are required for different objects of attention, such as domestic prudence in regard to the home, political prudence in regard to the state, and regnative prudence, fit for one who rules a city or kingdom.[99] However, even political prudence is exercised by servants, in a certain manner, insofar as they direct themselves to obey their superiors through free will.[100]

Attention to Circumstances

According to Aquinas, one of the facts of the moral life that necessitates prudence—and defines its work—is the need of rational creatures for insight into circumstances. Aquinas teaches repeatedly that understanding abstract matters of morality is not enough. Instead, the prudent person must take cognizance both of universal principles of reason and of the singular matters about which action is concerned.[101] Aquinas writes that prudence needs "circumspection," the comparison of the means to an end with the circumstances. The reason for this is that singular matters of action involve many combinations of circumstances, and certain circumstances can make something good *per se* unsuitable to attaining the desired end.[102] For similar reasons, Aristotle said that political prudence must consider what is best under the circumstances.[103]

Aquinas again follows Aristotle when he identifies the many circumstances that may affect the quality of moral action: who, what, where, by what aids, why, how, when, and about what.[104] Aquinas lists three specific reasons why a theologian must consider the circumstances of human acts, one of which is that "the theologian considers human acts according as they are found to be good or evil, better or worse: and this diversity depends on circumstances…."[105] Later, he explains that while some matters of action are easily understood from the general principles of natural law, other matters require that circumstances be considered.[106] This displays an inherent flexibility in Aquinas's natural law that is often overlooked, yet has been increasingly recognized in contemporary scholarship.[107] Such flexibility in moral reasoning arising out of the various turns of circumstances is a central aspect of Aquinas's broader Aristotelian conviction that ethics is an inexact science.

He specifically identifies the mutability of circumstances as a reason why we cannot fully know what is for our good.[108]

Aquinas speaks in various ways of the effect of circumstances on the many aspects of the moral life. He asserts in several places that circumstances are one factor that determines an action's goodness or evil.[109] Likewise, circumstances shape the essence of virtue, which consists in hitting the appropriate mean between extremes, for the identity of the mean itself is partly determined by circumstances.[110] In addition, Aquinas makes circumstances an important factor in his consideration of sin. He writes that sin can be caused by a defect in some circumstance, and that the gravity of a sin can be aggravated by circumstances.[111] At every turn, therefore, moral reasoning is drawn away from the abstract and universal and toward the concrete and indefinite by the need to consider the circumstances attending each action.

Instruction from Others

One of the most important ways in which the virtue of prudence is acquired is receiving instruction from other people. As noted above, prudence requires the trait of docility, or teachability, especially toward the elderly. Aquinas explains that no one can consider matters of action in a quick or sufficient manner, since there are an infinite variety of them.[112] Hence, each person must rely upon the knowledge and skill of others for training. As Cristina Traina notes, this means learning not only from individual teachers, but also from the wisdom accumulated through generations of communal life.[113]

People do not learn all that they know from others, of course. Aquinas comments that those skilled in human affairs may appropriate their working principles either by acquiring them from others or by discovering them by themselves.[114] Nevertheless, at least as to the intellectual virtues, such as prudence, more people learn truth through instruction than learn it by their own discovery.[115] Success in attaining intellectual and moral growth requires that special attention be given to those who are old and experienced, as well as to all people who are prudent in their actions. For such people, truth and morality have become instinctual, a second nature. Following Aristotle, Aquinas concludes that one ought to heed the mere opinions of the old, experienced, and prudent even more than their reasoned demonstrations of truth.[116]

Age and Experience

The importance of age and experience for Aquinas, following Aristotle, is worth further exploration. As noted above, prudence concerns matters of action, for which people are not directed by absolutes that are necessarily true, but by concrete things that happen a majority of the time. Aquinas says that the ability to reduce the infinite number of particulars down to a finite number that can serve as regular guides for action requires experience, which is the result of many memories.[117] He states elsewhere that the elderly possess prudence in greater degree, in part because of their lifetime of experience.[118] Likewise, the instruction that is necessary in order to gain prudence ought to come particularly from the old.[119] As many scholars have observed in Aquinas, prudence is obtained and perfected through practice.[120]

Like Aristotle, Aquinas is skeptical about the ability of young people to study moral and political science profitably because of their lack of experience.[121] A person needs experience to understand the moral principles that these fields entail.[122] Formation of the intellectual virtues, like prudence, takes time and experience.[123] As discussed above, Aristotle and Aquinas advise their readers to heed the opinions of the old and experienced more than their intellectual arguments, since such people have an "eye" for the truth that comes only through experience.[124] This way of thinking shaped some of the practical teaching that Aristotle offered elsewhere in his corpus. For example, he urged private people who seek to acquire the art of legislation to learn from legislators rather than from theorists, for practitioners learn more about legislation through experience in legislating than do theorists who only think about it.[125] Aristotle and Aquinas claim that experience normally gets better results than theory; therefore, prudence depends more upon familiarity with the particulars of actions than upon understanding general principles.[126] According to Aristotle, even the general public is skeptical that youths can be prudent.[127]

Commentators on Aquinas's ethics emphasize these points. For example, Traina notes that practical reason does indeed draw on some *a priori* principles, but draws primarily on experience and memory of how effects follow from causes.[128] Hall's appropriation of Aquinas moves along similar lines. For Aquinas, promulgation of the natural law is accomplished by a *process* of learning by individuals and communities. According to Hall, Aquinas presupposes an understanding of temporality and a model of practical reasoning engaged with the material of experience that supports a narrative explanation of human action and history. Only by reflection upon one's predecessors' and one's own desires, choices, mistakes, and successes is the natural law learned, and what is learned is expressed in each society's customs, beliefs, and laws. Hall explains that learning the natural law by experience entails making mistakes and requires the corrigibility of individual and community goals.[129] The human journey to God is ongoing and historical, always requiring time, experience, and the support of others.[130] Aquinas says this best when he comments that Aristotle's ethical method is such because "it is according to man's nature to proceed by the steps of reason to a knowledge of the truth. Reason has this peculiar characteristic that it grasps the truth gradually, and as a consequence man properly perfects himself in knowledge little by little." He continues:

> He says that time seems to be, as it were, a discoverer of things well suited to sketch a subject and to be of special assistance in the work. The meaning is not that time itself contributes anything but that this help comes with time. If someone should busy himself investigating the truth for a period, he will be aided in the discovery of the truth by the passage of time. This is true in the case of the same person who will understand subsequently what he had not understood before, and also for different persons, as in the case of a man who learns the things discovered by his predecessors and adds something himself. But if, on the contrary, application to study be neglected, time is rather a cause of forgetfulness.... We see indeed that the negligent individual forgets what he knows, and in human history we observe that many sciences which flourished among the ancients have been lost when interest in them ceased.[131]

The Limitations of Reason and the Implications for Human Law

Thus far, this chapter has described the limitations of human reason and the consequent inexactness of ethics in the thought of Aquinas, in order to set the fuller context for Aquinas's theology of custom. The final step in this task before dealing again with custom specifically is to describe the implications of the limitations of reason for the development of human law. As explored in some detail above, valid human law is identified by its conformity to reason just as morality in general is.[132] As an aspect of the rational moral life, then, the development of human law bears all the marks of the limitations of reason and the inexactness of ethics.

Law and Utility

As observed above, the fact that moral reasoning has limits and is unable to grasp truth all at once means that moral conduct and virtue must be examined in the light of utility. As one aspect of moral reasoning, the development of human law depends upon utility in similar ways, for Aquinas. The proper shape of law is not immediately obvious, but one discovers it by testing the utility of various courses of action. In the "Treatise on Law," Aquinas repeatedly teaches that utility is a central standard for the legitimacy and justice of human laws. It is not simply this fact itself, but the emphasis that Aquinas puts upon it, that deserves notice.

One example is found in Aquinas's defense of the existence of divine law. Aquinas identifies four reasons why a divine law is necessary for the directing of human conduct, and the fourth is relevant here. Aquinas assumes that nothing evil should "remain unforbidden and unpunished." However, human laws cannot eradicate all bad things, because "while aiming at doing away with all evils, it would do away with many good things, and would hinder the advance of the common good [*utilitas boni communis*], which is necessary for human intercourse."[133] Aquinas identifies here one limitation of human law: in solving one problem, new difficulties are created. In the face of this problem, Aquinas provides a standard for determining which (always imperfect) human laws ought to be enacted: the *utilitas boni communis*. This is the end that ought to be pursued, and civil laws that divert society from attaining this goal, even in pursuit of eradicating evil, have overreached. The utility of the common good thus establishes the requirements and bounds of human law.[134]

Another example of this relationship between human law and utility comes from the discussion of Isidore's criteria for what constitutes just law. Isidore's criteria, which were addressed in a different context above, are:

> Law shall be virtuous, just, possible to nature, according to the custom of the country, suitable to place and time, necessary, useful [*utilis*]; clearly expressed lest by its obscurity it lead to misunderstanding; framed for no private benefit, but for the common good.[135]

Utility is a requirement that all human laws must satisfy. As Aquinas explains, usefulness, and the requirements of necessity, clarity, and promotion of the common good, "mean that law should further the common weal [*refertur ad hoc quod expediat saluti*]." Usefulness accomplishes its part of this task by pointing to what is good: "*utilitas, [referatur] ad consecutionem bonorum.*" [136] The teleological nature of law is evident again here. Law presses on to attain what is good, and, by requiring law to be useful, Aquinas seeks to insure that law retains this focus. However, it is intriguing that Aquinas does not simply relegate utility to one criterion among others in this list of requirements for human law, but rather points to utility as the overarching consideration explaining why Isidore created the list that he did: "Now the end of human law is to be useful [*utilitas*] to man, as the jurist states. Wherefore Isidore in determining the nature of law, lays down, at first, three conditions...."[137] Hence, the reason that Isidore described law in precisely the way that he did is because the end of law is usefulness. According to Aquinas, Isidore's entire list of criteria for law is driven by a desire to explain how utility is the central purpose for human law's existence. In this context, Aquinas identifies three things to which human law ought to be "proportionate:" Divine law, natural law, and "the utility of mankind [*utilitati humanae*]." Utility is in heady company.

Aquinas's treatment of change in human law provides a third example of the connection between human law and utility. Aquinas defends the idea that law can be changed, and he identifies two instances in which this might be done justly: a change in reason or a change in the people regulated by the law. His explanation of the first calls attention to utility. He notes that reason advances from the imperfect to the perfect, and thus he argues that

> those who first endeavored to discover something useful [*utile*] for the human community, not being able by themselves to take everything into consideration, set up certain institutions which were deficient in many ways; and these were changed by subsequent lawgivers who made institutions that might prove less frequently deficient in respect of the common weal [*communi utilitate*].[138]

Here Aquinas speaks of the task of the first lawgivers as an attempt to discover what is useful for the people. Their legislation is deficient, to be sure, but the fault is not in the goal (finding what is *utile*), but in the legislators' inability to take all social factors into account. The standard that Aquinas offers for determining when a change in such laws is appropriate is whether the change might prove "less frequently deficient in respect of the common weal [*communi utilitate*]."[139] Again, Aquinas does not expect human law to do everything, but assumes that all laws have some deficiency. However, augmentation of the common utility is always a goal, and this is precisely what underlies the ongoing modification of civil law.

Aquinas sheds additional light on the interconnection of law and utility in answering an objection to the idea that law can be changed. The objection states: "Further, it is of the essence of law to be just and right [*iusta et recta*].... But that which is right once is right always. Therefore that which is law once, should be always law."[140] Aquinas does not challenge the premise that law is just and right, a truth that he has previously affirmed (Question 95, Article 2). Instead, he points again to the relative, non-absolute character of the specifics of human law:

> In corporal things, right is predicated absolutely: and therefore, as far as itself is concerned, always remains right. But right is predicated of law with reference to the common weal [*sed rectitude legis dicitur in ordine ad utilitatem communem*], to which one and the same thing is not always adapted, as stated above: wherefore rectitude of this kind is subject to change.[141]

It is the common utility, *utilitatem communem*, that determines the extent of a law's rectitude. Since particular laws may be just in one circumstance and unjust in another, the standard of utility is necessary to provide the requisite discernment.

Aquinas's later discussion of change in human law provides a fifth example of the relationship of law and utility. As discussed above, the fact that a proposed law is better than an existing law is not in itself sufficient reason for the proposed change to be implemented. The mere change of law is detrimental to the common good, and hence the benefits of the new law must outweigh the harm done by modifying the prevailing legal order. Again, utility is a necessary assistant in determining the correct course of action. In summary fashion, Aquinas explains that law is rightly changed "in so far as such change is conducive to the common weal [*communi utilitati providetur*]."[142] In the same article, he describes how to determine when the harm to the common weal is compensated by the improvement of the new law, thereby justifying the change in law:

> Such compensation may arise either from some very great and very evident benefit [*aliqua maxima et evidentissima utilitas*] conferred by the new enactment; or from the extreme urgency of the case, due to the fact that either the existing law is clearly unjust, or its observance extremely harmful. Wherefore the jurist says, that in establishing new laws, there should be evidence of the benefit to be derived [*evidens debet esse utilitas*], before departing from a law which has long been considered just.[143]

As discussed in a previous chapter, Aquinas sets a high bar for anyone proposing a change in law. The presumption is against change, given the intrinsic damage done to the common good by the mere fact that law is changed. But change in law is not prohibited, provided that the utility of the new law is very great and very evident.

The final, and perhaps most powerful, example of this interconnection between utility and human law relates to Aquinas's careful handling of the "dispensing power." The dispensing power refers to the ability of a ruler to declare a specific rule of law inapplicable in a given circumstance. Aquinas discusses this issue under the general heading of whether one who is under a law may act against the letter of the law, that is, whether the words of the law ought always to apply or instead can be bypassed in certain situations. Aquinas begins to answer this thorny jurisprudential question by citing the authority of Hilary, from which he concludes that "we should take account of the motive of the lawgiver, rather than of his very words."[144] In explaining this claim, Aquinas writes that every law is directed to the common good and obtains its force from it. This centrality of the common good has serious ramifications. Quoting the *CJC*, he writes: "By no reason of law, or favor of equity, is it allowable for us to interpret harshly, and render burdensome, those useful measures which have been enacted for the welfare of man [*salubriter pro utilitate hominum introducuntur*]."[145] Aquinas allows nothing to override the promotion of utility, which is the purpose of law. One might wonder how serious Aquinas is in laying down this (uncommonly) absolute legal precept. Legal theorists have argued that beneficial legal purposes are served by enforcing the letter of the law rather than granting exemptions when strict application leads to seemingly unjust results. A common rationale is that enforcing the letter of the law in unfortunate cases prods legislators to be more careful in anticipating scenarios and drafting legislative language. According to this line of thinking, strict enforcement actually enhances human utility in the long run.

Aquinas not only appears completely serious in rejecting all arguments advocating absolute enforcement of the letter of the law, but he also anticipates the counter-argument. To Aquinas, demanding laws that will never do injustice when strictly applied is asking legislators to provide the impossible. He notes the obvious fact that laws sometimes promote the common good in the majority of circumstances, yet are hurtful in other cases. But rather than blame the legislators for their carelessness, Aquinas says that this is the kind of laws that we expect: "Since then the lawgiver cannot have in view every single case, he shapes the law according to what happens most frequently, by directing his attention to the common good." In those minority cases where the letter of the law promotes injustice, it should not be observed. Aquinas offers the example of a city whose law requires the city gate to be kept closed. In most cases this law promotes the general welfare, but in case of a siege, when defenders of the city are being chased by their enemies, it would be a great loss to the city to follow the law strictly. Aquinas concludes that "in that case the gates ought to be opened, contrary to the letter of the law [*contra verba legis*], in order to maintain the common weal [*ut servaretur utilitas communis*], which the lawgiver had in view."[146] In stating again that the common utility trumps the letter of the law, he adds a new idea: one is to interpret laws assuming that the legislator intended them to promote the common utility. And this intention is to be honored at all costs.

It is true, as Aquinas goes on to say, that not just anyone can decide when a law should be inapplicable. In cases of emergency, when sudden danger requires a quick decision, anyone can make this judgment. Necessity knows no law. However, in non-emergency situations, this power ought to be entrusted to one with proper authority. In explaining his conclusion, Aquinas points to nothing else but utility. When there is no emergency, "it is not competent for everyone to expound what is useful and what is not useful to the state [*quid sit utile civitati et quid inutile*]."[147] To judge whether the letter of the law is to be applied is to make a judgment about utility.

Law and Virtue

As discussed earlier in this chapter, Aquinas recognized that an individual's moral action never takes place in a vacuum, but is ineluctably shaped by one's customs and habits—and particularly virtues and vices. As with utility, virtue and vice are issues that concern human law in particular, as well as the moral life in general. Specifically, Aquinas describes human law as an educator in virtue. The purpose of law is to accustom people to act in certain ways,[148] and he calls the principles of a community's law "nurseries of virtue."[149] In a number of places, Aquinas speaks of the responsibility of law to make people virtuous and to curtail the exercise of vice.[150] But Aquinas sets forth his teaching on this point most clearly in three sections of the "Treatise on Law."

In his treatment of the effects of law, Aquinas argues that law is to make men good:

> a law is nothing else than a dictate of reason in the ruler by whom his subjects are governed. Now the virtue of any subordinate thing consists in its being well subordinated to that by which it is regulated.... But every law aims at being obeyed by those who are subject to it. Consequently it is evident that the proper effect of law is to lead its subjects to their proper virtue: and since virtue is *that which makes its subject good*, it follows that the proper effect of law is to make those to whom it is given, good, either simply or in some particular respect.[151]

Elsewhere, Aquinas clearly advocates the necessity of this training in virtue that law provides. While not all people need the training provided by law in order to be virtuous, all do require training of some sort from another. Some receive all the training in virtue that they need from their fathers, but others are not so pliable. Of these, Aquinas says:

> But since some are found to be depraved, and prone to vice, and not easily amenable to words, it was necessary for such to be restrained from evil by force and fear, in order that, at least, they might desist from evil-doing, and leave others in peace, and that they themselves, by being habituated in this way, might be brought to do willingly what hitherto they did from fear, and thus become virtuous. Now this kind of training, which compels through fear of punishment, is the discipline of laws. Therefore, in order that man might have peace and virtue, it was necessary for laws to be framed.[152]

Aquinas qualifies these claims slightly. He argues that human law is not meant to repress every vice, nor to prescribe every act of virtue. The very attempt to do so is impossible, he reasons.[153] Nevertheless, Aquinas consistently concludes that the development of virtue in individuals, which is necessary for them to act in morally proper ways, depends in great measure on the training provided by human law.

Variation in Law

One of the defining characteristics of morality is its dependence upon circumstances, as discussed above. An act that is right under one set of conditions may be wrong under another. Again, what is true of morality in general is true of human law as well. To Aquinas, human law is nothing like a monolithic structure that is to be imposed once for all and that is equally suited to every community. Instead, Aquinas agrees with Isidore that law must be "adapted to time and place,"[154] and he adds that "law can be rightly changed on account of the changed condition of man."[155] Law is not at all absolute, but highly dependent upon the complex variations in human society.

This can be seen in part from Aquinas's identification of human law as a work of prudence. As noted above, prudence's task is largely defined as the discernment of circumstances as they bear upon the means for attaining an end. Aquinas asserts that those responsible for the formation of human law have need for prudence. For example, he says that a legal judgment, in order to be just, must be issued according to a right ruling of prudence.[156] Likewise, he calls law a rule of prudence that pre-exists in the mind as a particular just work.[157] In speaking this way, Aquinas once again follows Aristotle. Aristotle believed that the particular social circumstances attending a given form of government are to determine which laws are best, rather than vice versa, and he deemed political prudence necessary for this task.[158]

Aquinas is consistent, therefore, when he advises that the precepts of law must be diversified for different communities if the common good is to be attained.[159] Though the achievement of justice is a perpetual obligation for human beings, the substance of what is just must be determined according to the different conditions in which they live.[160] Likewise, a kingdom's justice consists in ruling each thing according to its own mode.[161] In regard to one particular type of justice, "distributive," Aquinas says that things ought to be accorded to individuals in proportion to their importance for the community as a whole. Yet, he explains that proper proportions vary from one kind of government to another.[162] For Aquinas, then, the various shapes of the organization of society demand various laws and various definitions of the content of justice. He observes that civil life and the administration of the state are not the same everywhere, and all laws are to be framed only as they are needed for the end of the state.[163] Even the government itself is to be structured according to the different conditions and purposes of the people.[164] As Anton-Hermann Chroust observes, Aquinas's descriptions of human law show a profound understanding of its social function.[165]

Since law takes different forms according to the nature of the societies that it governs, the range of what is deemed just law must be defined broadly. Indeed, Aquinas says that positive right has wide boundaries as long as it is consistent with natural right.[166] Similarly, Aristotle divided political justice into the natural and the conventional. While the former has universal validity, the latter is reached by agreement among people, without any inherent justification. Aristotle rejected the claim that all justice is conventional, but he admits that "in this world of ours, while natural justice undoubtedly exists, the rules under which justice is administered are everywhere being modified."[167] For Aquinas, as for Aristotle before him, law is just only as it fits circumstances and, therefore, universally applicable rules will remain elusive.

Law and Equity

The idea that universally applicable rules are elusive leads to another point that illustrates how the development of human law is a product of the indeterminate and inexact science of ethics. For Aquinas, law must be stated generally and must recognize that exceptions and the exercise of equity will at times be appropriate. In the "Treatise on Law," Aquinas carefully explains that established laws are not to be regarded as absolutely binding, but exceptions in the interest of justice are always legitimate:

> Now it happens often that the observance of some point of law conduces to the common weal in the majority of instances, and yet, in some cases, is very hurtful. Since then the lawgiver cannot have in view every single case, he shapes the law according to what happens most frequently, by directing his attention to the common good. Wherefore if a case arise wherein the observance of that law would be hurtful to the general welfare, it should not be observed.[168]

Aquinas proceeds to offer a concrete example that was discussed above in a different context. A law directing that the city gate be kept closed may promote the city's welfare as a general rule. However, if certain citizens who are defenders of the city are fleeing from enemies, the city would suffer loss were the gate not opened to them, and thus an exception to the rule is necessary. In replying to an objection in this same article, Aquinas clarifies that the need for exceptions to general laws does not imply that laws ought to be something other than general. As he says:

> No wise man is so wise as to be able to account for every single case; wherefore he is not able sufficiently to express in words all those things that are suitable for the end he has in view. And even if a lawgiver were able to take all the cases into consideration, he ought not to mention them all, in order to avoid confusion: but should frame the law according to that which is of most common occurrence.[169]

The fact that laws must be stated generally, and that exceptions inevitably attend such general laws, calls forth the need for equity. By "equity," Aquinas refers to the action of a judge in setting aside strict application of the law in favor of some more just outcome. He explains that equity, which is an aspect of justice, moderates the observance of the letter of the law.[170] A number of scholars have identified equity as a crucial aspect of Aquinas's moral and legal thought.[171] Aquinas specifically grounds the need for equity in the fact that human action—and hence human law—is of a contingent nature and concerns infinite possibilities. Legislators have no choice but to legislate for the majority of cases; conversely, judges have no choice but to set aside the letter of the law when the dictates of justice demand.[172] Aquinas explains that legislators in fact intend that judges should dispense from their laws when this serves the cause of justice.[173]

The Imperfection of Law

As an expression of the inexact and indefinite character of ethics, law is also inevitably imperfect. Certainly, this conclusion could be implied from many of the matters previously discussed, but Aquinas at times also draws this conclusion explicitly. Commenting on Aristotle, Aquinas states that not only the study of morality, but also the study of justice must content itself with a rough outline of the truth and broad conclusions, given the nature of the subject.[174] Elsewhere, Aquinas denies that there is demonstrative certitude in judging human acts, for they concern things that are contingent and variable. In the judicial context, the certitude of probability must suffice.[175]

As a concrete matter, one must live with the fact that law and legal processes are imperfect. For example, though Aquinas agrees that rebellion against tyranny is permissible, rebellion is to be avoided and the tyranny endured if rebellion would cause the tyrant's subjects to suffer more greatly than under the tyrant's rule,.[176] Likewise, Aquinas writes that resisting an unjust condemnation to death is morally right, unless perhaps the opposite course would avoid a scandal of some great disturbance to society.[177] Again, therefore, one might have to endure a grave injustice. Finally, Aquinas laments that Christians must sometimes tolerate unbelievers' religious rites, since human government, like the divine government, tolerates certain evils in order to avoid greater.[178] The imperfection of law is an inevitability.

Law and the Social Order

Finally, the inexactness and indefiniteness of ethics comes to expression in human law in the law's role of upholding the social order. For example, Aquinas understands the well-known but frequently under-appreciated concept of the rule of law to be an outworking of the limitations of human moral reasoning. This is evident in his response to the claim that "animate justice" (delivered by judges as cases arise without a predetermined standard) is superior to "inanimate justice" (determined in advance by laws). Aquinas appeals to Aristotle in support of the judgment that all things ought to be regulated by law rather than left to the free discretion of judges. He offers three reasons, all of which reflect the limitations of human reason and the indefinite character of morality. First, Aquinas notes that few men are wise, and hence it is easier to find a handful of wise men to frame laws than to find many wise men to serve as judges. Second, Aquinas appeals to the fact that right judgments are often not immediately evident, but take time and consideration of many facts. Thus, laws that are promulgated in leisure and after much deliberation are better than judicial decisions that must be made quickly. Finally, Aquinas is cognizant of the temptation to be swayed by passion and to slip into bias instead of being governed by reason. And thus he has greater confidence in the judgment of legislators, who judge in the abstract and for the future, than in that of judges, who must judge of present things toward which they feel love or hatred.[179]

The ideal of the rule of law was strongly and persuasively advocated already by Aristotle, whose influence on Aquinas is again evident here. Aristotle's rationales reflect the perspective of the limitations of human moral reasoning. He says that law, rather than human beings, should be our ruler, because law is a dictate of reason while people are inevitably swayed by their own interests.[180] Unlike human beings, law is free from passion.[181] Aristotle equates the idea that law rules with the idea that God or intellect rules.[182] The authority of the law is also a safeguard against human abuse. For example, a government ordered by law helps to prevent officials from profiting from their positions of authority.[183] Likewise, demagogues have no place where law rules. Aristotle goes so far as to say that where laws have no authority, there is, in truth, no government.[184]

Another point of relation between law and the broader social order emphasized by Aristotle and Aquinas is that law should not be changed except under the most pressing circumstances. Aristotle warned that traditional laws should not be frequently changed, even if new laws would be better. He reasoned that citizens develop habits when laws are obeyed, and that these take time to develop.[185] Aquinas issues similar warnings. He explains that a change in law is not justified simply by showing that a new law would be better than the old law. The new law must be so significantly better that it more than compensates for the harm that accrues from the mere fact that law is changed. He writes:

> Wherefore human law should never be changed, unless, in some way or other, the common weal be compensated according to the extent of the harm done in this respect. Such compensation may arise either from some very great and very evident benefit conferred by the new enactment; or from the extreme urgency of the case, due to the fact that either the existing law is clearly unjust, or its observance extremely harmful.[186]

Aristotle mentioned another reason why change in law should be avoided: replacing the law frequently weakens its power.[187] Likewise, Aquinas asserts that "when a law is changed, the binding power of the law is diminished."[188] For both thinkers, the rule of law is so important that any action that diminishes the respect in which law is held is to be avoided. Therefore, Aristotle exhorted rulers to guard against deviations in existing laws, and especially against small changes that tend to escape notice, but whose effects add up over time.[189] Aquinas discusses a concrete matter that seems to illustrate these points. He writes that non-Christians are not to be granted political authority over Christians, as an initial matter. However, he concedes that once an unbeliever's authority is settled, it is to be preserved as an institution of human law.[190]

Therefore, through acknowledging the limitations of human moral reason, Aquinas concludes that law is usually best left unchanged. Human beings need help in developing the habits that are necessary for right moral living, and they are also prone to disrespect the law, a tendency exacerbated by frequent tampering with legal rules. As this chapter has repeatedly argued, moral reasoning about the development of human law tracks more general moral reasoning. This is a crucial point for the present study because Aquinas's treatment of the legal authority of custom takes exactly this fact into consideration. The reasons that Aquinas offers for custom's role in the endeavor of human law are grounded not only in the rational, free, and social character of humanity, as discussed in the previous chapter, but also in the recognition that moral reasoning is always inexact and indefinite, and, therefore, that human law is the product of such moral reasoning. Therefore, I turn now to examine the importance of custom in accounting for the inevitable limitations that attend every human legal system.

The Limitations of Law and the Authority of Custom

As discussed in Chapter Two, Aquinas deems custom a central aspect of the development of human law. Part of the explanation for this view is that the formation of custom is an expression of the rational, free, social nature of human persons. This theme was explored in Chapter Three. The final section of the present chapter examines another part of Aquinas's explanation: the establishment and implementation of just law depends upon custom due to the limitations of human reason and the consequent inexactness of ethics. This is elucidated in how Aquinas describes the role of custom in terms of the moral and legal concerns that have been discussed earlier in this chapter. It becomes evident that Aquinas's Aristotelian conviction that ethics is an inexact science calls forth the need for the legal authority of custom.

Custom as Filter from Natural Law to Human Law

One of the most noteworthy characteristics of legitimate human law is that it is derived from the natural law and, as such, is a product of human reason. For Aquinas, as seen above, a human law not derived from natural law—that is, from reason—is not really a law at all. However, this chapter has also observed the difficulty of attempts to concretize the general principles of the natural law into specific rules applicable to the particular circumstances of life. The basic problem is that finite minds cannot completely grasp the infinitely complex world that they must try to understand. Aquinas identifies custom as one of the aids that human beings have as they seek to cope with this situation. Specifically, Aquinas speaks of custom as a sort of filter from natural law to human law that refines the general principles into specific rules.

Aquinas describes custom as a filter from natural law to human law in his numerous references to the claim by Tully that "justice has its source in nature; thence certain things came into custom by reason of their utility; afterwards these things which emanated from nature and were approved by custom, were sanctioned by fear and reverence for the law."[191] This remarkable statement grants to custom a central function in implementing the law of nature in the mundane situations of life. It leaves human law itself with a surprisingly secondary role, that of sanctioning [*sanxit*] the applications of the natural law that custom has already tested [*probates*]. The picture portrayed is striking. Custom does the difficult work of probing the usefulness of particular applications of natural law. Law then confers legal force upon those rules that survive the challenges that custom has mustered. Law is not described as creating something wholly new, but as confirming the results that have emerged out of the refining fires of the development of custom. Hall correctly interprets Aquinas in saying that the customs of a society reveal its understanding of what the natural law is.[192] The subsections that follow present several reasons why Aquinas describes the work of custom in this way.

Custom, Law, and Utility

Previous sections of this chapter have discussed the significance of the concept of utility for both morality in general and for human law in particular. One of the implications of the limitations inherent in finite human reason is that answers to moral problems are often not immediately obvious. For Aquinas, utility is one important factor in determining the moral course of action in the face of difficult choices. Aquinas demonstrates the importance of custom for human law by speaking of custom as a means for determining utility.

Aquinas's quotation of the passage from Tully makes this point: "Justice has its source in nature; thence certain things came into custom by reason of their utility; afterwards these things which emanated from nature and were approved by custom, were sanctioned by fear and reverence for the law." [193] In adopting these sentiments as his own, Aquinas points to utility as the driving force behind the development of custom. Things become part of custom, he says, "by reason of their utility [*ex utilitate rationis*]." The customary practices of communal interaction emerge out of the complex of human relationships because they prove themselves useful. Yet these useful patterns of behavior are not simply useful in the bare sense of the word; they are the expressions of justice derived from the natural law itself. According to Tully and Aquinas, these customary expressions of justice are fittingly sanctioned by human law.

However, Aquinas does not view the development of custom as a testing ground of utility only for determining which social practices are to be granted legal force initially. He also regards the perpetual development of custom as an ongoing refiner of existing human law. Though Aquinas's remarks on this issue were briefly mentioned in Chapter Two, it is important to revisit them from the perspective of the present section. Aquinas believes it morally permissible to act against a law when the purpose of the law fails in a particular situation. If a law begins to fail repeatedly, and, as a consequence, a custom of contrary conduct develops, "then custom shows that the law is no longer useful [*manifestatur per consuetudinem quod lex ulterius utilis non est*]."[194] At this point, Aquinas makes the case that custom can effect a change in law, and does this precisely by displaying that a law has lost its *utility*. Custom tests the utility of laws, and, when the laws are found wanting, custom supercedes them as to legal force.

As observed above, Aquinas does qualify his conclusion slightly, though even the qualification depends upon reasons of utility. He writes: "If, however, the same reason remains, for which the law was useful [*utilis*] hitherto, then it is not the custom that prevails against the law, but the law overcomes the custom." This claim may seem to undermine the connection of custom and utility, for it assumes that a custom may develop contrary to a law when the interests of utility still favor the law's retention. Even here, however, Aquinas hesitates to separate utility from custom. He cautions: "perhaps the sole reason for the law seeming useless [*inutilis*], be that it is not possible according to the custom of the country, which has been stated to be one of the conditions of law. For it is not easy to set aside the custom of a whole people."[195] In such circumstances, says Aquinas, the custom should still prevail over the previously-existing law. The mere fact that a prevailing law is contrary to custom may be enough to strip the law of its utility.

Custom and Virtue

Another of the issues examined earlier in this chapter is the relationship of morality and law with virtue. Though rationality and freedom are two of the great sources of human dignity, Aquinas does not look at reason as though it operates in a vacuum. It is always a human person with a package of characteristics—especially of virtues and vices—that reasons about moral issues. Those persons with the appropriate virtues are able to excel as moral reasoners; those persons without them are inevitably poor moral reasoners. Aquinas highlights this importance of virtue for the moral life by speaking of the duty of law to promote virtue. In this context, Aquinas also attributes a role to custom.

To begin, it may be helpful to revisit briefly Aquinas's denial that all virtuous acts are directly and absolutely derived from the natural law, even though all virtuous acts are required by the natural law from a certain perspective. Reason understands some acts to be virtuous in and of themselves. There are other acts that are not inherently virtuous, but which reason nevertheless understands to be good and useful in light of specific circumstances.[196] Thus, all virtuous acts are judged to be such by reason, and hence are derived from the natural law, yet the virtuous character of many acts is mutable. This dynamic is simply another expression of Aquinas's persistent conviction that there is often no straight, abstract line to be drawn from the general principles of the natural law to specific applications in ordinary life. To know which acts are virtuous, reason must inquire about circumstances. Custom plays an important role in this process.

In the first question he asks about human law, namely, whether it is useful for people to frame laws, Aquinas speaks of custom as a trainer in virtue. In addressing this question, Aquinas assumes that people are to be virtuous and to live in peace with one another. Although people possess a "natural aptitude" for virtue, he argues that training is necessary in order to attain the perfection of virtue. Aquinas does not think that people can train themselves, due to inclination toward undue pleasures. Hence, a person must be trained by another and, as discussed above, those who are more prone to vice and less easily instructed through words need human law to provide this training.[197]

However, Aquinas concedes that not all people fit this category. Some young people, he says, "are inclined to acts of virtue, by their good natural disposition, or by custom [*vel consuetudino*],[198] or rather by the gift of God." For these, "paternal training suffices, which is by admonitions."[199] The basic difference between the two sorts of people is that one needs to be trained by force and fear while the other needs only gentle instruction. The latter require a less rigorous training because they are already inclined to acts of virtue, and this inclination can come either by naturally good disposition, by custom, or, especially, by a divine gift. Custom, therefore, is portrayed as a noncoercive influence on young people inclining them to act virtuously. It functions as a subtle, pre-legal constraint on human natural instincts toward indulgence in improper pleasures. This insight casts additional light on the ability of custom to concretize the requirements of natural law in particular human situations. Custom is an irenic, silent pedagogue of the next generation, teaching how to live in accord with the natural law. Understandably, from this perspective, law ought to sanction the requirements of nature approved by custom, for coercive law is meant to shape people toward exactly the same end as that toward which non-coercive custom shapes them. Hall is perceptive here again in saying that both a society's customs and its laws inculcate individual and community goals.[200]

Custom and the Discernment of Social Circumstances

One of the points emphasized earlier in this chapter is Aquinas's sensitivity to how circumstances affect moral judgments. The importance of circumstances is perhaps the most prominent manifestation of the inexact and indefinite character of ethics. In the realm of human law, as seen above, rules must be framed in general ways, to fit the majority of occasions, and application of the letter of the law must sometimes be bypassed in favor of a more just course. The task of understanding the relevant circumstances is obviously very important for the formation of human law, and Aquinas assigns to custom a significant role in this endeavor. Two statements in particular display his conviction that custom provides necessary information about social particulars. The first speaks of custom as a gauge for determining a people's character and the second views custom as an expression of what is suitable to time and place.

Aquinas assumes that human law should repress vice, but denies that it should repress all particular vices, as noted above. The central consideration pointing Aquinas in this direction emerges from a quotation from Aristotle: "Now a measure [in this case, law] should be homogeneous with that which it measures."[201] From this, Aquinas concludes that "laws imposed on men should also be in keeping with their condition." This has very important implications. Just as one does not expect the same kinds of actions from a child as from an adult, so one does not expect the same things from one who is imperfect in virtue as from one who is perfect. Some actions that are possible for the latter are simply impossible for the former. Since human law must be applied to many people, most of whom are not perfect in virtue, only the worst vices, the presence of which threaten the very preservation of civil society, ought to be prohibited. In short, laws must be appropriate for the particular people that they will bind.[202]

When Aquinas states that "laws imposed on men should also be in keeping with their condition," he cites as proof part of a quotation from Isidore that has already been discussed: laws must be "possible both according to nature, and according to the customs of the country."[203] Here, Aquinas interprets the requirement that law be according to custom as implying that law should fit the condition of the people. A people's customs, it seems, indicate what their character is. Since the context of these statements concerns the legal enforcement of virtues and the prohibition of vices, Aquinas implies that a virtuous people have certain sorts of customs and a non-virtuous people others. Their customs, then, by reflecting their character, indicate what kinds of laws are appropriate. Custom is like a reference book that provides information necessary for the proper formation of law.

Another statement by Aquinas in the "Treatise on Law" reiterates these thoughts on custom and the discernment of social circumstances. This returns attention to Aquinas's defense of Isidore's list of what constitutes positive law. As seen above, Aquinas identifies the need for law to be "helpful to discipline" as one of three general concerns of Isidore's extended list of criteria. The elements of the list that Aquinas groups under the heading of "helpful to discipline" are that law should be "just, possible to nature, according to the customs of the country, adapted to place and time."[204] Aquinas, following Isidore, sandwiches the requirement of custom between two requirements that deal directly with the concern that law take account of particular situations. Law must be "possible to nature" because "discipline should be adapted to each one according to his ability, taking also into account the ability of nature (for the same burdens should be not laid on children as on adults)." Likewise, law is to be "adapted to place and time" because discipline "depends on certain circumstances."[205] Aquinas is concerned that law be helpful to discipline, and effective discipline demands that those subject to the discipline are dealt with according to their real situation, not according to abstract considerations. The requirement that law be according to custom, then, is again framed within the context of understanding the condition of the people who must live under the law.

Custom and Respect for the Law

This chapter previously discussed the role of law in upholding the social order. Aquinas, following Aristotle, describes the rule of law as necessary for the just governance of society, and both men warn of the dangers of frequent change in the law. The passions and self-interest that cloud human moral reasoning call forth the need that law rule, and refusal to change the law frequently promotes the regular observance of the law. Again, Aquinas draws on the idea of custom in order to explain these important points fully. This subsection explores how custom encourages respect for law, and the next describes how neglect of custom disturbs social peace and the endurance of the social order.

The relevant passages concerning custom and respect for the law come from an article in the *Summa Theologiae* that is certainly one of the most crucial for appreciating Aquinas's high view of custom as a legal authority. In this article, Aquinas asks whether a human law should always be changed when a better law could be enacted. As seen above, Aquinas denies that law should always be changed in such circumstances. In fact, he sets a heavy burden upon those advocating a change. He reminds his readers of the general rule that human law is rightly changed when this promotes the common good. However, because the common good is damaged to some degree every time the law is changed, a new law must be so much better than the old that the harm to the common good that the mere change in law causes is offset.[206]

Aquinas supports this position in large part by appealing to the significance of custom. First, he explains why a change of law itself is detrimental to the common good:

> But, to a certain extent, the mere change of law is of itself prejudicial to the common good: because custom avails much for the observance of laws, seeing that what is done contrary to general custom, even in slight matters, is looked upon as grave. Consequently, when a law is changed, the binding power of the law is diminished, in so far as custom is abolished.[207]

Two very significant things about custom deserve to be highlighted in this short passage. First, Aquinas says that "custom avails much for the observance of laws." In the context, in which Aquinas speaks about harm and benefit to the common good, he treats the general observance of laws as a beneficial practice. Therefore, when a change of law (and hence also the effect on the common good) is contemplated, one must take account of how the change would influence people's adherence to the law. According to Aquinas, observance of the law is not automatically achieved by its promulgation, but must be cultivated. For this purpose, "custom avails much." That is, laws are most faithfully observed not when they are simply "on the books," but when they are repeatedly practiced by the people and hence incorporated into their broader custom. For Aquinas, exactly this process of the incorporation of law into popular custom is stunted when the law is frequently changed. Second, Aquinas says that "when a law is changed, the binding power of the law is diminished, in so far as custom is abolished." This is the reverse side of what was just discussed. Just as remaining with an old law promotes observance of the law, precisely because it promotes customary behavior, so also changing to a new law detracts from the binding power of law, precisely because it hinders customary behavior. Aquinas considers human law not as an isolated series of rules, but as a whole fabric that itself is to be an essential aspect of a community's customs. To remove even one stitch (a "slight matter") from the legal fabric is to damage the whole. It demeans the law and inhibits people from developing customary adherence to particular laws and to law in general, thus making social life less certain, less predictable, less to be trusted. For the rule of law to flourish, the law must be observed; for the law to be observed, the people must obey it out of custom and as part of their custom; to cultivate this custom the law must not be frequently changed.

Aquinas reinforces these ideas elsewhere in this same article of the *Summa Theologiae*. Aquinas poses an objection stating that human laws should always be changed when there seems to be a better course of action, because "human laws are devised by human reason, like other arts." As in other arts, the old gives way to the new and improved.[208] Aquinas responds by contrasting law with the rules of other arts. While the rules of art "derive their force from reason alone...laws derive very great force from custom." From this he concludes that laws "should not be quickly changed."[209] Again, the role of custom in promoting observance of law is emphasized. Though law is indeed a product of reason, a point that Aquinas has repeatedly asserted, its authority is reinforced by custom. Laws are more greatly respected as aspects of the prevailing custom than as merely products of an abstract rational mind. And laws are obeyed more easily when people not only assent to them by reason but also incorporate them into their customary practices. Respect for custom promotes law-keeping.

Custom and the Maintenance of Society

Another example of custom's role in upholding the social order is observed in Aquinas's discussion of the power of human law to bind the conscience. Aquinas implies that overturning custom inevitably disturbs the peace of society. He asserts that civil laws are either just or unjust, and that the just laws bind conscience because of their derivation from the eternal law. Laws are considered just based upon three factors, their end (being ordained to the common good), their author (a competent authority), and their form (laying proportionate burdens on people with a view to the common good). Conversely, unjust laws are contrary to either human good or divine good, and are deficient in their end, author, or form. Aquinas claims that laws contrary to the divine good—meaning anything opposed to divine law—do not bind the conscience and must never be observed. Similarly, laws contrary merely to human good are violence rather than true laws. They too, generally speaking, do not bind the conscience.[210]

Contrary to expectations, however, the conscience may indeed be bound by laws that are opposed to human good, under certain circumstances: "Wherefore such laws do not bind in conscience, except perhaps in order to avoid scandal or disturbance, for which cause a man should even yield his right...."[211] Implicit in Aquinas's claim is that a law opposed to human good in the ways he delineates may still promote a higher good. As observed above, human laws are frequently ambiguous for Aquinas. The bad are seldom completely bad, and even the good are provisional and approximate. Laws may be opposed to human good in a number of significant ways, yet still obligate the members of society because they promote the higher goods of peace and order. Just as laws should not be automatically changed when they are perceived to be deficient, so also they should not be automatically disobeyed. A seemingly better alternative may not really be better. No matter how deficient a law is, the fact that it is *law* is of great moment. Because prevailing laws become part of the fabric of social custom, and since custom "avails much for the observance of laws,"[212] these prevailing laws carry within themselves an obligating force that is derived from their customary nature. Following custom averts disturbance. Thus, unjust laws may bind the conscience simply because adhering to custom is such an outstanding social good.

These points are well-illustrated in Aquinas's discussion of tyrannical rulers in *De Regno*. Since a tyrant's laws are more like violence than true laws, Aquinas finds the removal of tyrants to be morally permissible. Yet, he warns that if the tyranny is not excessive, the expedient course is to tolerate it. The rationale rests in the relative character of all human law and government. A relatively bad law or ruler may still be better than the alternatives, for overthrowing a tyrant may bring on a dissolution of social order that is far worse than the tyrant's injustice. Aquinas reasons:

> For it may happen that those who act against the tyrant are unable to prevail and the tyrant, thus provoked, rages the more. Even if one should be able to prevail against the tyrant, from this fact itself very grave dissensions among the people frequently ensue: the multitude may be broken up by factions either during their revolt against the tyrant, or, concerning the organization of the government, after the tyrant has been overthrown. It also happens that sometimes, while the multitude is driving out the tyrant by the help of some man, he, having received the power, seizes the tyranny, and fearing to suffer from another what he did to his predecessor, oppresses his subjects with a more grievous slavery. For this is wont to happen in tyranny, namely, that the second becomes more grievous than the one preceding, inasmuch as, without abandoning the previous oppressions, he himself thinks up fresh ones from the malice of his heart.[213]

The prevailing laws and social institutions—which are considered part of the social custom, as seen above—are to be overturned only with the greatest caution, lest the social order disintegrate and ever greater difficulties ensue.

A related point adds a new twist to, yet also reinforces, the above. For Aquinas, upsetting custom not only works social disorder, but upsetting the social consensus (upon which custom presumably rests) also carries within it the seeds of its own destruction, and cannot be continued indefinitely.[214] He writes:

> Therefore it is no easy task to shake the government of a prince whom the people so unanimously love.... But the government of tyrants cannot last long because it is hateful to the multitude, and what is against the wishes of the multitude cannot long be preserved.... Consequently it can scarcely come to pass that the government of a tyrant will endure for a long time.[215]

Social order depends upon social consensus. Social consensus, and through it social order, tends to assert itself over time, meaning that a (widely-despised) tyranny will inevitably collapse. Similarly, Aquinas writes elsewhere that "a nation is a body of men united together by consent to the law and by a community of welfare."[216] Without the social consensus, there can be no nation. When all people are given a proper share in government, on the other hand, it "ensures peace among the people, commends itself to all, and is most enduring, as stated in [Aristotle's] *Polit.* ii. 6."[217]

Aquinas develops these issues further in the second book of *De Regno*, where he describes how a king ought to establish his city. One requirement is that the king find a location that is fertile, in order that the city may be agriculturally self-sufficient. This is important for the maintenance of social order because lack of self-sufficiency requires a city to engage in foreign trade and, hence, to interact with those of other kingdoms. Aquinas explains why this is dangerous:

> Now, intercourse with foreigners, according to Aristotle's *Politics*, is particularly harmful to civic customs. It follows inevitably that strangers, brought up under other laws and customs, will in many cases act as the citizens are not wont to act, and thus, since the citizens are drawn by their example to act likewise, their own civic life is upset.[218]

The close connection between adherence to custom and the preservation of social order is again patent. Interaction with foreigners compromises obedience to laws and customs, which upsets civic life. Custom is therefore virtually identified with the sacrosanct order of the community.

One final reflection on this connection between custom and social order may be pertinent. As observed above, Aquinas believes both that law must be according to custom and that law actually becomes custom.[219] In reciprocal relationship, custom determines what law is and law determines what custom is. This mutual determination is certainly highly appropriate. Law must be in accord with custom if law itself is to become part of custom; otherwise, there would be no internally coherent and harmonious social custom, and hence no vibrant and peaceful social order. Yet finite and fallible moral reasoners need the support and guidance that a well-defined social order provides, a point similar to that made recently by Alisdair MacIntyre.[220] Law must be according to custom, in the mind of Aquinas, because the pressing requirement of social order depends upon it.

Conclusion

This chapter has investigated the limitations of human reason, the inexactness of ethics, the implications for the development of human law, and especially the role of custom in the development of human law. The previous chapter argued that custom is an effective, and even necessary, expression of humanity's rational, free, and social nature in the task of creating and implementing a legal order. This chapter has also shown the effectiveness and necessity of custom, though here in the context of accounting for and dealing with the inexactness of human law, which in turn is an aspect of the inexactness of moral reasoning more generally. For Thomas Aquinas, granting legal authority to social custom was an expression of his Aristotelian perspective on ethics.

A serious objection to imputing legal authority to custom is that custom is sometimes evil, a fact too obvious to dispute and one acknowledged by Aquinas. From Aquinas's perspective, however, this fact is hardly insuperable to a close dependence of law upon custom. Ethics is an inexact and indeterminate science, and law, therefore, must always be imperfect. Law can only embody general principles, which inevitably fail on occasion, and it must give way to equity when justice demands. To expect law to be perfect is to ask the impossible. Thus, for Aquinas, the mere fact that custom itself is imperfect is far from a definitive argument against ascribing legal authority to it. To ask whether custom is a *perfect* resource or standard for law is never an appropriate question. Reasoning to moral conclusions is a gradual, organic process and, as an important aspect of moral reasoning, the development of human law must follow the same process. This characteristic of human law manifests the appropriateness of custom as a legal resource and standard. The ongoing development of custom is nothing if not gradual and organic. Custom does not originate in a moment, nor is it independent, at any point in time, of past customary practices. By its very nature, it can never escape its historical and organic roots. Custom embodies what moral reasoning ought always be, according to Aquinas.

For Aquinas, the limitations of human moral reasoning consist principally in the fact that finite minds cannot comprehensively grasp the infinite number of circumstances and moral choices that confront them. Likewise, the limitations in human legal reasoning consist essentially in the fact that finite human minds cannot grasp the infinite complexities of the social order and the relationships among the people in it. Aquinas portrays society as consisting of many parts and many concerns, yet united by a single, overarching common good. This unified *telos* of society and of its laws does not nullify the laws' particularity. For Aquinas, such a complex relationship of parts to whole is unable to be grasped by a finite mind. Those attempting to construct a just system of human laws face an acute difficulty: laws must aim at particular actions and particular goods, yet each must contribute to the betterment of a common order, the parts and interconnections of which no one can fully understand. Everything that Aquinas says about custom indicates that it is precisely to custom that one must look in order to make the necessary judgments. In the face of a complex society that nevertheless needs to be governed justly by finite minds, social custom provides necessary resources. Though no single person is able to understand the relationship of parts to the whole, the small, inscrutable, and mysterious contributions of each individual freely interacting with others can weave a beautiful tapestry that could be produced in no other way. Confronted with an overwhelmingly complicated task, the governors of society are not left solely to their own resources, nor to those of a handful of advisors, nor even to those of a body of legislators. The order of custom, in which all members of society have contributed, provides the necessary matrix within which all future legislating and judicial decision-making are to be done. For finite human minds in an infinite world, thought Thomas Aquinas, custom is indeed a necessary legal authority.

Chapter 5

Aquinas, Custom, and the Future of the Common Law

Thomas Aquinas's view of the relationship of custom and law is of more than simply historical interest. His advocacy of custom's role within a legal system, as well as the profound theological and ethical reasons by which he supports his position, provoke important questions about the state of civil law today. The dominance of statutes and administrative regulations in contemporary legal culture gives the development of custom little opportunity to shape the law, and Aquinas's thought suggests that something rather important is lost thereby. In the English-speaking world, this prompts the question whether the common law, in some form or another, is worthy of revival. This chapter follows the lead of Aquinas and argues that indeed a reinvigoration of the common law is needed. Aquinas grounded his view of custom and law in the fact that human beings are rational creatures, that human beings are free creatures, that human beings are social creatures, and that ethics is an inexact science. Precisely these four insights provide the framework for the argument of this chapter that the relationship of law and custom ought to be strengthened through reestablishing the prominence of the common law.

Aquinas and the Common Law

The argument that this chapter makes may seem to be hindered by certain popular conceptions of the Anglo-American common law that suggest that it is something quite different from the sort of dynamic relationship of law and custom envisioned by Aquinas. Such conceptions are important to acknowledge, because they cut to the heart of the present claim that an appreciation for Aquinas's insights demonstrates the need for a revival of the common law. Though the historical discussion of the common law in Chapter One should put to rest some of the most serious objections to the customary basis of the common law, these potential challenges to the present argument should be taken seriously. Certainly the practice of the common law has not always perfectly mirrored the theory of the common law, and it is also true that the theory of the common law does not precisely mirror Aquinas's theology of law and custom. The idea that the common law itself may require certain reforms if it is to capture Aquinas's concerns is one to which the present argument is open.

There are at least four popular conceptions of the common law that stand in some tension with Aquinas's vision of the relationship of law and custom. First, the idea that the common law is "judge-made law" could imply that it is definitively non-customary. Law that is legislated—albeit by the judiciary rather than by the legislature—has its origin in the will of its enactors rather than in the practices of the people. While legal positivists, such as Jeremy Bentham, may be inclined to assert that all law is necessarily legislated by someone, those who recognize the reality of non-legislated, customary law might use the term "judge-made law" as the simple equivalent of "judge-recognized." Second, certain conceptions about who creates the customs underlying the common law are also in tension with Aquinas's perspective. Some scholars suggest that it is the customs of the *courts* that constitute the common law, and hence that the members of the legal profession are the creators of the customary common law. There is no reason to think that Aquinas would deny the need for customary practices of courts, but he located the ultimate source of the customary laws in the people as a whole. Though these two sources of customs are not mutually exclusive, some conception that customs blossom from popular soil is essential to capture Aquinas's primary concerns. Third, the attitude toward legal change and development is another potential source of difference between the common law and Aquinas's vision. While Aquinas treats the customs of the people as if they are always changing and developing, and never simply static, some scholars have defined the customs that constitute the common law as those that have existed from "time immemorial" or "time out of mind"—which, by a quirk of history, technically means prior to 1189, the year of the death of Henry II. According to this latter view, common law courts enforce those customs that have been acknowledged as law as far back as legal memory extends. This is, undoubtedly, a caricature of the common law, but openness to the continual evolution of custom is crucial for appropriating Aquinas's concerns. Fourth, and finally, is the matter of consensus. For Aquinas, the customs from which law emerges must rest upon a genuine consensus of the people. Customs do not necessarily require consensual support in order to become well-established, and the common law has undoubtedly enforced such non-consensual customs.

These four considerations provide caveats about making too simplistic an identification between the common law and Aquinas's view of law and custom. Empirical investigation of the degree to which the common law is a customary law along the lines assumed by Aquinas would be a helpful project on another occasion. Whatever the precise conclusions of such an investigation, certainly the similarities are great enough to justify the general association of these two things for purposes of the present argument. Not only does much of the material in Chapter One support this conclusion, but also does the fact that several scholars in recent years have also defended the common law on the basis of its customary origin.

This case has been made perhaps most comprehensively by F. A. Hayek, who is best known as the Nobel laureate, free market economist, but was also a legal scholar.[1] Hayek's philosophy of law reflects a moral perspective that is difficult to categorize, on the one hand advocating the "liberal" society and on the other hand anticipating important critiques of liberalism.[2] Hayek's basic argument in the first volume of *Law, Legislation and Liberty* is that the advanced society of today is not the product of any individual's planning or will, but emerged spontaneously as people interacted and discovered rules of conduct that enabled them to survive. Unlike an organization (such as the business corporation), or *taxis*, in which superiors give orders to subordinates for the accomplishment of certain set purposes, a spontaneous order, or *kosmos*, is not the result of any person's planning. Due to the vast complexity of a spontaneous order, no one can comprehend how specific social goals will be attained. Therefore, the laws governing it must be no more than rules of general conduct, most of which will have been formed by customs, but which may be modified by legislation that fits into the matrix of the prevailing rules. To legislate in the hope of attaining substantive social goals is inherently irrational, for no one can know how to attain whatever goals are set. For Hayek, the fact that a spontaneous order develops only by the ongoing utilization of the knowledge of all the members of society demands the existence of a vibrant customary law, of which the Anglo-American common law is an example.

Other Europeans have joined Hayek, a native Austrian, in defending the common law due to its customary nature. For example, Bruno Leoni argues that a conventional, customary, spontaneous legal order, in which *all* people participate (in imperceptible ways), is a better way to make law than by legislation, in which only a *few* participate (though they may be called "representatives" of the people). Leoni advocates a customary legal order as a noncoercive alternative to legislation, which inherently entails coercion of a majority against a minority. He cites many historical examples of his model that have functioned and flourished, particularly, for present purposes, the English common law. Also, he sees an analogous process governing the development of science, fashion, and language, and notes that these things could only have developed into their modern forms by such a spontaneous process. Another example is French political theorist Bertrand de Jouvenal, who argues that the supremacy of law ought to be the central issue of political science. Jouvenal sees the flood of legislation of modern times as unambiguously destructive of law's supremacy and views the new mass of legislation as only a parody of law, the product of the fancies and passions of one interest group after another, and therefore as inherently anti-social. The supremacy of law requires a law that is older than the state and that is sustained by the common beliefs and feelings of the members of the community. Jouvenal points to the common law as an example, and claims that the strength of the American constitutional system can be traced to its roots as a natural offspring of the common law.[3]

Some of these same concerns can be found in American legal scholars such as Alexander Bickel, Robert Cover, and Harold Berman. Bickel, though not as explicit about the need for the common law as such, joins Jouvenal in calling for law based not on coercion, but on consent. Drawing inspiration from Edmund Burke, Bickel seeks a law not imposed from on high, but developed especially through local processes where broad-based consent can emerge. Legislation or judicial decisions that seek to solve social controversies once and for all, however well intentioned, are fundamentally misguided. Retaining the moral basis of law requires contentment with an imperfect justice, says Bickel.[4] Cover argues that there are a plethora of *jurisgenerative* (that is, law-creating) communities in society. For Cover, law is a normative universe in which people live, far broader than any collection of legal rules or institutions of justice, not even requiring a state. He views courts of the state as *jurispathic*, in that their primary function is to "kill" law or, in other words, to resolve conflicts among different laws and legal interpretations produced by the *jurisgenerative* communities by choosing one or some and suppressing the rest, under threat of coercion.[5] With some similar concerns, Berman describes the contemporary "crisis" of the Western legal tradition in part in terms of the law's increasing interest in expediency at the expense of morality. He decries the contemporary tendency to define the law wholly in terms of the will of the lawmaker instead of also in terms of the customs and usages of the community.[6]

In addition to these scholars' broad concerns about the creation of a moral social order through local, spontaneous processes, other American legal scholars have explicitly highlighted various aspects of the common law necessary for a sound legal system. For example, M. Stuart Madden likes the common law's "enlightened gradualism" and "polycentric justice," which have effectively pursued objectives of law like corrective justice, individual autonomy, instrumentalism, and efficiency.[7] Guido Calabresi, concerned about the "petrification" of statutes (that is, their tendency to grow obsolete as they age) and aware that legislatures have difficulty in keeping statutes current, admires the traditional ability of the common law to balance the needs for continuity and change in the law. He argues that judicial precedents that interpret statutes should be treated just as common law precedents have been traditionally treated, with a combination of respect and flexibility, thereby creating a new common law of statutes.[8] Daniel Farber and Philip Frickey, drawing on republicanism and social choice theory, perceive a continuing need for common law when the existence of a statute affects judicial policymaking outside of the statute's domain.[9]

Custom, Law, and Rationality

As described at the beginning of this chapter, Thomas Aquinas provides four primary insights that indicate the benefits that would accrue through a reinvigoration of the relationship of law and custom. To conclude this book, I develop these four insights to argue for the renewal of the customary basis of the law. A development of Aquinas's insights has the benefit of systematizing many of the concerns of the scholars considered in the previous paragraphs who have more recently advocated an important role for custom and a renewed appreciation for the common law. The first insight, then, is that the reinvigoration of the customary basis of law enhances law's rational character. There is a long tradition of seeing the common law as embodying a rational system of legal practice.[10] Though such claims have also been challenged,[11] there are reasons to see truth in them. In this section, I argue that a thick customary basis enriches law's coherence and internal integrity, accounts more fully for all of the relevant facts in the process of adjudication, promotes the generality and equality of the law, and enhances its certainty and predictability.

First, therefore, the rationality of the legal system might be enriched through the ability of common law to promote the coherence and integrity of the legal order. To be rational, law must undoubtedly be coherent and possess an internal integrity. A body of law that leaves areas of conduct undefined and unaddressed, or, even worse, that consists of contradictory elements, falls short of rational coherence. In a wholly statutory legal order, law is merely a finite series of rules and, as such, cannot well account for this desired rational coherence. This is because any series of finite rules must inevitably come short of addressing the whole of a social order that approaches infinite complexity. This problem, ironically, seems to worsen as society grows more complex—it is ironic because statutory law has exponentially increased in this past century that has also seen an exponential rise in social complexity.

A number of legal scholars have recognized, sometimes with alarm, the inability of statutory law by itself to produce law that is a cohesive and integral whole. The confidence of writers such as Bentham and Rantoul in the ability of legal codes to produce cohesive and integrated law[12] is not shared by many who have viewed aggressive attempts to codify the law in hindsight.[13] Eisenberg insightfully observes that positivist theories of law leave the law full of gaps.[14] In between the series of posited rules are inevitably vast areas of human interaction to which the "law" does not speak. When controversies arise concerning conduct that falls within such gaps, statutes themselves cannot provide a verdict. Judges must either apply a statute to a set of circumstances that the statute was not intended to address, or they must turn to non-statutory sources of law. Insofar as one looks only to statutes to define what constitutes the law, then, the law is silent in regard to many patterns of conduct and hence fails to achieve a comprehensive, integrated coherence.

To address this limitation of statutory law, a number of scholars have looked to common law for help. In various ways, they recognize that a legal landscape dominated by statutes lacks a significant degree of coherence, consistency, and uniformity. They also recognize that the common law, as a kind of customary law, helps to remedy such difficulties.[15] This is true in one respect because customs, the product of innumerable people over long periods of time, address the manifold nuances and shades of the whole of human life in a way naturally more comprehensive than any attempt to address them all through posited acts of legislation. This is not to say that common law itself never has gaps; to take but one example, the pace of recent technological change makes unlikely the possibility of finding established customs to answer every dispute.

Nevertheless, common law provides resources for dealing with gaps that are missing from statutory codes standing alone. In an exclusively statutory law, as mentioned above, gaps in areas of conduct covered by statutes are by definition not governed by law at all. In common law, on the other hand, law is not a series of isolated rules, but a web of interlocking ways of defining proper conduct.[16] Rules do not constitute the totality of the common law; they are simply aids for identifying where certain actions performed under certain circumstances fit in the vast network of acceptable social activity. Even the common law "rules" embedded in case precedents are not taken as the law itself, but as evidence of what the law is.[17] Each situation is evaluated by analogizing it to other similar situations that have been more clearly defined. Leon Sheleff, a sociologist, points out that most people do not look to legal minutiae or seek advice from lawyers to learn how they ought to conduct themselves day by day, activity by activity. Instead, they rely on their understanding of prevailing communal norms, which have been imperceptibly forged in the development of social customs. It is only by acknowledging this fact and incorporating its reality into the law that a fluid normative system can exist.[18]

A second way in which common law may enhance the rationality of the legal system is through its ability to account more fully for all of the relevant facts in the process of adjudication. As discussed above, Aquinas concluded that people are able to act intelligently only by singling out and considering a small number of relevant facts in their moral decision-making. It is an act of reason (specifically, of prudence) to choose the right facts to single out, but, no matter how well this is done, moral acts are exercised without all of the relevant information. Hayek, in the midst of his defense of customary law, makes the identical point.[19] This situation raises acute problems for any attempt to construct absolute rules of conduct. Aquinas, therefore, argued that legislative statutes ought to set forth only general rules applicable to most circumstances. Because all particular nuances and circumstances can never be foreseen, judges must retain the option of abandoning the letter of the law through the power of equity when the generally applicable rule produces an unjust verdict.

Customary law is in many ways sensitive to this aspect of moral and legal reality. One important reason for this is that bodies of customary law like the Anglo-American common law are specified only in actual legal controversies.[20] Rantoul lambastes the common law precisely at this point,[21] but it is a characteristic that seems propitious in light of the limitations of human knowledge. Statutes lay down ahead of time firm rules applicable to defined circumstances but, as Madden has noted, are limited in their ability to distinguish the hues and nuances of different situations.[22] The relevant facts, as Aquinas taught, must be identified if one is to make morally rational decisions, yet one cannot define ahead of time what all of the relevant facts will be. As more truly relevant facts in a legal controversy are identified, the possibility of finding a statute that was promulgated to address just such facts decreases. In comparison, common law does not limit judges ahead of time to a certain set of factual scenarios into which each case must be plugged. As mentioned above, common law is more like an interconnected web of acceptable conduct rather than a specified series of rules. In traditional common law adjudication, for example, judges are called upon to identify the relevant facts for each particular case, and then to find, or discover, the just resolution through analogizing the factual situation to other factual situations for which just resolutions are known. A vast matrix of judicial precedents, each grounded in its own particular set of facts, provides the pool of analogies from which to draw. In such a process, the more relevant facts that are identified, the greater the possibility of finding the best analogy. The existence of vibrant common law, then, may expand the ability to account for all of the relevant facts in the application of law. And thus, insofar as the ability to account for all of the relevant facts is a mark of law's rationality, common law may be a means for promoting the rationality of the legal system.

A third area in which common law may enhance the rationality of the legal order pertains to the generality and equality of the law. The generality and equality of the law refers here to the idea that laws should not be aimed only at a particular person or class of persons, but rather should apply to all people engaging in certain forms of conduct. The insight that a flourishing common law promotes the generality and equality of the law depends upon the ideal that the customs underlying it are the product of genuine social consensus. This ideal is certainly not always true in fact, though it is a goal to be pursued. In thinking about the generality and equality of the law, it may be helpful to apply Cover's thesis that there are multiple norm-creating communities in any society. The smaller and more tightly-knit a *jurisgenerative* community is—in terms of religion or ethnicity, for instance—the more likely it may be to produce customs that systematically discriminate against those outside that community. In many cases, such discriminatory customs are perfectly understandable and justifiable (e.g., a church's custom of excluding non-members from its sacraments). Such customs may very well represent the consensus of those who participate in the particular *jurisgenerative* community, and hence bear the marks of generality and equality in that context.

In contrast, broader and less voluntary *jurisgenerative* communities, such as the city or nation, encompass a wide range of people and their interests, and hence the laws of these communities that discriminate against their members on account of factors such as ethnicity or religion fail the test of generality and equality. However, the discriminatory practices of such communities are not likely to exact the consensus of those who are threatened by the discrimination, and thus ought not to become incorporated into the common law.[23] Therefore, when common law acknowledges customs that rest upon genuine consensus, it possesses a built-in check against failures in generality and equality and, consequently, further bolsters the rationality of the law.

A final matter in which the rationality of the legal system may be enhanced through common law concerns the certainty and predictability of law. Perhaps the most significant reason why a rational legal system must be certain and predictable is that otherwise attempts to conduct oneself according to the law become to some degree a matter of guesswork. A reasonable law is one that can be understood by those living under it by the exercise of their reason. When law is reasonable, effects follow from causes according to a regular pattern, so that one may know that certain patterns of behavior are acceptable and certain patterns are not. However, to the degree that the law lacks certainty and that people cannot predict with some degree of accuracy what will be received by others as lawful, attempts to live by the law are irrational. In such circumstances, there is no fact or reality upon which to base decisions about action. When the law lacks certainty and predictability, planning for one's career and investing one's resources and any number of other things become more a matter of guesswork than of rational judgment.

The common law's ability to promote the certainty and predictability of the law has in fact been denigrated. Both Bentham and Rantoul portrayed the common law as indeterminable, and hence as radically unpredictable and uncertain. For them, one cannot determine what the common law is before an action is executed or a matter adjudicated, nor can one know after the fact exactly what an adjudication decided.[24] They asserted that only statutory, codified law could remedy these problems. Even Hayek speaks of his own deep-rooted bias, cultivated in his upbringing and training under the continental civil law and only overcome relatively late in life, toward the idea that written law is inherently more certain and predictable than unwritten law.[25]

Perhaps there is at least one sense in which written, statutory law is more clear and certain than unwritten, customary law. Leoni makes the perceptive observation that the notion of the greater certainty of written law rests upon an understanding of certainty as that of *precision*.[26] Written laws tend to be precisely formulated in a way that unwritten, customary law is not. Whatever the value of precision in the formulation of law, it is also not without its drawbacks. In line with previous discussion, the precision of statutes may increase gaps in the law, for the more precisely each statute defines what conduct it addresses, the greater the range of conduct that each statute fails to address. The problem is that if gaps in the law increase, the law's certainty and predictability tend to decrease. Neither Leoni nor Hayek believed that the certainty and predictability of law are exhausted by its precision. Their insights suggest three ways by which a vibrant system of common law may promote the certainty and predictability of law beyond the precision provided by statutes.

First, vibrant common law might moderate the pace and degree of change in the law. Law that is static and unchanging is certainly not desirable. For law to be useful and just, it must be appropriate for the conditions of society, and because social conditions change, the law must change too. However, the very fact that law is changeable detracts from it certainty and predictability. The possibility that a given area of law will change means that people cannot make their plans around its continuing applicability with full confidence. What is needed are mechanisms that balance the potentially disharmonious facts that law must change and that change in law strips the law of some degree of its certainty and predictability. Statutory law presents certain difficulties in attaining this goal. In part, this is because of the possibility of *sudden* change in statutory law. At least theoretically, any given statute is potentially never more than a moment away from being altered or even eliminated. In reality, the demands for legislative process and the existence of a free and open press diminish the possibility that statutes will change abruptly or without warning. Perhaps more problematic is the possibility that statutes can be changed without any necessary continuity over time. Statutes may change by significantly altering the kind of conduct that they reward and punish, and hence greatly affect the way people make their plans.[27]

Common law offers possibilities for stability in the midst of change beyond that offered by mere statutes. Though common law, like statutory law, changes, its means of change tend to be more gradual and fluid. Statutes can and do change overnight and, by their very nature, are either on or off, in effect or abolished.[28] Customs, insofar as they are the achievement of a social consensus, ordinarily neither appear nor disappear overnight. This is due to the fact that consensus-building generally takes time, since it requires dialogue, mutual experience, and the like. (Though there are exceptional cases, to be sure, when some notorious event takes place that generates an immediate and widespread reaction from a community and a correspondingly swift change in community practice—the response of the American people to the terrorist acts of September 11, 2001 may provide something of a recent, concrete example.) Furthermore, the common law not only has the advantage of changing gradually, but also that of changing organically. Insofar as individuals and groups tend to have relatively stable opinions and practices, their consensual customs will bear significant resemblance to each other over time. Leoni comments that customary law in the Roman world "did not mean absence of change, but it certainly meant that nobody went to bed at night making his plans on the basis of a present rule only to get up the next morning and find that the rule had been overturned by a legislative innovation."[29]

Second, common law contributes to the rational certainty and predictability of the legal system because, when the law changes, it seeks the consent even of those threatened to be harmed by the change. Because of the consensual nature of common law, a potential change in law that would sour the plans that certain individuals have made will actually take place only if these people themselves agree to it. This is, indeed, somewhat idealistic. The customs underlying the common law will rarely achieve consensus in the sense of unanimous approval. Nevertheless, to the extent that common law strives to recognize customs that have been achieved by something at least very close to consensus, change in the law occurs in consultation and agreement among the various individuals and groups that have stake in the change. Statutory law, which can change by mere majority agreement, does not have these same advantages.

Third, and finally, common law may enhance the rationality of the legal system because people are simply better attuned to customs than to statutory law. In light of the character of customary law as a reflection of the common practices that have developed through the formation of social consensus, Hayek's comment is insightful: "It seems to me that judicial decisions may in fact be more predictable if the judge is also bound by generally held views of what is just, even when they are not supported by the letter of the law, than when he is restricted to deriving his decisions only from those among accepted beliefs which have found expression in the written law."[30] The point is that the law, as expressed in judicial decisions, is easier to predict when it accords with commonly-held notions than when it accords simply with a precisely-worded statute that one finds "on the books." The truth of this observation is echoed in Sheleff's point that most people, most of the time, conduct themselves in relation to others not according to their lawyer's advice or their investigation of legal documents, but according to their assumptions about the right and wrong ways of dealing with others.[31] No matter how precisely a statute is worded, its application is neither certain nor predictable if no one reads it. And, generally speaking, people do not read statutes—the very proliferation of statutes in the past century makes it prohibitive. Attempting to adjudicate according to the customs of the people, on the other hand, is likely to increase the odds of a result that people would predict.

In light of all of these considerations, I suggest that common law is able to make great contributions to the rationality of the legal system. One important consequence of these matters is that common law is an expression of the rule of law. The various contributions of common law that I have identified (upholding the integrity of the legal order, accounting for all of the relevant facts of judicial controversies, upholding the generality and equality of the law, and promoting the certainty and predictability of the law) are conventionally regarded as requisites for the rule-of-law ideal.

Custom, Law, and Freedom

As observed in Chapter Three, Aquinas advocated the close relationship of law and custom not only for the sake of the rationality of the legal system, but also for the sake of freedom. For Aquinas, the freedom of the human person is a consequence of human rationality. While the rest of the corporeal creation can participate in divine, providential reason only determinedly and necessarily, human beings participate in it freely, with the capacity for self-determination. Human beings are not merely acted upon, but themselves act upon other things, for, although God is the first cause of everything, human persons act as secondary causes. They have the freedom, under God's providence, to shape the world for themselves. Chapter Three argued that Aquinas grounds his view of custom and law in part in this theology of human freedom. Aquinas explains that either a prince or the people as a whole may be the supreme law-maker in a community, and that, when the people are free to make their own laws, it is through their customs that the people express their legal authority. For Aquinas, therefore, customary law is a means for rational creatures to enjoy their divinely-endowed freedom, and vibrant customary law thus manifests the dignity of the human person.

In many ways, Aquinas's understanding of human freedom as expressed through customary law is likely to sound strange to contemporary ears. Though today's life in Anglo-American lands boasts of a measure of civil freedom beyond that of most other peoples and most previous ages, this civil freedom is exercised in regard to law-making primarily through the right to vote for legislative representatives. However, some recent commentators have adopted a more Thomistic perspective in searching for the provenance of Anglo-American freedom. Jouvenal, a Frenchman, made the provocative suggestion that Parliamentary supremacy was not the real source of the social liberty for which the English became famous. Rather, the real source was the common law. Looking at the United States, Jouvenal claimed that the American political and legal system has worked as well as it has because, again, it is grounded in the common law tradition.[32] Like Aquinas, Jouvenal points to customary law rather than to notions of universal suffrage and representation as the chief expression of the freedom to make law.

This unfamiliar perspective is in many ways compelling. A living body of common law may certainly deepen the opportunities for a people to exercise their freedom in the creation of legal norms. The existence of political elections and deliberative legislative assemblies, especially when joined with the notions of freedom of speech and freedom of the press, does allow for some widespread participation in the development of civil law. But this participation also has distinct limitations. Jouvenal and Leoni go so far as to claim that legislation is inherently coercive.[33] Whether such an extreme conclusion is justified, it is true that legislation, in whatever form, involves a tiny fraction of the population making (judicially enforceable) decisions for the rest. The power to change the law is granted to a small group of individuals. Whatever participation the people as a whole may have in the selection of legislative representatives (an issue to be addressed at further length below), only a few people engage in the actual deliberation and enactment of statutory law.

The existence of vibrant common law provides opportunities, beyond those provided solely by statutory law, for directly engaging the whole of society in the work of creating law. As Aquinas implied, customary law draws forth the manifestation of the divine image in each human being, insofar as each image-bearer seeks to express an active role in the ongoing development of creation and not to be simply acted upon. The connection of customary law and freedom is developed at length in Leoni's work, whose very title, *Freedom and the Law*, reflects his interest in the subject. In a system of customary law, as Leoni believes has existed under the common law and even under much of the history of the Roman law, *each person* is directly involved in the creation of law. He claims that human freedom best flourishes "where the law-making process is directly performed by each and all of the citizens."[34] This is not meant to imply that each person is left as an autonomous being bereft of any responsibility toward anyone else, which is a perverted and unreal understanding of freedom. Life under law implies a measure of constraint upon people's actions; nevertheless, law may either set necessary bounds within which human persons are allowed to develop their God-given nature as shapers of the world around them—in a sense, creators by analogy—or law may inhibit and squelch this nature.

Common law is the product of the immeasurable contribution of all parties involved. When it is based upon consensual customs, it is the people's own creation rather than something imposed upon them. As Leoni suggests, the ideal of democracy—that is, a government of the people—is capable of fuller realization when people are allowed to order society through their own customs.[35] Sheleff's sociological studies lead him to agree. He writes, commenting on Oliver Wendell Holmes Jr.'s famous dictum that "the life of the law has not been logic, it has been experience:"

> It may equally be said that the logic of life is not law but custom, an appreciation of the manner in which people will strive for the ultimate realization of their democratic right to express themselves as autonomous beings—by moving beyond the formal reaches of the law to lay down the rules that will govern their lives, beyond that which is contained in enacted codes, judicial pronouncements and learned treatises.[36]

He goes on to call this self-ordering function of custom a "pristine form of democracy" where norms are determined "at the grass-roots level" by people sensitive to every nuance of everyday needs.[37] It is this sort of recognition that promotes respect for each and every person, in all of his or her mundane activities. It treats people as active subjects rather than as passive objects and upholds the dignity of the weak in the face of constant threats from the strong to impose their own and supposedly better ways upon the rest. In this sense, therefore, the flourishing of common law allows for the incorporation of the free, rational conduct of *all* human beings, rather than of just a few.

Custom, Law, and Sociality

According to Thomas Aquinas, the role of custom in civil law is important not only for taking account of human rationality and freedom, but also for taking account of the social nature of human beings, as explored in Chapter Three. Like Aristotle and many others before and after him, Aquinas described human persons as social animals, meant to live and act with one another. For Aquinas, human rationality is a social rationality—people are to reason with each other and for each other in a mutual quest for human flourishing. In light of this, Aquinas believed that keeping all law within the bounds of the community's customary practices was an important way to acknowledge humanity's social nature. Several recent defenders of customary law have also looked to it as an expression and consequence of our sociality, insofar as legal order is created through the shared activity of the members of society. Considerations along these lines add additional support to the claim that an increasingly statutory legal system would benefit by a renewal of common law.

The notion of *consensus* is critical for the present discussion, and thus it needs further attention here. If human beings are social creatures, and indeed if human reason is the sort of thing that ought to be exercised in community, with the guidance and constraints provided by other people, then the rational process of law-making ought to occur by communal activity. Law that is imposed by the one or the few upon the many fails this test. Creating law in such manner is an anti-social rather than social process, and is therefore a matter of power rather than of reason. As people from many different philosophical perspectives agree, the legal order ought to rest on the consent of the people. Charting the community's course through consent is a social activity, while forcing the community's course on an unwilling people is a rejection of rational, social activities such as discussion, learning, and compromise.

Therefore, in establishing law-making mechanisms, a primary goal must be to achieve as great a degree of consensus in the development of civil law as possible. One obvious possibility for attaining this desired consensus is through the enactment of statutes by democratically elected representatives. In the particularly American version of this process, the people of a given geographical area vote, and the candidate that receives the majority (or even the plurality) of the votes cast is sent to the legislature as the representative of these people. This representative then participates in the activity of the legislature and casts his or her vote on measures designed to create statutory law. The consensual nature of this representative law-making process rests in the idea that all of the people to be governed by the statutes have genuinely participated in the statutes' creation: they have spoken directly in electing their representatives, and through their representative they have spoken indirectly on each of the statutes that come to govern them. The merits of such claims are at least twofold. First, the very fact that laws are enacted by a group of legislators rather than by an autocrat captures part of the concern that law be a product of social reasoning. Second, by subjecting legislators to periodic re-election, there is some check on the activity of the representatives that keeps their patterns of voting within certain bounds that are acceptable to society more broadly.

Nevertheless, if law is made solely through the legislative activity of elected representatives, the process of attaining social consensus on legal matters is cut short in unfortunate ways. On one level, though this is not the main interest here, the meaning of the idea that legislators "represent" their constituencies is disputed and rather puzzling. Are legislators to vote as they think the members of their constituency would vote were the matter put to popular election; in other words, is legislation through representation a means of reproducing the results of direct democracy more practically and efficiently? Or, on the other hand, are legislators those who are designated by their constituencies to gather the appropriate information and to use their best judgment in assessing and voting on given matters? Both are plausible theories and both have been advocated, but they produce different ideas about the nature of "representation."[38] Therefore, precisely how representation is supposed to reflect the social consensus has never been definitively articulated.

In the quest for social consensus, there is another and more important limitation of creating law through the legislation enacted by representatives. Granting momentarily that a statute, upon its enactment by a representative assembly, does indeed reflect the consensus of the represented people, a statute does not seem to express more than a *momentary* consensus. Society is always in flux and any consensus attainable in society is always developing, never static. One reason for this is that popular sentiments are constantly changing as people alter their opinions, broaden or restrict their outlook, and confront new circumstances. Even if the consent of a given set of people to an act of legislation through representation is attained, there is no guarantee that this set of people would reach the same consensus a decade, a year, or a day after enactment. Complicating this difficulty even further is the fact that there is also no society that consists of a static, set group of people. The membership of society is always in flux as people are born and die, come of age and become incompetent, emigrate and immigrate. There is no assurance at any point after a statute is enacted that whatever consensus once existed still endures. This difficulty would be overcome if statutes were enforced only so long as the consensus holds. However, to do this not only statutes but also the membership of the legislature would require constant adjustment. Election of representatives and especially reconsideration of the corpus of statutory law cannot take place too frequently, practically speaking. On the contrary, statutes are ordinarily put into effect indefinitely, and, no matter how diligently legislators try to account for future contingencies, statutes "age" and often become inapplicable to new circumstances. Legal theorists have proposed numerous solutions to deal with the difficulties that emerge from this fact.[39]

All this being true, there even seems reason to question the assumption granted in the last paragraph, namely, that statutes enacted by a legislature of representatives constitute even a momentary, let alone an enduring, consensus. The issue that provokes this question is that the whole process of elections and statutory enactment advances by the principle of majority, if not plurality, decision. First, representatives are elected by garnering a majority—or simply a plurality—of the vote, and then legislation is enacted by another majority vote. At neither level is consensus necessary, or usually even sought. At the first level, a minority, or perhaps even a majority, of the electorate has not voted in favor of their representative. Even many members of the majority or plurality that did vote for the representative probably did so as the lesser of evils. Undoubtedly, many people do not feel that their "representatives" speak for them in any particularly meaningful way.[40]

The difficulty in envisioning how representatives could embody the consensus of their voting districts perhaps lies precisely in the fact that the election process is simply not a mechanism designed to form or express consensus. Electing representatives by majority or plurality vote is an easier, more efficient route for shaping social rules than the long task of consensus-formation. The goal of consensus is that there be no winners or losers, while the process of electing representatives who legislate is built specifically on the idea that some win and others lose. For such reasons, Jouvenal calls legislation "anti-social."[41] Whatever its insight, this verdict must ultimately be judged an exaggeration, however, for there are many issues for which consensus is extremely difficult to attain. In the resolution of such issues the virtues of the election-legislation process are manifest, for this process is far superior to bloodshed, a far more "anti-social" solution.

However, though the election-legislation process may be a benevolent one when consensus is unattainable, building consensus ought still to be preferred. Due to the inherent limitations of legislation, other legal processes are necessary if such consensus is to be formed and expressed. A system of customary law, as envisioned by Aquinas, is designed precisely to meet this goal of consensus. Insofar as common law embraces consensual customs, as Aquinas thought law should do, it provides an important complement to legislation, with its relative non-interest in consent. In some important sense, the process of forming customs by consent forces people to be the right sort of human beings: socially rational creatures who, if they are to order their interlocking lives rationally, must do so socially and not anti-socially, preferably by enduring consensus rather than by momentary majority. In the on-going creation of common law, the process of social reasoning promises to be a continually ongoing phenomenon in which people are ordering and reordering their communal relations, with the legal system giving present recognition to the ever-evolving shape of the consensus. The customary consensus can account for shades and nuances of opinion that the up-or-down, black-or-white nature of voting cannot or need not.

The theoretical plausibility of such claims may be more convincing than their practical plausibility. It is one thing to advocate a common law built upon consensual customs, but it is another thing to suggest that significant social consensus, particularly in a complex, pluralist society, can be attained through custom and be perceived in judicial decision-making. To demonstrate that the common law processes can work in the way that they are supposed to is an arduous task, and one that the present study must largely leave for another occasion. However, it is worth noting that many scholars have already made serious arguments that the development of consensus and a corresponding customary legal order is indeed possible, and in fact has happened throughout history. From a sociological perspective, Sheleff claims that people conduct most aspects of their lives according to their own understanding of community norms, without reference to official legal authorities. Along these lines, Sheleff asserts, on empirical grounds, that custom must be an essential part of a law that is to be willingly accepted by the people.[42] He believes it possible for, and indeed calls for, law to be administered by judges who give verdicts on the basis of customs that have emerged from the people and emanated from a consensus that is continually determining norms.[43] From a jurisprudential perspective, Bickel too suggests ways in which social consensus can and must be attained if law is not to be simply coercive.[44] Similarly, recent disciples of Thomas Aquinas, such as eminent theologians John Courtney Murray and Bernard Lonergan, have also appealed to ideas of consensus as important and realizable aspects of a morally sound social life.[45]

Leoni has provided several helpful, practical examples of how consensus has been attained in non-legal matters through spontaneous social interaction.[46] By analogy, these examples support the idea that attaining a consensual body of common law in many areas of conduct is indeed possible. Leoni points to the development of language as one example. None of the world's languages was created through the conscious planning or theoretical invention of any individual or group of people. What is more, these spontaneously-developed, unplanned languages are immensely useful and capable of supporting effective communication on a practically infinite complex of matters. It is unthinkable that a person or small group of persons *could* create a language such as present-day English. Language has developed by an indefinitely long process of social consensus. Vocabulary and rules of grammar have not been determined by majority vote, but by an inscrutable process of communal interaction, experimentation, and agreement. Undoubtedly, the great complexity and consequent usefulness of contemporary languages like English were and could only be brought about by a spontaneous process of attaining social consensus.[47] By analogy, it is not unreasonable to conclude that a similar process could create law. If people have been able to develop spontaneously an infinitely complex and useful mode of communication, and one that is constantly in flux, people are surely not unable to develop spontaneously complex and useful modes of social relationships that themselves are always in flux.[48] As customary language requires interpretation and is sometimes unintelligible, yet is generally understandable and useful, customary law may also be generally understandable and useful, despite inevitable points of indeterminacy. Just as those interpreting language have dictionaries and books of grammar, so those interpreting law, such as judges, have case precedents and legal textbooks—none of these "authorities" give official answers, but they do serve as very useful aids for interpretive difficulties, even as they are themselves being constantly adapted to fit changing conditions.

In fact, this analogy of law with language might suggest, contrary to common opinion, that a complex and advanced society needs a consensual law just as it needs a consensual language. A language planned and developed by a group of people who enact it into existence would almost inevitably be far from comprehensive and only of limited use. Analogously, a law planned and developed by a group of people who enact it into existence is inevitably far from comprehensive and therefore of limited use (as discussed above in regard to gaps in statutory law). Building on these realizations, Hayek argues in *Rules and Order* that our complex and advanced society has in fact become what it is through a spontaneous development of consensual rules of social conduct. According to Hayek, the "great society" never was and never could have been planned by anybody or any discrete group, claims that will be considered below at greater length. Though cutting short the consensual development of language and attempting to legislate it is possible, it is not the case that language can be formed only through legislation. Likewise, Leoni suggests, though cutting short the consensual development of law and legislating it by majority vote is possible, it is not the case that law can be formed only through legislation. If the development of consensual law through custom is indeed possible, then it affords the prospect of enhancing the social character of the legal system, beyond what can be accomplished by statutory law alone.

Custom, Law, and the Inexact Science of Ethics

Chapter Four explored at length Aquinas's Aristotelian perspective on ethics as an inexact science and its relationship to his views on custom and law. The limitations of human reason that Aquinas recognized entailed many consequences for ethics, such as the always indefinite character of moral reasoning and the need for experience, instruction from others, attention to circumstances, and the cultivation of prudence and other virtues. As observed in Chapter Four, Aquinas grounded many of his defenses of customary law in the inexact nature of ethics. In this section, I argue that Aquinas, once again, provides important insights regarding not only the limitations of ethics, but especially their consequences for law. By considering these consequences, the potential contribution of common law for the legal system is better appreciated.

One of the motivating factors of Aquinas's view of ethics as an inexact science is the simple fact that human reason is finite and that, consequently, knowledge of the world is extremely limited. As amazing as the human mind is, it can know only a finite number of things, a tiny fraction of all the knowledge that might possibly be acquired. In a sense, this is an indisputable observation that perhaps needs little discussion. However, as Hayek marveled, it is a point that requires emphasis since it is very often ignored, perhaps in large part because it is so disappointing. In discussing "the necessary and irremediable ignorance on everyone's part of most of the particular facts which determine the actions of all the several members of human society," Hayek comments:

> This may at first seem to be a fact so obvious and incontestable as hardly to deserve mention, and still less to require proof. Yet the result of not constantly stressing it is that it is only too readily forgotten. This is so mainly because it is a very inconvenient fact which makes both our attempts to explain and our attempts to influence intelligently the processes of society very much more difficult, and which places severe limits on what we can say or do about them. There exists therefore a great temptation, as a first approximation, to begin with the assumption that we know everything needed for full explanation or control.[49]

Aristotle and Aquinas, who would have acknowledged Hayek's point, did not succumb to the temptation that he describes. They taught that people do not know all that is necessary in order to possess a comprehensive understanding of ethics and law, and that ethical and legal endeavors must reflect the limitations inherent in human knowledge. Hayek, in a similar spirit to Aristotle and Aquinas, emphasizes that the complex rules by which society functions are those that have gradually evolved and have been handed on by tradition, teaching, and imitation. People do not know them by instinct or by abstract reason.[50] It is interesting to note that Rantoul, in his polemics against the common law, contrasted negatively the historically-developed, ever-evolving common law with the idea of an abstract and absolute justice that can be known and applied by enlightened thinkers.[51]

Acceptance or rejection of the general view that the concrete applications of moral and legal concepts like justice can never be intuitively and comprehensively grasped by a finite human mind, but must always be learned gradually and partially, is bound to affect a philosophy of law. Indeed, it is quite coherent that Rantoul, with his confidence in the ability of enlightened thinkers to perceive an absolute justice, extols statutory law and excoriates common law, while Aristotle, Aquinas, and Hayek uphold the virtues of customary law. Hayek speaks extensively of the need for customary law as a consequence of the limitations of human reason and knowledge. At the heart of his argument is the point that all the facts that must be known in order to understand how and why the social and legal order operates the way it does and how particular actions affect the shape of this order are unknown to any individual person or discrete group of persons. Hayek does not say that the entirety of these facts is completely unknown—rather, they are comprehended only in the pooled knowledge of all the people in the society. The immeasurably numerous circumstances that mutually constitute and determine the social and legal order "are known to all the members of that society taken together but...are not known as a whole to any one person."[52] The upshot, according to Hayek, is that statutory law, even when enacted by a group of legislators acting with genuine integrity, proceeds on the basis of only a miniscule amount of the information needed to understand what the statute will actually accomplish. Hence, an inevitable randomness and arbitrariness accompanies even the best legislation. Whether a statute has a definite purpose or not, the full consequences of the statute cannot be known either ahead of time or in hindsight. Whatever particular problem it may succeed in solving, it will have an unknown number of other, unintended effects.[53]

Another potential benefit of a revival of the common law is its ability to account for the limitations of human knowledge in ways that statutory law alone cannot. Insofar as it is grounded in consensus, common law utilizes a greater share of the pool of the available knowledge belonging to members of society.[54] Whereas legislation utilizes the knowledge that only a small group of legislators is able to get into its grasp, the common law utilizes the knowledge of the many members of the *jurisgenerative* communities from which it emerges. In the development of the customs from which common law emerges, every person is called upon to give input into the formation of legal rules. The content of common law takes shape only when ways of social ordering are established that account for the mass of information that each person provides. Much of the practically infinite amount of information that the legislative process must ignore cannot be ignored in the development of custom and hence of common law.

A closely related matter that reinforces these considerations is the complexity of society and of the *jurisgenerative* communities that constitute it. In large part, this is the reverse side of discussions about the limitations of human reason: human reason is so limited in part because the range of possible knowledge is so vast. An aspect of this vastness of potential knowledge is the complexity of society. Comprehensive knowledge of *jurisgenerative* communities that are relatively simple, such as families or small businesses, may be more or less attainable by the human mind. But the intricate relationships that constitute even many relatively small *jurisgenerative* communities, let alone a vast *jurisgenerative* community such as a nation, can never possible be grasped comprehensively. This issue constantly grows more acute, for the globalization of culture and economic relationships means that genuine knowledge of even small *jurisgenerative* communities requires knowledge of the communities world-wide that interact with them and hence shape them. If the conclusion of the preceding paragraphs is sound, and the common law is indeed able to account for more of the knowledge and information necessary to make effective law than statutory law alone is able to account for, then this contribution of common law seems to be growing more important every day with the constant expansion of global communication. At an ever-quickening pace, knowledge is becoming increasingly diffused, and the input of every person possessing bits and pieces of the pool of information is needed if law based on fact and reality is to be created. The development of common law can procure and incorporate this input in ways that the development of statutory law cannot.

This conclusion is certainly ironic. Common law is frequently assumed to be unfit for an advanced and rapidly changing society, at best capable of functioning in societies that remain primitive. Rantoul, the champion of statutory law, debunked the common law as fit only for stationary nations and as unable to respond to social change.[55] On the contrary, Milsom argues more persuasively that codified law is what has difficulty responding to change in society.[56] In and of themselves, codes are unchanging, and the legislators entrusted with updating them possess only a fraction of the information about how society is evolving, especially as the pace of change quickens. Exactly for such reasons Hayek and Leoni assert that customary law is *more*, not less, necessary in an advanced society.[57] The very complexity of society makes the loss of common law to be felt more acutely. For good reason, Hayek labels as "paradoxical" the view that "we must deliberately plan modern society because it has become so complex."[58]

Energizing Hayek's discussion of complexity and the need, among other things, for customary law, is his analysis of the concept of "spontaneous order." At length in *Rules and Order*, Hayek distinguishes the concepts of *kosmos* and *taxis*; the former being a spontaneous or self-generating order and the latter a deliberately planned organization. According to Hayek, spontaneous orders, such as modern Western societies, not only developed apart from anybody's planning, but also are of such a complex and inscrutable nature that nobody *could have* planned them nor can anybody today know enough to be able to control them. On the other hand, organizations such as business corporations are planned and can be controlled in large part. Since a social order does not develop apart from a legal order, Hayek associates the development and existence of the legal order with the same spontaneous processes that have animated society as a whole. Other scholars have come to similar conclusions about the spontaneous nature of the growth of the common law. Milsom, for example, on numerous occasions writes of the unplanned character of the common law, even speaking of this characteristic as a condition of its progress.[59] In short, an unplanned, spontaneously generated common law represents a legal order that parallels the unplanned and spontaneously generated features of advanced society as a whole. In this, it does what a code of statutory law cannot do.

Though every connection established in Chapter Four between Aquinas's views on customary law and the inexact character of ethics cannot be explored here, one more issue is worth discussing, namely, the common law as a product of time. Aquinas believed that the inexact character of ethics calls forth the need for experience, not only the moral reasoner's own experience but also that of others, especially one's elders. This, in turn, requires docility, the ability to learn from others' efforts to grow in moral wisdom. Insofar as this perspective is accurate, the merits of common law are again impressive. Common law is the product of the cumulative experience of innumerable generations. Because society is in constant flux, the customs of today are not identical to the customs of yesterday. Nevertheless, the customary law of today is in basic continuity with the customs of yesterday and of the many generations preceding. It is never created anew. Common law seems to hold in balance two potentially competing, but nevertheless critical aspects of good law: it keeps in step with the constant change of society while remaining rooted in the consensuses formed in past ages. Its progressive character is countered by its conservative character. As argued by many of the advocates of common law, its provisions are the result of long experience and worthy of respect because they reflect the test of time.[60]

Conclusion

In the context of political and legal centralization in his own day, Thomas Aquinas reasoned that civil law is best served when shaped by custom. In spite of the lapse of many centuries, Aquinas's insights remain lucid and compelling today in the face of the triumph of statutory law over common law in the past century. Aquinas advocated the role of custom in the creation of human law in light of the dignity of rational, free, and social human beings and in light of the limitations inherent in human knowledge and moral reasoning. This chapter has developed Aquinas's ideas and concluded that a renewal of the customary common law promises to bring an integrity, generality, equality, certainty, predictability, and consensus to the law that a statutory code cannot by itself provide. The desire to solve social problems quickly through swift legislative action is a constant temptation, yet the prospects for a just and sound civil law are better served when the process of consensus-building is allowed to run its full and often long course. Legislation need not and certainly ought not be prohibited, but it is perhaps better viewed as an alternative form of law-making when consensus is truly unattainable rather than the form of first resort. Aquinas himself did not repudiate legislation, but did require that all law be "according to custom." Certainly he is correct that making and interpreting statutes in ways consistent with the matrix of custom serves as a means for keeping majoritarian legislation in touch with the social consensus that does exist.[61] As Hayek warned, echoing Aquinas, any government or legal arrangement that does not rest upon some real social consensus is inherently self-destructive and not likely to survive for the long-term.[62] The need for consensual, customary law is not only a matter of human rational and moral dignity; it is also a very practical matter of the flourishing and even survival of our society and its cultures.

Notes

Introduction

1. Some writers see this older reading as exemplified in works such as Harry V. Jaffa, *Thomism and Aristotelianism* (Chicago: University of Chicago Press, 1952); and Leo Strauss, *Natural Right and History* (Chicago: University of Chicago Press, 1950).
2. E. A. Goerner, "On Thomistic Natural Law: The Bad Man's View of Thomistic Natural Right," *Political Theory* 7 (February 1979): 101–122; E. A. Goerner, "Thomistic Natural Right: The Good Man's View of Thomistic Natural Law," *Political Theory* 11 (August 1983): 393–418; Daniel Mark Nelson, *The Priority of Prudence: Virtue and Natural Law in Thomas Aquinas and the Implications for Modern Ethics* (University Park: Pennsylvania State University Press, 1992); Pauline C. Westerman, *The Disintegration of Natural Law Theory: Aquinas to Finnis* (Leiden: Brill, 1998), 21–73.
3. For example, see Jean Porter, *The Recovery of Virtue: The Relevance of Aquinas for Christian Ethics* (Louisville: Westminster/John Knox Press, 1990); Jean Porter, "Contested Categories: Reason, Nature, and Natural Order in Medieval Accounts of the Natural Law," *Journal of Religious Ethics* 24 (1996): 207; Pamela M. Hall, *Narrative and the Natural Law: An Interpretation of Thomistic Ethics* (Notre Dame: University of Notre Dame Press, 1994); Daniel Westberg, *Right Practical Reason: Aristotle, Action, and Prudence in Aquinas* (Oxford: Clarendon, 1994); Ralph McInerny, *Ethica Thomistica: The Moral Philosophy of Thomas Aquinas*, rev. ed. (Washington, D. C.: Catholic University of America Press, 1997); Cristina Traina, *Feminist Ethics and Natural Law: The End of the Anathemas* (Washington, D. C.: Georgetown University Press, 1999), 56–99; and Kevin L. Flannery, S. J., *Acts Amid Precepts: The Aristotelian Logical Structure of Thomas Aquinas's Moral Theory* (Washington, D.C.: Catholic University of America Press, 2001).
4. For example, see John Bowlin, *Contingency and Fortune in Aquinas's Ethics* (Cambridge: Cambridge University Press, 1999); Anthony J. Lisska, *Aquinas's Theory of Natural Law: An Analytic Reconstruction* (Oxford: Clarendon, 1996), 253–255; John Boler, "Aquinas on Exceptions in Natural Law," in *Aquinas's Moral Theory: Essays in Honor of Norman Kretzmann*, eds. Scott MacDonald and Eleonore Stump (Ithaca: Cornell University Press, 1998), 161–204.

5. For example, Daniel Westberg, "The Relationship between Positive and Natural Law in Aquinas," *Journal of Law and Religion* 11, no. 1 (1994–1995): 1–22. Westberg discusses how civil law is rooted in natural law, and considers the relationship of natural law and legislation, but does not deal with custom.
6. For example, see Anton-Hermann Chroust, "The Philosophy of Law of St. Thomas Aquinas: His Fundamental Ideas and Some of His Historical Precursors," *American Journal of Jurisprudence* 19 (1975): 33. Here Chroust tantalizingly speaks of Aquinas's view of customary law as "quite interesting," but offers no real analysis of it. See also John Finnis, *Aquinas: Moral, Political, and Legal Theory* (Oxford: Oxford University Press, 1998), 270 (footnote 94). R. W. Carlyle and A. J. Carlyle identify custom as a chief source of law for Aquinas; see *A History of Mediaeval Political Theory in the West*, vol. 5 (New York: Barnes & Noble, n.d.), 47–48. J. M. Kelly concludes that statutes were more important for him than custom; see *A Short History of Western Legal Theory* (Oxford: Clarendon, 1992; reprint, Oxford: Clarendon, 1996), 139.
7. Alasdair MacIntyre, "Natural Law as Subversive: The Case of Aquinas," *Journal of Medieval and Early Modern Studies* 26 (Winter 1996): 70.

Chapter 1

1. Sir Matthew Hale, *The History of the Common Law of England*, ed. Charles M. Gray (1713; reprint, Chicago: University of Chicago Press, 1971), 37; Sir William Blackstone, *Commentary on the Laws of England* (1765; reprint, Chicago: University of Chicago Press, 1979), 1:67.
2. Arthur R. Hogue, *Origins of the Common Law* (Bloomington: Indiana University Press, 1966; reprint, Indianapolis: Liberty Fund, 1985), 186–190.
3. Blackstone, *Commentary*, 1:63–64.
4. Ibid., 1:73.
5. The very notion of a *customary* law has occasionally been challenged. For example, see J. P. B. de Josselin de Jong, "Customary Law: A Confusing Fiction," in *Folk Law: Essays in the Theory and Practice of the* Lex Non Scripta, eds. Alison Dundes Renteln and Alan Dundes (Madison: University of Wisconsin Press, 1994), 111–117; originally published in *Koninklijke Vereeniging Indisch Instituut* (Amsterdam: Het Indisch Instituut, 1948), 1:3–8. Much more frequently, scholars have defended the validity of the idea of customary law. See the recent extensive study of customary law by Leon Sheleff, *The Future of Tradition: Customary Law, Common Law and Legal Pluralism* (Portland, OR: Frank Cass, 2000).
6. Hale, *History of the Common Law*, 17.
7. John Hudson, *The Formation of the English Common Law: Law and Society in England from the Norman Conquest to Magna Carta* (London: Longman, 1996), 6–8.
8. Ibid., 6 (footnote 25).

9. Sir Frederick Pollock and Frederic William Maitland, *The History of English Law before the Time of Edward I*, 2d ed. (Cambridge: Cambridge University Press, 1923), 1:184.
10. Ibid., 1:xxiv. Maitland frequently expressed sentiments suggesting that customary law is more primitive and written law more advanced, a point also noted by John Hudson in "Maitland and Anglo-Norman Law," in *The History of English Law: Centenary Essays on 'Pollock and Maitland'*, ed. John Hudson (Oxford: Oxford University Press, 1996), 28. Maitland's observations about the written character of law in his own day should perhaps be read with this in mind.
11. M. Stuart Madden, "The Vital Common Law: Its Role in a Statutory Age," *University of Arkansas at Little Rock Law Journal* 18 (Summer 1996): 573–574.
12. A. W. B. Simpson, "The Common Law and Legal Theory," in *Folk Law*, ed. Renteln and Dundes, 1:119–139 (originally published in *Oxford Essays in Jurisprudence*, ed. A. W. B. Simpson [Oxford: Oxford University Press, 1973]); Melvin Aron Eisenberg, *The Nature of the Common Law* (Cambridge: Harvard University Press, 1988), 146–151.
13. Hogue, *Origins of the Common Law*, 192–200; Mary Ann Glendon, Michael Wallace Gordon, and Christopher Osakwe, *Comparative Legal Traditions*, 2d ed. (St. Paul: West, 1994), 709–710.
14. Blackstone, *Commentary*, 1:69–70.
15. Ibid., 1:76–79.
16. Ibid., 1:67.
17. On this point, see Hale, *History of the Common Law*, 31.
18. Pollock and Maitland, *History of English Law*, 1:183.
19. S. F. C. Milsom, *Historical Foundations of the Common Law*, 2d ed. (Toronto: Butterworths, 1981), 6.
20. S. F. C. Milsom, *Studies in the History of the Common Law* (London: Hambledon, 1985), 152.
21. Ibid., 209–222.
22. Ibid., 171–189.
23. See Pollock and Maitland, *History of English Law*, 1:20, 88; Milsom, *Historical Foundations*, 11; Hudson, *Formation of the English Common Law*, 18, 21; and Paul Brand, *The Making of the Common Law* (London: Hambledon, 1992), 325.
24. For various perspectives on Henry II's contribution to English law, see Brand, *The Making of the Common Law*, 77–102; Milsom, *Historical Foundations*, 12; Pollock and Maitland, *History of English Law*, 1:136; and Hudson, *Formation of the English Common Law*, 19–21.
25. Hogue, *Origins of the Common Law*, 191.
26. See Pollock and Maitland, *History of English Law*, 1:175–188. For a critical reading of Maitland on Bracton and his accomplishments, see Paul Brand, "The Age of Bracton," in *History of English Law: Centenary Essays*, ed. Hudson, 65–89.
27. Hudson, *Foundations of the English Common Law*, 236–237.
28. See Brand, *The Making of the Common Law*, 135–168, 325; Hogue, *Origins of the Common Law*, 68–70; and Hale, *History of the Common Law*, 44.

29. Milsom, *Historical Foundations*, 417–418.
30. Quoted in Friedrich A. Hayek, *Law, Legislation and Liberty*, vol. 1, *Rules and Order* (London: Routledge & Kegan Paul, 1973; reprint, Chicago: University of Chicago Press, 1983), 173–174.
31. Hale, *History of the Common Law*, 3–4.
32. Ibid., 16–17.
33. Ibid., 44–45.
34. See Blackstone, *Commentaries*, 1:64.
35. Ibid., 1:73.
36. Ibid., 1:70.
37. For example, see Charles Covell, *The Defense of Natural Law: A Study of the Ideas of Law and Justice in the Writings of Lon L. Fuller, Michael Oakeshot, F. A. Hayek, Ronald Dworkin, and John Finnis* (New York: St. Martin's, 1992), 2.
38. Milsom, *Historical Foundations*, 7.
39. See Jeremy Bentham, *Of Laws in General*, ed. H. L. A. Hart (London: Athlone, 1970). Though this work was published only posthumously, it provides an excellent systematic treatment of the views on law that Bentham also expressed elsewhere.
40. Robert Rantoul, "Oration at Scituate," quoted in Stephen B. Presser and Jamil S. Zainaldin, *Law and Jurisprudence in American History: Cases and Materials*, 3d ed. (St. Paul: West, 1995), 255–257.
41. Maitland, *History of English Law*, 1:26–27.
42. For example, see A. V. Dicey, *Introduction to the Study of the Law of the Constitution*, 10th ed. (London: MacMillan & Co., 1961), 27–28.
43. Ellen Ash Peters, "Common Law Judging in a Statutory World," *University of Pittsburgh Law Review* 43 (1982): 995.
44. Ibid., 996.
45. Guido Calabresi, *A Common Law for the Age of Statutes* (Cambridge: Harvard University Press, 1982), 5.
46. Winston Churchill, *A History of the English–Speaking Peoples*, vol. 1, *The Birth of Britain* (New York: Dodd, Mead & Company, 1956), 223.
47. Peters, "Common Law Judging," 996–998. Peters' analysis of the decline of the common law's importance was confirmed more recently in Madden, "The Vital Common Law," 556. See also Calabresi, *Common Law*, 1. In spite of what has happened to the predominance of the common law, there are those who still perceive real life in it. See, for example, Madden, "The Vital Common Law," 559, and Daniel A. Farber and Philip P. Frickey, "In the Shadow of the Legislature: The Common Law in the Age of the New Public Law," *Michigan Law Review* 89 (1991): 875–906, who claim that the common law retains some vitality and that there remains a symbiotic relationship between statutes and the common law, despite the predominance of the former.
48. See, for example, Hayek, *Law, Legislation and Liberty*, vol. 1, *Rules and Order*, 84–87; Bruno Leoni, *Freedom and the Law*, 3d ed. (Indianapolis: Liberty Fund, 1991), 11, 143.
49. Lenoi, *Freedom and the Law*, 145–146.

50. John Edward Murray, Jr., *Contracts: Cases and Materials*, 4th ed. (Charlottesville: Michie, 1991) 8–9. For the text of the UCC, see, e.g., *The Portable UCC: 1995 Official Text*, Corinne Cooper, ed. (Chicago: American Bar Association, 1996).
51. On these and other matters regarding the history and implementation of the UCC, see James J. White and Robert S. Summers, *Uniform Commercial Code*, 5th ed. (St. Paul: West, 2000), 1–21.
52. Ibid., 21.
53. Quirinus Breen makes this interesting observation on Aquinas's use of the *CJC*: "As to the Roman law, it is evident from his works that Thomas had read it diligently. When he quotes Justinian…, it is under the name of 'the Jurist,' just as he quotes Aristotle under the name of 'the Philosopher.' It appears that he shares the common high regard for the civil studies; at least he quotes Justinian with the same complimentary casualness which he uses in quoting Aristotle" ("The Twelth Century Revival of the Roman Law," in *Christianity and Humanism: Studies in the History of Ideas*, ed. Nelson Peter Ross (Grand Rapids, MI: Eerdmans, 1968), 136). On the importance of the *CJC* for medieval jurisprudence more generally, see Chroust, "The Philosophy of Law," 5.
54. For example, see Peter Stein, *Roman Law in European History* (Cambridge: Cambridge University Press, 1999), 3; Wolfgang Kunkel, *An Introduction to Roman Legal and Constitutional History*, trans. J. M. Kelly, 2nd ed. (Oxford: Clarendon, 1973), 25; Paul Frederic Girard, *A Short History of Roman Law*, trans. Augustus Henry Frazer Lefroy and John Home Cameron (Toronto: Canada Law Book Company, 1906), 32; Andrew Stephenson, *A History of Roman Law* (Boston: Little, Brown, and Company, 1912; reprint, Littleton, CO: Fred B. Rothman, 1972), 8.
55. Ibid., 24; Stein, *Roman Law*, 3–4.
56. For example, Olga Tellegen–Couperus describes both the constitutional and non–constitutional law of this period as largely based on custom; see *A Short History of Roman Law* (New York: Routledge, 1993), 12, 17–19. On the other hand, Kunkel claims that legal development during this period was mostly interpretation of the Twelve Tables (*Introduction*, 30). Stein also highlights this point, and notes that this interpretation was sometimes quite progressive (*Roman Law*, 7–8). A third opinion is offered by Fritz Schulz, who claims that the jurists' casuistry made both legislation and custom of limited use; see *History of Roman Legal Science* (Oxford: Clarendon, 1946), 24.
57. This view is expressed by Girard (*Short History*, 71) and Stephenson (*History*, 246). But even among these older writers the opinion is not unanimous. Charles Phineas Sherman , for example, does not include custom on his list of the sources of law in the late Republic and early Empire; see *Roman Law in the Modern World* (Boston: Boston Book Company, 1917; reprint, Littleton, CO: Fred B. Rothman, 1993) 1:44–45, 96–99.
58. See Schulz, *History*, 61; and Alan Watson, *Law Making in the Later Roman Republic* (Oxford: Clarendon, 1974), 169–70.
59. For the older opinion, see Girard, *Short History*, 71. This view is countered by Schulz, *History*, 137; and A. Arthur Schiller, "Custom in Classical Roman Law," in

Folk Law, ed. Renteln and Dundes, 1:33–47 [originally published in *Virginia Law Review* 24 (1938): 268–282].

60. For example, see ibid., 286; O. F. Robinson, T. D. Fergus, and W. M. Gordon, *An Introduction to European Legal History* (Abingdon: Professional Books Limited, 1985), 6; Tellegen–Couperus, *Short History*, 124; Kunkel, *Introduction*, 154–55.
61. Stein, *Roman Law*, 26–27.
62. Schulz, *History*, 278–79.
63. Fritz Schulz, *Principles of Roman Law*, trans. Marguerite Wolf (Oxford: Clarendon, 1936), 17–18.
64. See Robinson, et al., *Introduction*, 6.
65. Kelly, *A Short History*, 67.
66. See Watson, *Law Making*, 3; and Alan Watson, *The Spirit of Roman Law* (Athens: University of Georgia Press, 1995), 195–200.
67. There is a great deal of modern scholarly consensus on this point. See Watson, *The Spirit of Roman Law*, 57; Kunkel, *Introduction*, 97–99; Stein, *Roman Law*, 12–13, 16–18; and Tellegen–Couperus, *Short History*, 49.
68. Watson, *The Spirit of Roman Law*, 245–45; Schulz, *Principles*, 83–106; Kunkel, *Introduction*, 83.
69. See R. W. Carlyle and A. J. Carlyle, *A History of Mediaeval Political Theory in the West* (Edinburgh and London: William Blackwood & Sons, 1930), 1:64, 79.
70. A useful, brief survey of the production of the *CJC*, on which this paragraph relies, is found in Tellegen–Couperus, *Short History*, 141–47.
71. On the compilers as plunderers, see the rather amusing comments of Kunkel, *Introduction*, 164–65.
72. On this point, G. C. J. J. van den Bergh claims that Justinian's codification provided later generations of lawyers with no clear doctrine of the relationship of custom and law. See "The Concept of Folk Law in Historical Context: A Brief Outline," in *Folk Law*, ed. Renteln and Dundes, 1:11.
73. *CJC, Inst.*, 1.2.1 [Hereafter, English translations of the *Institutes* are taken from *The Institutes of Justinian*, trans. Thomas Collett Sanders (Westport CN: Greenwood, 1970); English translations of the *Digest* are taken from *The Digest of Justinian*, trans. and ed. Alan Watson, rev. ed., vol. 1 (Philadelphia: University of Pennsylvania Press, 1998); the original Latin texts are cited from *Corpus Iuris Civilis*, ed. Paulus Krueger and Theodorus Mommsen, vols. 1–2 (Berlin: Weidmannos, 1954).
74. Ibid., 1.2.3.
75. "This kind of law is held to be of particularly great authority, because approval of it has been so great that it has never been necessary to reduce it to writing." *CJC, Dig.*, 1.3.36.
76. *CJC, Inst.*, 1.2.9.
77. *CJC, Dig.*, 1.3.32.
78. Ibid., 1.3.35.
79. Ibid., 1.3.38.
80. *CJC, Inst.*, 1.2.11.
81. *CJC, Dig.*, 1.3.32.
82. Ibid., 1.3.37.

83. *CJC, Code.* 8.52(53).3 (translation mine). (*Leges quoque ipsas antiquitus probata et servata tenaciter consuetudo imitatur et retinet.*)
84. In light of some of the discussion above, perhaps the choice of *lex* here, rather than *jus*, indicates how this passage might be reconciled with other statements about custom as a source of law. As seen above, it is *jus* that was taken as the generic term for law, while *lex* was a specific kind of *written* law. Hence, to say that the emperor's will was *lex* may not impinge the least on the validity of other sorts of *jures*.
85. *CJC, Inst.*, 1.2.6.
86. For comments on Isidore's influence, see Stein, *Roman Law*, 41.
87. See Carlyle and Carlyle, *A History of Mediaeval Political Theory in the West*, vol. 2 (New York: Barnes & Noble, n.d.), 96.
88. Ibid., 98–100.
89. See Kelly, *Short History*, 121; Kunkel, *Introduction*, 181.
90. See Breen, "The Twelth Century," 147.
91. Ibid., 143. For a brief history of and statement of the importance of the rediscovery of the Digest, see Stein, *Roman History*, 43–45.
92. Breen, "The Twelth Century," 131, 180. See also Stein, *Roman Law*, 43–45.
93. Breen, "The Twelth Century," 156.
94. Kunkel, *Introduction*, 181–82.
95. Breen, "The Twelth Century," 137–38.
96. For reflections on Irnerius's contributions, see ibid., 148–51.
97. For example, see ibid., 180; and Kunkel, *Introduction*, 183–84.
98. Breen, "The Twelth Century," 136.
99. Ibid., 151, 179. On the relationship of the new study of Roman law with other academic disciplines, see also Stein, *Roman Law*, 46.
100. Carlyle and Carlyle, *History*, 2:53.
101. Ibid., 52, 58–59.
102. Ibid., 52, 59–67; Kelly, *Short History*, 138.
103. Gratian, *The Treatise on Laws with the Ordinary Gloss*, trans. Augustine Thompson, O.P. and Katherine Christensen (Washington, D.C.: Catholic University of America Press, 1993), D.1, c.2–5; D.8, c.2–9; D.11, c.1–8; D.12, c.3–12. On the relationship of civil and canon law in Gratian's day, see Stein, *Roman Law*, 49–52.
104. R. W. Carlyle and A. J. Carlyle, *A History of Medieaval Political Theory in the West* (New York: Barnes & Noble, n.d.), 3:45, 51; Carlyle and Carlyle, *History*, 5:64–65.
105. Carlyle and Carlyle, *History*, 5:48–49.
106. Susan Reynolds, *Kingdoms and Communities in Western Europe, 900–1300*, 2[d] ed. (Oxford: Clarendon, 1997), 1, 7.
107. Ibid., 15–16; also see Kelly, *Short History*, 101; Carlyle and Carlyle, *History*, 3:41, 45, 51.
108. Reynolds, *Kingdoms*, 18, 36, 38.
109. Ibid., 22.
110. Ibid., 39. Also see Robinson, et al., *An Introduction*, 67, 69.
111. Reynolds, *Kingdoms*, 42–51.
112. Ibid., 64.

Chapter 2

1. There are many sources that recount the details of Aquinas's life. See especially Jean–Pierre Torrell, O.P, *Saint Thomas Aquinas*, vol. 1, *The Person and His Work*, trans. Robert Royal (Washington, D.C.: Catholic University of America Press, 1996). A standard account is James A. Weisheipl, *Friar Thomas D'Aquino: His Life, Thought, and Work* (Garden City, NY: Doubleday, 1974;). Also see Thomas Franklin O'Meara, O.P., *Thomas Aquinas Theologian* (Notre Dame: University of Notre Dame Press, 1997); Jan A. Aertsen, "Aquinas's philosophy in its historical setting," in *The Cambridge Companion to Aquinas*, eds. Norman Kretzmann and Eleonore Stump (Cambridge: Cambridge University Press, 1993), 12–37; James A. Weisheipl, *Thomas d'Aquino and Albert His Teacher* (Toronto: Pontifical Institute of Mediaeval Studies, 1980); and Anthony Kenny, *Aquinas* (New York: Hill and Wang, 1980), 1–31.
2. O'Meara, *Thomas Aquinas Theologian*, 2.
3. Ibid.
4. Torrell, *Saint Thomas Aquinas*, 141.
5. For treatment of the eventful life of Frederick II, see David Abulafia, *Frederick II: A Medieval Emperor* (New York: Allen Lane, 1988); Thomas Curtis Van Cleve, *The Emperor Fredrick II of Hohenstaufen:* Immutator Mundi (Oxford: Clarendon, 1972); and Ernst Kantorowicz, *Frederick the Second: 1194–1250*, trans. E. O. Lorimer (London: Constable, 1931; reprint, New York: Frederick Ungar, 1957). (Scholars spell the Emperor's name differently; in my own references I call him "Frederick," but I have retained the spellings used by others as I find them)
6. For treatment of the life and reign of Louis IX, see Jean Richard, *Saint Louis: Crusader King of France*, trans. Jean Birrell (Cambridge: Cambridge University Press, 1992); William Chester Jordan, *Louis IX and the Challenge of the Crusade: A Study in Rulership* (Princeton: Princeton University Press, 1979); Margaret Wade Labarge, *Saint Louis: Louis IX Most Christian King of France* (Boston: Little, Brown and Company, 1968).
7. MacIntyre, "Natural Law as Subversive," 61–83.
8. Ibid., 70–71.
9. See Van Cleve, *Emperor Fredrick II*, 139, 142, 242–43.
10. Abulafia, *Frederick II*, 210–14.
11. See Van Cleve, *Emperor Fredrick II*, 145, 237–40; Abulafia, *Frederick II*, 202–03, 214; and Kantorowicz, *Frederick the Second*, 230–36.
12. Van Cleve, *Emperor Fredrick II*, 243.
13. Ibid., 142, 251.
14. Ibid., 139–42.
15. Abulafia, *Frederick II*, 207.
16. Van Cleve, *Emperor Fredrick II*, 244.
17. Ibid., 157.
18. Richard, *Saint Louis*, 155.

19. See ibid., 155, 177, 213.
20. Ibid., 172, 175–76.
21. Labarge, *Saint Louis*, 169.
22. Richard, *Saint Louis*, 245.
23. See ibid., 9.
24. See Labarge, *Saint Louis*, 170, 181.
25. Richard, *Saint Louis*, 176. See also Labarge, *Saint Louis*, 169, 174.
26. See Richard, *Saint Louis*, 332.
27. See Richard, *Saint Louis*, 174–75; Labarge, *Saint Louis*, 172. For some comment on Louis' overturning of custom on a matter related to the promulgation of law, see Jordan, *Louis IX*, 40.
28. Richard, *Saint Louis*, 20–21.
29. Ibid., 214–17.
30. MacIntyre, "Natural Law as Subversive," 70.
31. *Summa Theologiae* (henceforth, *ST*), 1a2ae 90.4. English translations from the *ST* are taken from *Summa Theologica*, trans. Fathers of the English Dominican Province, rev. ed., vols. 1–3 (1920; reprint, Allen, TX: Christian Classics, 1981). Quotations from the original Latin are from *Summa Theologiae*, vols. 1–2 (Rome: Marietti, 1950) and *Summa Theologiae*, vol. 3 (Rome: Marietti, 1948).
32. *ST*, 1a2ae 90.1. Aquinas speaks similarly of law as a certain rational plan (in a governing capacity) and rule of operation in several places in his *Summa Contra Gentiles* (henceforth *SCG*), 3.114.3; 3.115.3; 3.128.1. English translations from the *SCG* are taken from *On the Truth of the Catholic Faith* [*Summa Contra Gentiles*], trans. Anton C. Pegis, vol. 1 (Garden City, NY: Hanover House, 1955); *On the Truth of the Catholic Faith* [*Summa Contra Gentiles*], trans. James F. Anderson, vol. 2 (Garden City, NY: Hanover House, 1956); *Summa Contra Gentiles*, trans. Vernon J. Bourke, vol. 3 (Garden City, NY: Hanover House, 1956; reprint, Notre Dame: University of Notre Dame Press, 1975); *Summa Contra Gentiles*, trans. Charles J. O'Neil, vol. 4 (Garden City, NY: Hanover House, 1957; reprint, Notre Dame: University of Notre Dame Press, 1975).
33. *ST*, 1a2ae 90.2.
34. *ST*, 1a2ae 90.3.
35. *ST*, 1a2ae 90.4.
36. *ST*, 1a2ae 91.1–4.
37. *ST*, 1a2ae 91.4–5.
38. *ST*, 1a2ae 91.1.
39. *ST*, 1a2ae 91.1 ad.2. Aquinas states that this promulgation occurs either by word of mouth or by writing. He explains that the eternal law is promulgated in both ways, through the eternal existence of the Divine Word and of the Book of Life.
40. *ST*, 1a2ae 93.1.
41. Ibid.
42. *ST*, 1a2ae 93.2.
43. *ST*, 1a2ae 93.3.
44. *ST*, 1a2ae 93.5.

45. *ST*, 1a2ae 93.6.
46. *ST*, 1a2ae 91.2. Elsewhere, in the same vein, Aquinas says that by divine providence human beings participate in a likeness of divine providence through governing themselves, their acts, and other people, and that it is *law* that governs these activities (*SCG*, 3.114.2).
47. *ST*, 1a2ae 94.1 ad.2.
48. *ST*, 1a2ae 94.1.
49. *ST*, 1a2ae 94.2.
50. *ST*, 1a2ae 94.3. For other discussions of how moral knowledge of the law is evident to various degrees, see, e.g., *ST*, 1a2ae 100.3; 1a2ae 100.11.
51. *ST*, 1a2ae 94.4. See also *ST*, 1a2ae 99.2 ad.2; 100.1. These issues are central to an understanding of Aquinas's legal and moral thought, and especially critical to the present investigation of his work on human law and custom. For some extended treatment of this issue, see Boler, "Aquinas on Exceptions in Natural Law," 161–204.
52. *ST*, 1a2ae 94.5.
53. *ST*, 1a2ae 94.6.
54. *ST*, 1a2ae 98.1; 1a2ae 99.3. See also *SCG*, 3.128.1.
55. *ST*, 1a2ae 95.1. For further treatment of law's function as a trainer in virtue, especially for those not naturally disposed toward it, see Aquinas, *SCG*, 3.116.4; 3.128.8; and his *Commentary on Aristotle's Nicomachean Ethics* (henceforth, *CNE*), trans. C. I. Litzinger, O. P. (Chicago: Regnery, 1964; reprint, Notre Dame: Dumb Ox Books, 1993), 1.9. This idea is characteristically Aristotelian: see Aristotle, *Nicomachean Ethics* (henceforth, *NE*), 1.9; 10.9. English translations of the *NE* are taken from *Ethics*, trans. J. A. K. Thomson (New York: Penguin, 1971).
56. For example, see *NE*, 5.6; and Aristotle *Politics*, 3.15; 4.4; 5.8. Translations from the *Politics* are taken from *Politics*, trans. Hippocrates G. Apostle and Lloyd P. Gerson (Grinnell, IA: Peripatetic, 1986).
57. *CNE*, 5.6.
58. *ST*, 1a2ae 95.4.
59. *ST*, 1a2ae 91.3. Aquinas also refers to such determinations as having only the force of "positive law," rather than of natural law (*ST*, 1a2ae 99.4 ad.2).
60. *ST*, 1a2ae 95.2. See also *ST*, 2a2ae 60.5 ad.1.
61. *ST*, 1a2ae 96.1. See also *ST*, 1a2ae 98.1.
62. *ST*, 1a2ae 96.2. On human law and the prohibition of only certain vices, see also *ST*, 1a2ae 71.6 ad.4; 1a2ae 100.2; 2a2ae 77.1 ad.1.
63. *ST*, 1a2ae 96.3.
64. *ST*, 1a2ae 96.4.
65. *ST*, 1a2ae 96.5; 1a2ae 100.8.
66. *ST*, 1a2ae 96.6; 1a2ae 97.4. See also *ST*, 2a2ae 60.5 ad.2.
67. *ST*, 2a2ae 120.1.
68. For two examples, see Goerner, "Thomistic Natural Right," 400–12; and Chroust, "The Philosophy of Law," 34.
69. On this important matter of the contingent nature of law and the consequent need that laws express only general rules, see *CNE* 5.7; 5.10.

70. *ST*, 2a2ae 120.1 ad.2; 2a2ae 120.2 ad.3.
71. Aristotle, *NE*, 5.10. In his commentary on this passage, Aquinas emphasizes that legislators intend equity to be applied to their laws in appropriate circumstances, and that legislation is not self–executing, but always requires the action of a judge (*CNE*, 5.10). On legislative intent and the dispensation from laws, see also *ST*, 1a2ae 100.8.
72. *ST*, 1a2ae 97.1.
73. *ST*, 1a2ae 97.2.
74. *ST*, 1a2ae 97.3.
75. Ibid.
76. Aquinas uses language similar to that in the "Treatise on Law" in *ST*, 2a2ae 79.2 ad.2. Here he writes that a laudable custom has the force of a precept [*Consuetudo etiam honesta habet vim praecepti*].
77. *ST*, 1a2ae 97.3 ad.3.
78. Ibid.
79. *ST*, 2a2ae 71.4.
80. *ST*, 2a2ae 77.2 ad.2.
81. *ST*, 1a2ae 97.3 ad.2. Immediately after this quotation, Aquinas proceeds to explain that if the same reason for which the law was originally instituted still holds, then the old law should prevail over the custom. In other words, custom is not infallible in demonstrating failures in prevailing laws. Even here, however, Aquinas admits that there may be reason to allow the custom to abolish the law, though the original reason for the law remains valid. This discussion is addressed and explored in more detail below.
82. *ST*, 1a2ae 95.1 ad.2.
83. *ST*, 1a2ae 95.3. See also *ST* 1a2ae 96.2.
84. *ST*, 1a2ae 96.6 sed contra.
85. *ST*, 1a2ae 96.6.
86. See *ST*, 1a2ae 96.6; 1a2ae 97.4.
87. For a few examples, see *ST*, 1a2ae 95.3; 1a2ae 96.2; 1a2ae 97.3 ad.2.
88. *ST*, 1a2ae 95.3 obj.1.
89. *ST*, 1a2ae 95.3.
90. *ST*, 1a2ae 95.3 obj.3.
91. *ST*, 1a2ae 95.1.
92. *ST*, 1a2ae 97.2.
93. Aquinas here follows the opinion of Aristotle very closely. Aristotle taught that existing, traditional laws should not be frequently changed, even for the sake of laws that are better *per se* (*Politics*, 2.8). He said that rulers were to take special care in this matter, giving particular regard to small changes in the law that tend to escape notice, yet add up in importance over time (*Politics*, 5.8).
94. *ST*, 1a2ae 94.4.
95. *ST*, 1a2ae 94.6.
96. *ST*, 1a2ae 97.3 ad.1. Similarly, see *ST*, 1a2ae 99.2 ad.2: "It was fitting that the Divine law should come to man's assistance not only in those things for which reason is insufficient, but also in those things in which human reason may happen to be impeded. Now human reason could not go astray in the abstract, as to the universal

principles of the natural law: but through being habituated to sin [*propter consuetudinem peccandi*], it became obscure in the point of things to be done in detail. But with regard to the other moral precepts, which are like conclusions drawn from the universal principle of the natural law, the reason of many men went astray, to the extent of judging to be lawful, things that are evil in themselves. Thus among the articles of faith not only are those things set forth to which reason cannot reach…; but also those which right reason can attain…, in order to remove the manifold errors to which reason is liable."

97. *ST*, 1a2ae 97.3 ad.2.
98. Ibid.
99. On this point, see Porter, *Recovery of Virtue*, 121, 134–35. Porter properly reminds her readers that Aquinas does not raise custom to an absolute standard, though she does not seem to take enough account of the deference that Aquinas pays to custom even when it does not seem to be the preferable rule of conduct *per se*, as considered in the present paragraph.
100. *ST*, 1a2ae 90.4 ad.3.
101. Ibid.
102. *ST*, 1a2ae 90.4; 1a2ae 90.4 ad.2.
103. *ST*, 1a2ae 90.4 ad.1.
104. *ST*, 1a2ae 91.1 ad.2.
105. The same concern seems to lie behind Aquinas's assertion that, as a judicial matter, legal accusations should be in writing. Words by themselves are apt to escape memory, he explains. See *ST*, 2a2ae 68.2. The right functioning of legal processes depends upon knowledge of the relevant legal data on the part of all concerned parties.
106. See *ST* 1a2ae 97.3 ad.2 ("*consuetudinem multitudinis*").
107. The matter of applying local law against visitors to the locality is really not a problem unique to customary law. Visitors are ordinarily less likely to read the laws of a place of travel than they are to observe its customs. The application of *any* sort of law particular to a given community against an outsider must face the serious moral and jurisprudential challenge that it is unjust to enforce a law against a person who could not reasonably be expected to know it.
108. The authorship of this work was the subject of long dispute, though the scholarly consensus today attributes it to Aquinas. However, he left the work unfinished and a later writer took the liberty to complete it for him. See Torrell, *Saint Thomas Aquinas*, 169–171. The material from *De Regno* considered here is taken from sections that are recognized as genuinely Aquinas's.
109. *On the Governance of Rulers* [*De Regno*] (henceforth, *DR*), trans. Gerald B. Phelan (New York: Sheed & Ward, 1938), 1.1.
110. *DR*, 1.2. Aquinas has a similar emphasis in his *SCG*, 1.42.20. Here he grounds his view of monarchy as the principal form of government in the desire for social unity.
111. *DR*, 1.12.
112. *DR*, 1.13–14.
113. *DR*, 2.1.
114. *DR*, 2.2.
115. *DR*, 2.3–4.

116. *ST*, 1a2ae 92.1 sed contra.
117. *ST*, 1a2ae 92.1.
118. *ST*, 1a2ae 95.1.
119. *ST*, 1a2ae 90.1.
120. *ST*, 1a2ae 90.1 obj.3.
121. *ST*, 1a2ae 90.1 ad.3.
122. *ST*, 1a2ae 96.5.
123. *ST*, 1a2ae 96.5 obj.3.
124. *ST*, 1a2ae 96.5 ad.3.
125. *ST*, 1a2ae 90.3 ad.2; 1a2ae 97.3 ad.3.
126. *ST*, 1a2ae 97.3 ad.3.
127. In *Man and the State* (Chicago: University of Chicago Press, 1951), chapter 2, Maritain identified the concept of sovereignty with absolutism. He defined "sovereignty" to mean two things: the natural and inalienable right of the ruler to supreme independence and power, and the ruler's holding this right as something absolute, transcendent, and separate from the body of people who are ruled.
128. *ST* 1a2ae 97.3 ad.3.
129. See *ST*, 1a2ae 90.1 ad.3; 1a2ae 96.5 ad.3; 1a2ae 97.3 ad.3.
130. *DR*, 1.6.
131. Ibid.
132. Paul E. Sigmund describes Aquinas as a believer in limitation of governmental powers, and even claims that he was one of the first to promote popular participation in government, though he wrote before the emergence of representative institutions. Sigmund holds that Aquinas's social thought reflected elements of the neo–Platonic view of a hierarchical universe and society, yet also learned from Aristotle a view of government as the rule over free men able to direct themselves ("Law and Politics," in *The Cambridge Companion*, eds. Kretzmann and Stump, 220). Aristotle did indeed display considerable flexibility as to what form of government was best. He noted that there are many forms of government because of the inability of people to agree how to apply their shared desire that justice be done (*Politics*, 5.1), and he viewed political prudence as necessary both for considering which form of government is best in the abstract and for determining which is possible under given circumstances (*Politics*, 4.1).
133. *ST*, 1a2ae 17.7.
134. *ST*, 1a2ae 105.2.

Chapter 3

1. *ST*, 1a 79.8.
2. *ST*, 1a 79.4.
3. *ST*, 1a 79.11. For a contemporary discussion that makes a similar distinction in the human intellect, by one working within the Thomistic tradition, see Timothy E.

O'Connell, *Principles for a Catholic Morality*, rev. ed. (San Francisco: Harper & Row, 1990), 58–61.

4. The relationship between morality and rationality as a distinctive feature of Aquinas's ethics is explored by many authors. For a few examples, see Jan A. Aertsen, "Thomas Aquinas on the Good: The Relation between Metaphysics and Ethics," in *Aquinas's Moral Theory*, ed. MacDonald and Stump, 248; D. J. O'Connor, *Aquinas and Natural Law* (New York: St. Martin's, 1968), 32; and James Oscar Brown, *Natural Rectitude and Divine Law in Aquinas: An Approach to an Integral Interpretation of the Thomistic Doctrine of Law* (Toronto: Pontifical Institute of Medieval Studies, 1981), 15–20.
5. *SCG*, 2.23.6.
6. *ST*, 1a2ae 19.3–6; 1a2ae 21.1.
7. *CNE*, 1.7.
8. *ST*, 1a2ae 64.1; 1a2ae 66.4.
9. *ST*, 1a2ae 64.2. On the idea of virtue as hitting the mean between extremes, see *ST*, 1a2ae 64.1–4. The idea was classically propounded by Aristotle: *NE*, 2.6–9.
10. *SCG*, 3.63.3.
11. *ST*, 1a2ae 71.6; 1a2ae 75.1.
12. For detailed argumentation that human autonomy must be understood in terms of human participation in the divine, see Martin Rhonheimer, *Natural Law and Practical Reason: A Thomist View of Moral Autonomy*, trans. Gerald Malsbury (New York: Fordham University Press, 2000).
13. The Platonic elements in Aquinas's thought, especially in his *Summa Contra Gentiles*, are given extensive review in Thomas S. Hibbs, *Dialectic and Narrative in Aquinas: An Interpretation of the* Summa Contra Gentiles (Notre Dame: University of Notre Dame Press, 1995). In summary, O'Meara writes that the neo–Platonic intellectual current "moved from the philosophy of nature through the knowing and praying human being to the divine ideas. It elaborated the motifs of a divine fullness of being and of God giving birth to words which were creatures, finite beings set free in the realms of existence and knowledge" (*Thomas Aquinas Theologian*, 15).
14. Torrell, *Saint Thomas Aquinas*, 25; Weisheipl, *Thomas d'Aquino and Albert his Teacher*, 5–6.
15. Writing a commentary on Lombard's *Sentences* was a formal requirement for those progressing toward the position of master of theology in Aquinas's day (and for a long time afterwards). The *Sentences* were organized collections of different opinions of the Church Fathers on a variety of theological matters. Many commentators on this standard work were innovative, using the text as a springboard for their own ideas. As noted above, Aquinas followed this path. Both the Aristotelian and Platonic strains in Aquinas's thought appeared in his commentary, as may be illustrated by the authors that he quoted: the top three spots were claimed by Aristotle, Augustine, and Pseudo–Dionysius, in that order. The value that Aquinas attributed to Lombard's work itself may not have been great. He cited it relatively few times in his great mature work, the *Summa Theologiae*. See Torrell, *Saint Thomas Aquinas*, 41–42, 47.

16. For a discussion of the debates concerning the *exitus/reditus* organization of the *Summa Theologiae*, see Torrell, *Saint Thomas Aquinas*, 151–53. Among those perceiving a clear *exitus/reditus* theme, see for example Nelson, *Priority of Prudence*, 29; and M.-D. Chenu, *Toward Understanding Saint Thomas* (Chicago: Regnery, 1964), 304–313.
17. Aersten, "Aquinas's philosophy," 16.
18. Hall, *Narrative and the Natural Law*, 31.
19. Paul E. Sigmund, "Law and Politics," in *Cambridge Companion*, eds. Kretzmann and Stump, 220.
20. See Aersten, "Aquinas's philosophy," 22. Also see Jan Aersten, *Nature and Creature: Aquinas's Way of Thought* (Leiden: Brill, 1988), 123–27; and Ralph McInerny, *St. Thomas Aquinas* (Notre Dame: University of Notre Dame Press, 1982), 110. On the relationship of human understanding of truth and Aquinas's metaphysics of participation, see John Milbank and Catherine Pickstock, *Truth in Aquinas* (New York: Routledge, 2001), chapter 1.
21. John F. Wippel, *The Metaphysical Thought of Thomas Aquinas: From Finite Being to Uncreated Being* (Washington, D.C.: Catholic University of America Press, 2000), 96–97.
22. *SCG*, 1.92.1–2.
23. *ST*, 1a2ae 18.1.
24. For a few examples, see *SCG*, 1.31.1–3; 1.32.2; 1.35.2; 1.54.5; 1.77.5; *ST*, 1a 13.4–5.
25. *SCG*, 1.70.4; 1.71.8.
26. *SCG*, 1.66.3.
27. *SCG*, 1.56.1–2; 1.57.1–2, 8–9; 1.61.4; 1.69.14.
28. *ST*, 1a 46.1.
29. *ST*, 1a 47.1–2.
30. On these points, see the excellent studies of Oliva Blanchette, *The Perfection of the Universe According to Aquinas: A Teleological Cosmology* (University Park: Pennsylvania State University Press, 1992); and of John H. Wright, *The Order of the Universe in the Theology of St. Thomas Aquinas* (Rome: Universitatis Gregorianae, 1957).
31. *ST*, 1a 22.1–2; 1a 65.2.
32. *SCG*, 3.64.9. See Blanchette, *Perfection of the Universe*, 15, 98, 107, 196; and Wright, *Order of the Universe*, 17.
33. *ST*, 1a 49.1.
34. *ST*, 1a 44.3; 1a 47.3.
35. Blanchette, *Perfection of the Universe*, 4–5.
36. *ST*, 1a 22.4; 1a 47.1; 1a 48.2.
37. *ST*, 1a 22.1.
38. *ST*, 1a 22.2.
39. *ST*, 1a 22.3–4.
40. *ST*, 1a 103.1; 1a 103.5.
41. Brown, *Natural Rectitude and Divine Law*, 74–81.

42. *SCG*, 3.100.6.
43. *SCG*, 2.42.6.
44. *SCG*, 3.94.10.
45. *SCG*, 3.97.1; 3.97.14.
46. *SCG*, 2.46.1–7.
47. *ST*, 1a 15.1.
48. In Aquinas's own words: "Since every created substance must fall short of the perfection of divine goodness, in order that the likeness of divine goodness might be more perfectly communicated to things, it was necessary for there to be a diversity of things, so that what could not be perfectly represented by one thing might be, in more perfect fashion, represented by a variety of things in different ways. For instance, when a man sees that his mental conception cannot be expressed adequately by one spoken word, he multiplies his words in various ways, to express his mental conception through a variety of means" (*SCG*, 3.97.2).
49. *SCG*, 1.29.2, 5; 2.45.2.
50. *SCG*, 3.78.2; 3.144.2; 3.146.2.
51. *SCG*, 3.20.2.
52. *ST*, 1a 4.2–3. Aertsen describes the unity between creator and creature in Aquinas's thought in these terms. The creator is one who has being without limit, while the creature is one who has being with limit (*Nature and Creature*, 123–126).
53. Heinrich A. Rommen, *The Natural Law: A Study in Legal and Social History and Philosophy*, trans. Thomas R. Hanley (St. Louis: B. Herder, 1947), 45.
54. See *SCG*, 1.75.4; 1.96.3; 3.19.1; 3.19.4–5; 3.25.1; 3.25.8.
55. *ST*, 1a 93.1–3.
56. N. Max Wildiers, *Theologian and His Universe: Theology and Cosmology from the Middle Ages to the Present*, trans. Paul Dunphy (New York: Seabury, 1982), 57–58.
57. *ST*, 1a 65.2.
58. *ST*, 1a 93.2.
59. *ST*, 1a 93.3.
60. *ST*, 1a 93.6. Aquinas explains here that an "image represents something by likeness in species" while "a trace represents something by way of an effect."
61. *ST*, 1a 105.3.
62. *ST*, 1a 16.5; 2a2ae 52.2.
63. *ST*, 1a 12.2; 1a 79.4.
64. Westerman, *Disintegration*, 29–33.
65. *ST*, 1a 76.5 ad.3.
66. *ST*, 1a 6.1 ad.2.
67. Blanchette, *Perfection of the Universe*, 260, 266.
68. Ibid., 269, 272–275.
69. Ibid., 282.
70. Ibid., 64–65, 268, 280.
71. Ibid., 302.
72. *SCG*, 3.69.16.
73. *ST*, 1a2ae 6.1.
74. *ST*, 1a2ae 6.4–5.

75. Aquinas's understanding of freedom as discussed here is similar to that of some recent ethicists working in the Thomistic tradition. See O'Connell, *Principles for a Catholic Morality*, 57–58; and Richard M. Gula, S. S., *Reason Informed by Faith: Foundations of Catholic Morality* (Mahwah, NJ: Paulist, 1989), 75–83.
76. *ST*, 1a 83.1.
77. *ST*, 1a2ae 1.1.
78. *ST*, 2a2ae 25.3.
79. *SCG*, 3.69.17.
80. *SCG*, 3.71.3.
81. *SCG*, 3.70.7; *ST*, 1a 22.3.
82. *SCG*, 3.67.1–7.
83. *SCG*, 3.69.1–27; *ST*, 1a 19.8.
84. *SCG*, 3.72.1–8; 3.73.1; 3.74.1–7; *ST*, 1a 22.4; 1a2ae 11.4.
85. *ST*, 1a 19.8; 1a 23.6.
86. *SCG*, 3.77.1–7; *ST*, 1a 105.5.
87. *ST*, 1a 103.6.
88. For a recent extended treatment of Aquinas on human free action, see Stephen L. Brock, *Action and Conduct: Thomas Aquinas and the Theory of Action* (Edinburgh: T & T Clark, 1998), 137–196. For a popular discussion, see Montague Brown, *The Romance of Reason: An Adventure in the Thought of Thomas Aquinas* (Petersham, MA: Saint Bede's, 1991), 95–123.
89. *ST*, 1a 105.6.
90. *SCG*, 3.81.4–5.
91. *SCG*, 3.140.4.
92. *SCG*, 3.24.5.
93. *ST*, 2a2ae 31.3. Competing claims have been made on the precise relationship of Aquinas's cosmology and his ethics. For example, Wildiers, in looking at the cosmological background of the medieval view of morality, has spoken of morality as a transposition of cosmic order to human conduct (Wildiers, *Theologian and His Universe*, 75). However, his conclusions have been challenged as misleading by Porter in "Contested Categories," 222. The question of the relationship of the good in the different orders of natural things and human actions is discussed in a broader context in Aertsen, "Thomas Aquinas on the Good," 235–53. Aertsen writes: "What is most striking in Thomas's analysis is precisely the parallelism that he develops between the two orders [i.e., between the moral order and the order of things]" (246).
94. *SCG*, 1.1.1; 3.77.5; 3.78.1; *ST*, 2a2ae 10.11.
95. *SCG*, 2.24.4.
96. *SCG*, 3.76.7; 3.140.2.
97. *SCG*, 1.93.5–6, 10–11; 3.71.4; *ST*, 1a2ae 61.5.
98. *SCG*, 1.93.12; *ST*, 1a2ae 61.5.
99. *SCG*, 3.19.4–5.
100. *Politics*, 1.2.
101. For example, in *CNE*, 1.1.
102. *SCG*, 3.128.1; *DR*, 1.1.
103. *DR*, 1.1.

104. *ST*, 1a2ae 14.3.
105. Porter, *Recovery of Virtue*, 147–148.
106. *SCG*, 1.91.4; *ST*, 2a2ae 26.8; 2a2ae 31.3.
107. For Aquinas, even the cardinal virtues are social virtues, since they are possessed by social animals. See *ST*, 1a2ae 61.5.
108. *ST*, 2a2ae 47.12.
109. *ST*, 1a2ae 90.4.
110. *ST*, 1a2ae 90.1.
111. *SCG*, 3.114.3; 3.115.3; 3.128.1.
112. *ST*, 1a2ae 91.1.
113. *ST*, 1a2ae 91.2.
114. *ST*, 1a2ae 91.3.
115. *ST*, 1a2ae 95.1.
116. *ST*, 1a2ae 91.3.
117. *ST*, 1a2ae 95.2.
118. Ibid.
119. *ST*, 1a2ae 90.3.
120. *ST*, 1a2ae 90.2.
121. *ST*, 1a2ae 91.1.
122. *ST*, 1a2ae 91.2.
123. *ST*, 1a2ae 99.3.
124. *ST*, 1a2ae 105.2.
125. *ST*, 2a2ae 77.1. ad.2.
126. *ST*, 1a2ae 98.1.
127. *ST*, 1a2ae 99.3.
128. *NE*, 5.1.
129. *ST*, 2a2ae 58.7.
130. *ST*, 1a2ae 100.2; 2a2ae 57.1.
131. *SCG*, 3.34.2; 3.128.6.
132. *ST*, 1a2ae 97.3.
133. Ibid.
134. *ST*, 1a2ae 97.2.
135. *ST*, 1a2ae 90.3.
136. *ST*, 1a2ae 97.3 ad.3.
137. *ST*, 1a2ae 105.1.
138. *ST*, 1a2ae 97.3 ad.3.
139. *ST*, 1a2ae 95.3.
140. Ibid.
141. Ibid.
142. This hagiographical proclivity is evident in some of the works cited in the last chapter regarding Fredrick and Louis. For example, Van Cleve, *Emperor Fredrick II*; and especially Kantorowicz, *Frederick the Second*.

Chapter 4

1. *ST*, 1a2ae 5.3.
2. For example, see *SCG*, 3.38.3; 3.39.2; *ST*, 1a 32.1.
3. *ST*, 2a2ae 70.4 ad.1.
4. *ST*, 1a 101.1.
5. *ST*, 1a2ae 98.6.
6. *ST*, 1a2ae 99.2 ad.2. The concern that revelation is necessary because of both the insufficiency and the error of human reason is a common one in Aquinas's writings. For example, see *SCG*, 1.4.4–6; 4.1.1–5; *ST*, 1a 1.1; 1a 2.2 ad.3; 1a 12.12.
7. *SCG*, 3.81.1.
8. *ST*, 1a 1.8 ad.2. On this point, see the remarks of Arvin Vos in *Aquinas, Calvin, and Contemporary Protestant Thought: A Critique of Protestant Views on the Thought of Thomas Aquinas* (Washington, D.C.: Christian University Press, 1985), 62–84. He offers a summary of the limits of natural reason in knowing God, and why one only obtains a feeble knowledge of God through it (ibid., 96–97).
9. *SCG*, 3.91.5.
10. *ST*, 1a 77.2.
11. *SCG*, 1.69.14; *ST*, 1a 85.5.
12. *SCG*, 1.35.2.
13. *ST*, 1a 13.4.
14. *ST*, 2a2ae 8.1; 2a2ae 8.1 ad.1.
15. *SCG*, 1.61.4.
16. *CNE*, 1.7. See also *ST*, 1a 79.4.
17. *ST*, 1a 85.3.
18. *ST*, 2a2ae 47.1.
19. *ST*, 2a2ae 47.3 ad.2.
20. *SCG*, 1.61.4.
21. *ST*, 2a2ae 49.3; 2a2ae 47.3 ad.2.
22. *ST*, 2a2ae 49.8 ad.3.
23. *ST*, 1a 116.1.
24. *ST*, 1a2ae 100.11.
25. *ST*, 1a2ae 2.3.
26. *ST*, 1a2ae 14.1.
27. *ST*, 1a2ae 99.2 ad.2.
28. *ST*, 2a2ae 52.1 ad.1.
29. *ST*, 2a2ae 47.3 ad.2.
30. On this point, see Westburg, *Right Practical Reason*, 216. Westburg argues that Aquinas's psychology of action accounts for sin at every stage in the process of acting much more comprehensively than does the thought of most medieval theologians, who tended to make human will the crucial factor. McInerney claims that for

Aquinas human beings are more wounded in the moral than in the intellectual order, but that Aquinas also asserts the need for grace both to illumine the mind and strengthen the will. See McInerny, *Ethica Thomistica*, 119.

31. *ST*, 1a2ae 71.6; 1a2ae 75.1.
32. *ST*, 1a2ae 71.6 ad.5.
33. *ST*, 1a2ae 85.2.
34. *ST*, 1a2ae 109.2.
35. *ST*, 1a2ae 33.1; 1a2ae 37.1; 1a2ae 48.3; 1a2ae 77.2; 1a2ae 80.2; 2a2ae 15.1.
36. On Aquinas's theology of grace generally, see *ST*, 1a2ae 109.1–9.
37. For example, see *ST*, 2a2ae 8.1; 2a2ae 8.1 ad.1.
38. *ST*, 1a2ae 109.8–9.
39. *ST*, 2a2ae 2.4.
40. Aertsen comments: "Until that time medieval thought had been oriented mainly toward Augustine, Boethius, and Pseudo–Dionysius the Areopagite, who were all strongly influenced by Platonism. In Aristotelianism it was now furnished with a comprehensive, often technical philosophy, in which human beings and other things in the physical world were understood not in terms of their participation in ideal Forms but on the basis of their own inner principles or natures" ("Aquinas's philosophy," 20).
41. See O'Meara, *Thomas Aquinas Theologian*, 4. On the study of Aristotle at the University of Naples, also see Brian Davies, *The Thought of Thomas Aquinas* (Oxford: Clarendon Press, 1992), 2.
42. On these controversies over Aristotle in Paris, see Torrell, *Saint Thomas Aquinas*, 37–38.
43. O'Meara, *Thomas Aquinas Theologian*, 14. On the relationship of Aquinas and Albert generally, see Weisheipl, *Thomas d'Aquino and Albert his Teacher*.
44. Weisheipl, *Thomas d'Aquino and Albert his Teacher*, 16.
45. See Torrell, *Saint Thomas Aquinas*, 47.
46. See Aertsen, "Aquinas's philosophy," 21. For various opinions on the quality of Aquinas's commentaries on Aristotle, see McInerny, *St. Thomas Aquinas*, 32–33; Torrell, *Saint Thomas Aquinas*, 238–239; Mark D. Jordan, *The Alleged Aristotelianism of Thomas Aquinas* (Toronto: Pontifical Institute of Mediaeval Studies, 1990); and Vernon J. Bourke, "The *Nicomachean Ethics* and Thomas Aquinas," in *St. Thomas Aquinas 1274–1974 Commemorative Studies* (Toronto: Pontifical Institute of Mediaeval Studies, 1974), 1:253–59.
47. In regard to nature and the cosmos, see Leo Elders, *The Philosophy of Nature of St. Thomas Aquinas: Nature, the Universe, Man* (Frankfurt am Main: Peter Lang, 1997), 5; and Wildiers, *The Theologian and His Universe*, 51. In regard to law, see D. J. O'Connor, *Aquinas and Natural Law* (New York: St Martin's, 1968), 58; Brown, *Natural Rectitude*, 45–46; Goerner, "Thomistic Natural Right, 415–16; and Sigmund, "Law and Politics," 224–26. In regard to virtue, see Bowlin, *Contingency and Fortune*, 141–42. In regard to government, see Sigmund, "Law and Politics," 220. Also see the recent "Aristotelian" reading of Aquinas in Flannery, *Acts Amid Precepts*.

48. The most relentless critic is Mark Jordan, who claims that Aquinas's philosophy was not Aristotelian and that he did not consider himself a part of the Aristotelian school. See Jordan, *Alleged Aristotelianism*, 5–7.
49. Anton C. Pegis points to the influence of Augustine, though also acknowledging points at which Aquinas favored Aristotelian ideas over those of Augustine; see *At the Origins of the Thomistic Notion of Man* (New York: Macmillan, 1963). Vos (*Aquinas, Calvin, and Contemporary Protestant Thought*, 163–65) discusses the influence of the reforming movement of the mendicant orders.
50. Jordan, *The Alleged Aristotelianism*, 30; Pegis, *At the Origins*, 3–18.
51. Joseph Owens, C.Ss.R, "Aristotle and Aquinas," in *Cambridge Companion*, ed. Kretzmann and Stump, 38–39, 45–53, 57. Among the issues considered by Owens are their different philosophies of being and the different bases upon which their respective philosophies were built (for Aristotle, sensible natures; for Aquinas, sensible existents).
52. Aquinas believed that reason and the philosophers who employed it were like handmaidens appointed to serve the sacred science of theology by helping to clarify its teaching (*ST*, 1a 1.5 ad.2). He adds: "sacred doctrine makes use also of the authority of philosophers in those questions in which they were able to know the truth by natural reason....Nevertheless, sacred doctrine makes use of these authorities as extrinsic and probable arguments" (*ST*, 1a 1.8 ad.2).
53. *ST*, 1a2ae 2.3; 1a2ae 14.1.
54. *NE*, 1.3. See Aquinas, *CNE*, 1.3.
55. *NE*, 2.2. See Aquinas, *CNE*, 2.2.
56. *NE*, 5.10. See Aquinas, *CNE*, 5.10.
57. For example, see *ST*, 2a2ae 29.3 ad.2.
58. For example, see McInerney (*St. Thomas Aquinas*, 70) on the difficulties of making moral knowledge concrete. See also Boler ("Aquinas on Exceptions in Natural Law," 161–204) on the mutability of practical reasoning and of exceptions to practical principles. Finally, see Bowlin (*Contingency and Fortune*, xi [summarizing much of the argument of the entire book]) on the need of accounting for contingent matters and the unexpected events of fortune if the moral life is to be properly understood.
59. *NE*, 1.1.
60. *ST*, 1a2ae 1.1.
61. *ST*, 1a2ae 1.3.
62. *ST*, 1a2ae 7.2 ad.1.
63. *ST*, 1a2ae 94.3.
64. Ibid.
65. Ibid.
66. *ST*, 1a2ae 99.5.
67. *CNE*, 5.1.
68. *ST*, 1a2ae 50.3.
69. *ST*, 1a2ae 49.1–5.
70. *ST*, 1a2ae 50.1.

71. *ST*, 1a2ae 49.3.
72. *ST*, 1a2ae 51.1.
73. *ST*, 1a2ae 51.2–3.
74. *ST*, 1a2ae 53.1–3.
75. *SCG*, 1.11.1; 3.85.8.
76. *ST*, 1a2ae 58.1.
77. *ST*, 2a2ae 47.15 ad.2.
78. *SCG*, 3.65.7. See also *CNE*, 10.9 in regard to the difficulty of breaking habits and *ST*, 1a2ae 99.2. ad.2 in regard to habituation to sin.
79. *NE*, 3.5.
80. *ST*, 1a2ae 55.3.
81. *ST*, 1a 1.6 ad.3; 1a2ae 63.2; 1a2ae 65.1; *CNE*, 2.1. See also Porter, *Recovery of Virtue*, 103.
82. *ST*, 1a2ae 57.5; 1a2ae 58.4.
83. *ST*, 1a2ae 61.2.
84. *NE*, 6.13.
85. Goerner's two articles ("On Thomistic Natural Law" and "Thomistic Natural Right") were something of a harbinger of what was to come. The importance of prudence in Aquinas's ethics has been emphasized by Hall, *Narrative and the Natural Law*; Porter, *Recovery of Virtue*; Nelson, *Priority of Prudence*; and Westburg, *Right Practical Reason*.
86. Westburg, *Right Practical Reason*, 3, 189.
87. This is probably true of both Goerner and Nelson. Porter ("Contested Categories," 207) and Hall (*Narrative and the Natural Law*, 12–16, 19–22) concur with this verdict.
88. For example, see *SCG*, 1.93.5; 3.35.3; *ST*, 1a2ae 57.4; 2a2ae 47.1 ad.3; 2a2ae 47.2; 2a2ae 47.2 ad.1; 2a2ae 47.5; Aristotle, *NE*, 6.5.
89. *ST*, 2a2ae 47.6–8.
90. *SCG*, 3.35.4; *ST*, 2a2ae 47.3,15.
91. *CNE*, 6.7.
92. *SCG*, 3.35.3; *ST*, 2a2ae 4.8; 2a2ae 47.3.
93. *ST*, 2a2ae 47.3 ad.2; 2a2ae 49.1.
94. *ST*, 2a2ae 49.3.
95. *ST*, 2a2ae 51.1–4.
96. *ST*, 1a 22.1; 2a2ae 47.1; 2a2ae 47.1 ad.2; 2a2ae 49.1; 2a2ae 49.6.
97. *ST*, 2a2ae 49.8; 2a2ae 49.8 ad.3.
98. *ST*, 2a2ae 47.12.
99. *ST*, 1a2ae 57.6 ad.4; 2a2ae 47.11; 2a2ae 50.1–3.
100. *ST*, 2a2ae 50.2.
101. *ST*, 2a2ae 47.3.
102. *ST*, 2a2ae 49.7. For an examples of a commentator who notes the bearing of singular circumstances on the right functioning of prudence, see McInerney, *St. Thomas Aquinas*, 71.
103. *Politics*, 4.1.
104. *ST*, 1a2ae 7.3.

105. *ST*, 1a2ae 7.2.
106. *ST*, 1a2ae 100.1.
107. For example, see the comments of A. P. d'Entreves already some time ago: *Natural Law: An Historical Survey* (London: Hutchinson, 1951; reprint, New York: Harper & Row, 1965), 43–44 (d'Entreves has written a revised edition, *Natural Law: An Introduction to Legal Philosophy* [London: Hutchinson, 1970], though I cite the first edition because of its greater age).
108. *ST*, 1a2ae 109.9.
109. For example, see *ST*, 1a2ae 18.3; 1a2ae 18.9–11; 1a2ae 20.1; 1a2ae 20.4.
110. *ST*, 1a2ae 64.1 ad.2.
111. *ST*, 1a2ae 73.7.
112. *ST*, 2a2ae 49.3.
113. Traina, *Feminist Ethics and Natural Law*, 66–67.
114. *CNE*, 1.4.
115. *CNE*, 2.1.
116. *CNE*, 6.11.
117. *ST*, 2a2ae 47.3 ad.2; 2a2ae 49.1.
118. *ST*, 2a2ae 47.15 ad.2.
119. *ST*, 2a2ae 49.3.
120. For example, see Nelson, *Priority of Prudence*, 79–80; and Westerman, *Disintegration*, 65.
121. *CNE*, 1.3. See Aristotle, *NE*, 1.3.
122. *CNE*, 1.4; 1.7.
123. *CNE*, 2.1. See Aristotle, *NE*, 2.1.
124. *CNE*, 6.11. See Aristotle, *NE*, 6.11.
125. *NE*, 10.9.
126. *CNE*, 6.7. See Aristotle, *NE*, 6.7.
127. *NE*, 6.8.
128. Traina, *Feminist Ethics and Natural Law*, 64–66. See also Hall, *Narrative and the Natural Law*, 40.
129. Hall, *Narrative and the Natural Law*, 15, 93–95, 102.
130. Ibid., 16, 94, 99–100, 111.
131. *CNE*, 1.7.
132. See *ST*, 1a2ae 91.3; *ST*, 1a2ae 95.2.
133. *ST*, 1a2ae 91.4.
134. Tully's definition of a nation, which Aquinas borrows from Augustine, is instructive here: "A nation is a body of men united together by consent to the law and by a community of welfare [*populus est coetus multitudinis iuris consensus et utilitatis communione sociatus*]" (*ST*, 1a2ae 105.2).
135. *ST*, 1a2ae 95.3 obj.1.
136. *ST*, 1a2ae 95.3.
137. Ibid.
138. *ST*, 1a2ae 97.1.
139. Ibid.
140. *ST*, 1a2ae 97.1 obj.3.

141. *ST*, 1a2ae 97.1 ad.3.
142. *ST*, 1a2ae 97.2.
143. Ibid.
144. *ST*, 1a2ae 96.6 sed contra.
145. *ST*, 1a2ae 96.6.
146. Ibid.
147. Ibid. On utility as a reason for dispensing from laws, see also *ST*, 1a2ae 100.8.
148. *ST*, 1a2ae 105.2 ad.1; 1a2ae 105.2 ad.4.
149. *ST*, 1a2ae 51.1.
150. *SCG*, 3.116.4; 3.128.8; *CNE*, 1.9. Likewise, see Aristotle, *NE*, 1.9; 10.9.
151. *ST*, 1a2ae 92.1.
152. *ST*, 1a2ae 95.1.
153. *ST*, 1a2ae 96.2–3.
154. *ST*, 1a2ae 95.3.
155. *ST*, 1a2ae 97.1.
156. *ST*, 2a2ae 60.2.
157. *ST*, 2a2ae 57.1 ad.2.
158. *Politics*, 4.1.
159. *ST*, 1a2ae 100.2.
160. *ST*, 1a2ae 104.3 ad.1.
161. *SCG*, 3.71.4.
162. *ST*, 2a2ae 61.2.
163. *CNE*, 5.7.
164. *SCG*, 3.111.1.
165. Chroust, "The Philosophy of Law," 32.
166. *ST*, 2a2ae 57.2 ad.2.
167. *NE*, 5.7.
168. *ST*, 1a2ae 96.6.
169. *ST*, 1a2ae 96.6 ad.3.
170. *ST*, 2a2ae 120.2; 2a2ae 120.2. ad.3.
171. For example, see Chroust, "The Philosophy of Law," 34; Goerner, "Thomistic Natural Right," 400–415.
172. *ST*, 2a2ae 120.1; *CNE*, 5.10. See also Aristotle, *NE*, 5.10; and Brown, *Natural Rectitude and Natural Law*, 24.
173. *ST*, 1a2ae 100.8; 2a2ae 60.5 ad.2; *CNE*, 5.10. See also Aristotle, *NE*, 5.10.
174. *CNE*, 1.3. See Aristotle, *NE*, 1.3.
175. *ST*, 2a2ae 70.2.
176. *ST*, 2a2ae 42.2. ad.3; *DR*, 1.6.
177. *ST*, 2a2ae 69.4.
178. *ST*, 2a2ae 10.11.
179. *ST*, 1a2ae 95.1 ad.2.
180. *NE*, 5.6. See Aquinas, *CNE*, 5.6.
181. *Politics*, 3.15.
182. *Politics*, 3.16.
183. *Politics*, 5.8.

184. *Politics*, 4.4.
185. *Politics*, 2.8.
186. *ST*, 1a2ae 97.2.
187. *Politics*, 2.8.
188. *ST*, 1a2ae 97.2.
189. *Politics*, 5.8.
190. *ST*, 2a2ae 10.10.
191. *ST*, 1a2ae 91.3. See also 1a2ae 95.2 sed contra.
192. Hall, *Narrative and the Natural Law*, 16, 95.
193. *ST*, 1a2ae 91.3.
194. *ST*, 1a2ae 97.3 ad.2.
195. Ibid.
196. *ST*, 1a2ae 94.3.
197. *ST*, 1a2ae 95.1.
198. One might object that *consuetudino* in this passage refers to personal habit rather than to broader social custom. R. J. Henle, for example, translates *consuetudino* here as "habit;" see R. J. Henle, ed., *Saint Thomas Aquinas The Treatise on Law* (Notre Dame: University of Notre Dame Press, 1993), 282. As seen above, however, Aquinas himself distinguishes an individual's *consuetudo* from an individual's *habitus* (*ST*, 1a2ae 50.3), and thus the meaning of the two words should not be conflated. This does leave open the possibility that *consuetudo* in 1a2ae 95.1 refers to an individual's custom rather than to a social custom. However, given the social context of the passage and the fact that *consuetudo* consistently refers to social custom throughout the "Treatise on Law," I have adopted the social understanding of *consuetudo* here as the more likely reading.
199. *ST*, 1a2ae 95.1. See also *CNE*, 10.9.
200. Hall, *Narrative and the Natural Law*, 102.
201. *ST*, 1a2ae 96.2.
202. Ibid. See also *ST*, 1a2ae 99.6; 1a2ae 104.3 ad.1. Aquinas believes that laws should differ not only according to the degree of virtue in a people, but also according to their type of polity (see *ST*, 1a2ae 100.2; 1a2ae 104.3 ad.2).
203. *ST*, 1a2ae 96.2.
204. *ST*, 1a2ae 95.3.
205. Ibid.
206. *ST*, 1a2ae 97.2.
207. Ibid.
208. *ST*, 1a2ae 97.2 obj.1.
209. *ST*, 1a2ae 97.2 ad.1.
210. *ST*, 1a2ae 96.4.
211. Ibid.
212. *ST*, 1a2ae 97.2.
213. *DR*, 1.6.
214. Aquinas's belief that custom is grounded in social consensus is stated in *ST*, 1a2ae 97.3 ad.3.
215. *DR*, 1.10.

216. *ST*, 1a2ae 105.2.
217. *ST*, 1a2ae 105.1.
218. *DR*, 2.3. See Aristotle, *Politics*, 6.6.
219. *ST*, 1a2ae 95.3; 1a2ae 97.2.
220. See Alisdair MacIntyre, *Dependent Rational Animals: Why Human Beings Need the Virtues* (Chicago: Open Court, 1999).

Chapter 5

1. His most important works dealing with the rule of law are *The Constitution of Liberty* (Chicago: University of Chicago Press, 1960) and *Law, Legislation and Liberty*, vol. 1, *Rules and Order*; *Law, Legislation and Liberty*, vol. 2, *The Mirage of Social Justice* (London: Routledge & Kegan Paul, 1976; reprint, Chicago: University of Chicago Press, 1983); *Law, Legislation and Liberty*, vol. 3, *The Political Order of a Free People* (Chicago: University of Chicago Press, 1979).
2. The subtitle of Hayek's 1970s trilogy, *Law, Legislation and Liberty* (*A new statement of the liberal principles of justice and political society*), reflects his desire to defend the "liberal" society. As such, Hayek's interest in fortifying an open, pluralist, non–metaphysically based society seems to put him in line with other defenders of various versions of liberalism in the 1970s, such as John Rawls (see *A Theory of Justice* [Cambridge, MA: Harvard University Press, 1971; rev. ed., Cambridge, MA: Harvard University Press, 1999]) and Robert Nozick (see *Anarchy, State, and Utopia* [New York: Basic Books, 1974]). However, Hayek, unlike Rawls and Nozick, eschewed ideas such as social contracts and veils of ignorance. To Hayek, the principles of justice in society could not be reasoned out in the abstract, apart from social relations, the knowledge of the conditions of life, or the experience of time. In this sense, Hayek's work anticipates some of the critiques of liberalism that would animate the world of moral philosophy in the next decade, such as those of Alisdair MacIntyre (see *After Virtue: A Study in Moral Theory*, 2d ed. [Notre Dame: University of Notre Dame Press, 1984] and several later works, most recently *Dependent Rational Animals*, in which he treats the dependent, animal nature of human rationality in ways that I believe also cohere with some of Hayek's contentions) and Michael Sandel (see *Liberalism and the Limits of Justice* [Cambridge: Cambridge University Press, 1982]).
3. Bertrand de Jouvenal, *On Power: The Natural History of Its Growth*, trans. J F. Huntington (London: Hutchinson, 1948; reprint, Indianapolis: Liberty Fund, 1993), 334–347.
4. Alexander Bickel, *The Morality of Consent* (New Haven: Yale University Press, 1975).
5. Robert M. Cover, "The Supreme Court, 1982 Term—Foreword: *Nomos* and Narrative," *Harvard Law Review* 97 (November 1983): 4–68. Franklin G. Snyder develops Cover's ideas and makes two particularly helpful modifications or clarifications:

individuals participate in multiple *jurisgenerative* communities and that the state as well as small communities can be *jurisgenerative*; see "*Nomos*, Narrative, and Adjudication," *William and Mary Law Review* 40 (May 1999): 1623–1729.

6. Harold Berman, *Law and Revolution: The Formation of the Western Legal Tradition* (Cambridge: Harvard University Press, 1983), 11, 39.
7. Madden, "The Vital Common Law," 555–611.
8. Calabresi, *Common Law*; see also his additional reflections on the matter in Guido Calabresi, "The Non–Primacy of Statutes Act: A Comment," *Vermont Law Review* 4 (1979): 247–255.
9. Farber and Frickey, "In the Shadow of the Legislature," 888–906.
10. William Blackstone famously claimed that the common law was the "perfection of reason" and asserted that what was unreasonable was simply not part of the common law (*Commentaries*, 1:70). See Madden, "The Vital Common Law," 572–573, for a brief survey of the historic understanding of the natural law as a source of the common law, as well as the close association of customary law and natural law recognized by Hayek (*Law, Legislation and Liberty*, vol. 1, *Rules and Order*, 84) and Leoni (*Freedom and the Law*, 83–86, 186). Again, both Hayek and Leoni have contrasted customary law with the sort of law envisioned by legal positivists, for whom law is defined in terms of will rather than reason—see Hayek, *Law, Legislation and Liberty*, vol. 1, *Rules and Order*, 7, 28, 31–32, 73, 97, 118, 123; and Leoni, *Freedom and the Law*, 9, 11, 83–85, 146, 186. A similar contrast is made in Sheleff, *The Future of Tradition*, 3–4.
11. For example, Jeremy Bentham could understand the common law only as a series of autocratic orders emanating from judges (*Of Laws in General*, 1, 152), and Robert Rantoul conceived the common law as one *ex post facto* after another and ridiculed Blackstone by analogizing "common law is the perfection of reason" to "alcohol is the perfection of sugar" (Rantoul, "Oration at Scituate," in Presser, *Law and Jurisprudence*, 255).
12. See Bentham, *Of Laws in General*, 232–235, 246; and Rantoul, "Oration at Scituate," in Presser, *Law and Jurisprudence*, 257.
13. One example, beyond those mentioned in this paragraph and the next, are the wistful comments of Robert S. Summers, in regard to the reform of contract law, on the failure of the Uniform Commercial Code to meet any of the "romantic" expectations of many jurists at the time of its creation. See the first chapter of the present volume and White and Summers, *Uniform Commercial Code*, 21.
14. Eisenberg, *Nature of the Common Law*, 146–151.
15. See Calabresi, *Common Law*, 2, 6–7; Peters, "Common Law Judging," 1005–1011; Madden, "The Vital Common Law," 567; and Eisenberg, *Nature of the Common Law*, 44–47, 146–151, 159–160.
16. This understanding of law may in some ways resemble Jean Porter's characterization of the medieval view of law. Porter contrasts the contemporary notion of law as a set of rules with the medieval notion of law as "primarily an intrinsic principle of order" ("Contested Categories," 216).
17. See Blackstone, *Commentary*, 69–71.
18. Sheleff, *Future of Tradition*, 86–87.

19. Hayek, *Law, Legislation and Liberty*, vol. 1, *Rules and Order*, 30.
20. On this aspect of the common law, see, for example, Hogue, *Origins of the Common Law*, 189.
21. Rantoul, "Oration at Scituate," in Presser, *Law and Jurisprudence*, 255–256.
22. Madden, "The Vital Common Law," 561–566.
23. It is true that when the majority's hatred of a minority runs strong, the minority may give consent to practices that do discriminate against them, for fear of suffering something worse, if for no other reason. However, when such unfortunate situations arise, hated minority groups may in fact be better off on the whole when courts enforce less than ideal customs to which they have given consent than when courts enforce against them statutory laws presumably enacted by legislatures controlled by the prejudiced majority.
24. Bentham, *Of Laws in General*, 185–191; Rantoul, "Oration at Scituate," in Presser, *Law and Jurisprudence*, 255–256.
25. Hayek, *Law, Legislation and Liberty*, vol. 1, *Rules and Order*, 116.
26. Leoni, *Freedom and the Law*, 73.
27. Periodic debates about the federal income and estate tax law are an example. Many people do change their behavior to accommodate the tax code, and much of this behavior is oriented to the future (such as, should they sell their stocks now, or will capital gains rates be lowered sometime soon; or, must they give away assets to their heirs now in order to maximize their gifts, or may/should they wait until death?). The possibility, and even likelihood, of abrupt change in the tax code via legislation makes such planning in many ways a matter of guesswork, and by necessity something less than fully rational.
28. This is illustrated by the recent front–page headline of a local newspaper: "Hundreds of new state laws to take effect today" (*Escondido North County Times*, 1 July 2002, A1).
29. Ibid., 83.
30. Hayek, *Law, Legislation and Liberty*, vol. 1, *Rules and Order*, 116.
31. Sheleff, *Future of Tradition*, 86.
32. Jouvenal, *On Power*, 345–347.
33. There is something similar here to Cover's idea of the *jurispathic*, discussed above. Though Cover speaks of it in terms of the judicial branch of government, and Jouvenal and Leoni deal here in terms of the legislative branch, all three scholars are concerned about the effects of governmental decrees that are imposed upon often unwilling people (as Cover might say, upon *jurisgenerative* communities) under threat of force.
34. Leoni, *Freedom and the Law*, 103.
35. Ibid., 110–111.
36. Sheleff, *Future of Tradition*, 5.
37. Ibid., 7.
38. For consideration of various issues related to the concept of representation in the creation of legislation, see William N. Eskridge, Jr. and Philip P. Frickey, *Legislation: Statutes and the Creation of Public Policy*, 2d ed. (St. Paul: West, 1995), 123–237.

39. The key issue that Calabresi confronts in *Common Law* is what to do about the obvious problem of obsolete statutes that legislatures do not readdress but that judges are called upon to apply. His answer, considered above, consists in adopting a "common law" of statutes, and he interacts at length with answers suggested by other scholars.
40. It probably should be granted that this failure of representatives truly to speak for their constituency is lessened when the constituency is religiously, ethnically, and socio–economically very homogenous, in ways that most American geographic constituencies are not.
41. Jouvenal, *On Power*, 341.
42. Sheleff, *Future of Tradition*, 86–87.
43. Ibid., 14.
44. For example, Bickel writes: "For the basis of all law—judicial, legislative, or administrative—is consensual. We are willing, and ought to be willing, to pay only a limited price in coercing minorities. Whenever a minority is sufficiently large or determined or, as in the case of *Brown* [*v. Board of Education*], strategically placed, we do not quite have law. We must then generate a greater measure of consent, or reconsider our stance on the minority's position. We must, in such circumstances resort to methods other than coercive law; methods of persuasion and inducement, appeal to reason and shared values, appeal to interest, and not only material but political interest. We act on the realization that the law needs to be established before it can be effectively enforced, that it is, in a quite real sense, still provisional." See *Morality of Consent*, 110–111.
45. See John Courtney Murray, *We Hold These Truths: Catholic Reflections on the American Proposition* (Kansas City: Sheed and Ward, 1960), where Murray structures the bulk of his argument on the past existence of the "American consensus" and the need to renew it for the sake of the present and future prospering of American society. Also see Bernard Lonergan, "Dialectic of Authority," in *A Third Collection* (New York: Paulist, 1985), 5–12. Here Lonergan argues that authority belongs to the community, and emphasizes the need for social cooperation grounded in commonality, in regard to which he speaks specifically of the (difficult) formation of common consent.
46. Leoni, *Freedom and the Law*, 146–151.
47. This is not to say that spontaneously–generated languages such as English are as useful as they could possibly be. Nevertheless, any improvements that one might suggest are simply minor adjustments of a spontaneously–generated whole, something far different from the idea of creating a language from scratch. This is analogous to the ideas about customary and statutory law that I am suggesting in this chapter: customary law is not necessarily the best law that could be, and statutes may offer prospects for improving it in many instances; however, statutory law ought not create the entire legal order by itself, but ought to exist in the context of vibrant customary law.
48. Of course, part of the legal consensus will consist of agreements to disagree. The pluralist nature of our society in regard to religious belief, for example, and the con-

sequent failure to attain consensus on theological matters does not necessarily prohibit the establishment of a legal consensus in regard to freedom of worship.

49. Hayek, *Law, Legislation and Liberty*, vol. 1, *Rules and Order*, 12.

50. Hayek, *The Collected Works of F.A. Hayek*, vol. 1, *The Fatal Conceit: The Errors of Socialism*, ed. W. W. Bartley, III (Chicago: University of Chicago Press, 1989), 12. These and other similarities between Hayek's view of law and the general perspective of the Aristotelian–Thomistic tradition suggest that important qualifications must be made to the claim that Hayek's jurisprudence is fundamentally different from Aristotle's. This claim is made by Eugene F. Miller, "Prudence and the Rule of Law," *American Journal of Jurisprudence* 24 (1979): 181–206. Miller argues that Hayek's conception of the rule of law leaves little room for the use of prudence in the development and application of law, in contrast to the close relationship between law and prudence in the Aristotelian–Thomistic tradition. For critique, see David VanDrunen, "Aquinas and Hayek on the Limits of Law: A Convergence of Ethical Traditions," *Journal of Markets and Morality* 5 (Fall 2002): 315–337.

51. Rantoul, "Oration at Scituate," in Presser, *Law and Jurisprudence*, 255.

52. Hayek, *Law, Legislation and Liberty*, vol. 1, *Rules and Order*, 44.

53. On this point, also see Peters, "Common Law Judging," 1002–1005, 1008.

54. See Hayek, *Law, Legislation and Liberty*, vol. 1, *Rules and Order*, 48–49; and Hayek, *The Fatal Conceit*, 6.

55. Rantoul, "Oration at Scituate," in Presser, *Law and Jurisprudence*, 257.

56. Milsom, "The Past and Future of Judge–Made Law," in *Studies in the History of the Common Law*, 212.

57. See especially Hayek, *Law, Legislation and Liberty*, vol. 1, *Rules and Order*, 3, 14, 17–18, 50–51; and Leoni, *Freedom and the Law*, 153, 175–177.

58. Hayek, *Law, Legislation and Liberty*, vol. 1, *Rules and Order*, 50–51. On this point, it is noteworthy that another contribution of Sheleff's recent work is his combating the prejudice that customary law is primitive law; for example, see *Future of Tradition*, 83.

59. See Milsom, "Reason in the Development of the Common Law," in *Studies in the History of the Common Law*, 150–151; and Milsom, *Historical Foundations*, 6, 26–27. See also Dicey, *Introduction*, 3, in regard to the unwritten constitutional law of England. On the spontaneous nature of law, see again the recent contribution of Sheleff, *Future of Tradition*, 3.

60. See especially Hayek, *Law, Legislation and Liberty*, vol. 1, *Rules and Order*, 9, 74, 80, 99, 119; Hayek, *The Fatal Conceit*, 6, 20, 75; and Leoni, *Freedom and the Law*, 22, 88. See also Blackstone, *Commentaries*, 1:70; and Edmund Burke, *Reflections on the Revolution in France* (1790; reprint, New York: Penguin, 1986), 193.

61. See also Hayek, *Law, Legislation and Liberty*, vol. 1, *Rules and Order*, 65, 78, 111.

62. Ibid., 92.

Bibliography

Thomas Aquinas: Primary Sources

Thomas Aquinas. *Commentary on Aristotle's Nicomachean Ethics*. Trans. C. I. Litzinger, O.P. Chicago: Regnery, 1964. Reprint, Notre Dame: Dumb Ox Books, 1993.

———. *On the Governance of Rulers* [*De Regno*]. Trans. Gerald B. Phelan. New York: Sheed & Ward, 1938.

———. *On the Truth of the Catholic Faith* [*Summa Contra Gentiles*]. Trans. Anton C. Pegis. Vol. 1. Garden City, NY: Hanover House, 1955.

———. *On the Truth of the Catholic Faith* [*Summa Contra Gentiles*]. Trans. James F. Anderson. Vol. 2. Garden City, NY: Hanover House, 1956.

———. *Summa Contra Gentiles*. Trans. Vernon J. Bourke. Vol. 3. Garden City, NY: Hanover House, 1956. Reprint, Notre Dame: University of Notre Dame Press, 1975.

———. *Summa Contra Gentiles*. Trans. Charles J. O'Neil. Vol. 4. Garden City, NY: Hanover House, 1957. Reprint, Notre Dame: University of Notre Dame Press, 1975.

———. *Summa Theologica*. Trans. Fathers of the English Dominican Province. Rev. ed. Vols. 1–3. 1920. Reprint, Allen, TX: Christian Classics, 1981.

———. *Summa Theologiae*. Vols. 1–2. Rome: Marietti, 1950.

———. *Summa Theologiae*. Vol. 3. Rome: Marietti, 1948.

Thomas Aquinas: Secondary Sources

Aertsen, Jan A. "Aquinas's philosophy in its historical setting." In *The Cambridge Companion to Aquinas*, ed. Norman Kretzmann and Eleonore Stump, 12–37. Cambridge: Cambridge University Press, 1993.

———. *Nature and Creature: Aquinas's Way of Thought*. Leiden: E. J. Brill, 1988.

———. "Thomas Aquinas on the Good: The Relation between Metaphysics and Ethics." In *Aquinas's Moral Theory: Essays in Honor of Norman Kretzmann*, ed. Scott MacDonald and Eleonore Stump, 235–253. Ithaca: Cornell University Press, 1998.

Armstrong, R. A. *Primary and Secondary Precepts in Thomistic Natural Law Teaching*. The Hague: Martinus Nijhoff, 1966.

Blanchette, Oliva. *The Perfection of the Universe According to Aquinas: A Teleological Cosmology*. University Park, PA: Pennsylvania State University Press, 1992.

Boler, John. "Aquinas on Exceptions in Natural Law." In *Aquinas's Moral Theory: Essays in Honor of Norman Kretzmann*, ed. Scott MacDonald and Eleonore Stump, 161–204. Ithaca: Cornell University Press, 1998.

Bourke, Vernon J. "The *Nicomachean Ethics* and Thomas Aquinas." In *St. Thomas Aquinas 1274–1974 Commemorative Studies*, 1:239–259. Toronto: Pontifical Institute of Mediaeval Studies, 1974.

Bowlin, John. *Contingency and Fortune in Aquinas's Ethics*. Cambridge: Cambridge University Press, 1999.

Brock, Stephen L. *Action and Conduct: Thomas Aquinas and the Theory of Action*. Edinburgh: T & T Clark, 1998.

Brown, James Oscar. *Natural Rectitude and Divine Law in Aquinas: An Approach to an Integral Interpretation of the Thomistic Doctrine of Law*. Toronto: Pontifical Institute of Medieval Studies, 1981.

Brown, Montague. *The Romance of Reason: An Adventure in the Thought of Thomas Aquinas*. Petersham, MA: Saint Bede's, 1991.

Burrell, David B., C.S.C. "Aquinas and Islamic and Jewish Thinkers." In *The Cambridge Companion to Aquinas*, ed. Norman Kretzmann and Eleonore Stump, 60–84. Cambridge: Cambridge University Press, 1993.

Chenu, M.–D. *Toward Understanding Saint Thomas*. Chicago: Regnery, 1964.

Chroust, Anton–Hermann. "The Philosophy of Law of St. Thomas Aquinas: His Fundamental Ideas and Some of His Historical Precursors." *American Journal of Jurisprudence* 19 (1975): 1–38.

Davies, Brian. *The Thought of Thomas Aquinas*. Oxford: Clarendon, 1992.

d'Entreves, A. P. *Natural Law: An Historical Survey*. London: Hutchinson, 1951. Reprint, New York: Harper & Row, 1965.

———. *Natural Law: An Introduction to Legal Philosophy*. Rev. ed. London: Hutchinson, 1970.

Elders, Leo. *The Philosophy of Nature of St. Thomas Aquinas: Nature, the Universe, Man*. Frankfurt am Main: Peter Lang, 1997.

Finnis, John. *Aquinas: Moral, Political, and Legal Theory*. Oxford: Oxford University Press, 1998.

Flannery, Kevin, S. J. *Acts Amid Precepts: The Aristotelian Logical Structure of Thomas Aquinas's Moral Theory*. Washington, D. C.: Catholic University of America Press, 2001.

Goerner, E. A. "On Thomistic Natural Law: The Bad Man's View of Thomistic Natural Right." *Political Theory* 7 (February 1979): 101–122.

———. "Thomistic Natural Right: The Good Man's View of Thomistic Natural Law." *Political Theory* 11 (August 1983): 393–418.

Hall, Pamela M. *Narrative and the Natural Law: An Interpretation of Thomistic Ethics*. Notre Dame: University of Notre Dame Press, 1994.

Henle, R. J., S. J., ed. *Saint Thomas Aquinas The Treatise on Law*. Notre Dame: University of Notre Dame Press, 1993.

Hibbs, Thomas S. *Dialectic and Narrative in Aquinas: An Interpretation of the* Summa Contra Gentiles. Notre Dame: University of Notre Dame Press, 1995.

Hood, John Y. B. *Aquinas and the Jews*. Philadelphia: University of Pennsylvania Press, 1995.

Jaffa, Harry V. *Thomism and Aristotelianism*. Chicago: University of Chicago Press, 1952.

Jordan, Mark D. *The Alleged Aristotelianism of Thomas Aquinas*. Toronto: Pontifical Institute of Mediaeval Studies, 1990.

Kenny, Anthony. *Aquinas*. New York: Hill and Wang, 1980.

Lisska, Anthony J. *Aquinas's Theory of Natural Law: An Analytic Reconstruction*. Oxford: Clarendon, 1996.

MacIntyre, Alasdair. "Natural Law as Subversive: The Case of Aquinas." *Journal of Medieval and Early Modern Studies* 26 (Winter 1996): 61–83.

McInerny, Ralph. *Ethica Thomistica: The Moral Philosophy of Thomas Aquinas*. Rev. ed. Washington, D. C.: Catholic University of American Press, 1997.

———. *St. Thomas Aquinas*. Notre Dame: University of Notre Dame Press, 1982.

Milbank, John and Catherine Pickstock. *Truth in Aquinas*. New York: Routledge, 2001.

Nelson, Daniel Mark. *The Priority of Prudence: Virtue and Natural Law in Thomas Aquinas and the Implications for Modern Ethics*. University Park, PA: Pennsylvania State University Press, 1992.

O'Connor, D. J. *Aquinas and Natural Law*. New York: St. Martin's, 1968.

O' Meara, Thomas Franklin, O.P. *Thomas Aquinas Theologian*. Notre Dame: University of Notre Dame Press, 1997.

Owens, Joseph, C.Ss.R. "Aristotle and Aquinas." In *The Cambridge Companion to Aquinas*, ed. Norman Kretzmann and Eleonore Stump, 38–59. Cambridge: Cambridge University Press, 1993.

Pegis, Anton C. *At the Origins of the Thomistic Notion of Man*. New York: Macmillan, 1963.

Porter, Jean. "Contested Categories: Reason, Nature, and Natural Order in Medieval Accounts of the Natural Law." *Journal of Religious Ethics* 24 (1996): 207–232.

———. *Natural and Divine Law: Reclaiming the Tradition for Christian Ethics*. Grand Rapids, MI: Eerdmans, 1999.

———. *The Recovery of Virtue: The Relevance of Aquinas for Christian Ethics*. Louisville: Westminster/John Knox, 1990.

Rhonheimer, Martin. *Natural Law and Practical Reason: A Thomist View of Moral Autonomy*. Translated Gerald Malsbury. New York: Fordham University Press, 2000.

Rommen, Heinrich A. *The Natural Law: A Study in Legal and Social History and Philosophy*. Trans. Thomas R. Hanley. St. Louis: B. Herder, 1947.

Sigmund, Paul E. "Law and Politics." In *The Cambridge Companion to Aquinas*, ed. Norman Kretzmann and Eleonore Stump, 217–231. Cambridge: Cambridge University Press, 1993.

Strauss, Leo. *Natural Right and History*. Chicago: University of Chicago Press, 1950.

Torrell, Jean–Pierre, O. P. *Saint Thomas Aquinas*. Vol. 1, *The Person and His Work*. Trans. Robert Royal. Washington, D.C.: Catholic University of America Press, 1996.

Traina, Cristina. *Feminist Ethics and Natural Law: The End of the Anathemas*. Washington, D. C.: Georgetown University Press, 1999.

Vos, Arvin. *Aquinas, Calvin, and Contemporary Protestant Thought: A Critique of Protestant Views on the Thought of Thomas Aquinas*. Washington, D. C.: Christian University Press, 1985.

Weisheipl, James A. *Friar Thomas D'Aquino: His Life, Thought, and Work*. Garden City, NY: Doubleday, 1974. Second edition, Washington, D. C.: Catholic University of America Press, 1983.

———. *Thomas d'Aquino and Albert His Teacher*. Toronto: Pontifical Institute of Mediaeval Studies, 1980.

Westberg, Daniel. "The Relationship between Positive and Natural Law in Aquinas." *Journal of Law and Religion* 11 (1994–1995): 1–22.

———. *Right Practical Reason: Aristotle, Action, and Prudence in Aquinas*. Oxford: Clarendon, 1994.

Westerman, Pauline C. *The Disintegration of Natural Law Theory: Aquinas to Finnis*. Leiden: Brill, 1998.

Wildiers, N. Max. *The Theologian and His Universe: Theology and Cosmology from the Middle Ages to the Present*. Trans. Paul Dunphy. New York: Seabury, 1982.

Wippel, John F. *The Metaphysical Thought of Thomas Aquinas: From Finite Being to Uncreated Being*. Washington, D. C.: Catholic University of America Press, 2000.

Wright, John H. *The Order of the Universe in the Theology of St. Thomas Aquinas*. Rome: Universitatis Gregorianae, 1957.

Other Sources

Abulafia, David. *Frederick II: A Medieval Emperor*. New York: Allen Lane, 1988.

Aristotle. *Ethics*. Trans. J. A. K. Thomson. New York: Penguin, 1971.

———. *Politics*. Trans. Hippocrates G. Apostle and Lloyd P. Gerson. Grinnell, IA: Peripatetic, 1986.

Bentham, Jeremy. *Of Laws in General*. Ed. H. L. A. Hart. London: Athlone, 1970.

Berman, Harold. *Law and Revolution: The Formation of the Western Legal Tradition*. Cambridge: Harvard University Press, 1983.

Bickel, Alexander. *The Morality of Consent*. New Haven: Yale University Press, 1975.

Blackstone, Sir William. *Commentary on the Laws of England*. Vol. 1. 1765. Reprint, Chicago: University of Chicago Press, 1979.

Brand, Paul. "The Age of Bracton." In *The History of English Law: Centenary Essays on 'Pollock and Maitland'*, ed. John Hudson, 65–89. Oxford: Oxford University Press, 1996.

———. *The Making of the Common Law*. London: Hambledon, 1992.

Breen, Quirinus. "The Twelth Century Revival of the Roman Law." In *Christianity and Humanism: Studies in the History of Ideas*, ed. Nelson Peter Ross, 131–182. Grand Rapids: Eerdmans, 1968.

Burke, Edmund. *Reflections on the Revolution in France*. 1790. Reprint, New York: Penguin, 1986.

Calabresi, Guido. *A Common Law for the Age of Statutes*. Cambridge: Harvard University Press, 1982.

———. "The Non–Primacy of Statutes Act: A Comment." *Vermont Law Review* 4 (1979): 247–255.

Carlyle, R. W. and A. J. Carlyle. *A History of Mediaeval Political Theory in the West*. Vol. 1. Edinburgh and London: William Blackwood & Sons, 1930.

———. *A History of Mediaeval Political Theory*. Vols. 2–3, 5. New York: Barnes & Noble, n.d..

Churchill, Winston. *A History of the English–Speaking Peoples*. Vol. 1, *The Birth of Britain*. New York: Dodd, Mead & Company, 1956.

Cooper, Corinne, ed. *The Portable UCC: 1995 Official Text*. Chicago: American Bar Association, 1996.

Covell, Charles. *The Defense of Natural Law: A Study of the Ideas of Law and Justice in the Writings of Lon L. Fuller, Michael Oakeshot, F. A. Hayek, Ronald Dworkin,and John Finnis*. New York: St. Martin's, 1992.

Cover, Robert M. "The Supreme Court, 1982 Term—Foreword: *Nomos* and Narrative." *Harvard Law Review* 97 (November 1983): 4–68.

de Jong, J. P. B. de Josselin. "Customary Law: A Confusing Fiction." In *Folk Law: Essays in the Theory and Practice of the* Lex Non Scripta, ed. Alison Dundes Renteln and Alan Dundes, 1.111–117. Madison: University of Wisconsin Press, 1994. Originally published in *Koninklijke Vereeniging Indisch Instituut*, 3–8. Amsterdam: Het Indisch Instituut, 1948.

Dicey, A. V. *Introduction to the Study of the Law of the Constitution*. 10th ed. London: MacMillan, 1961.

Eisenberg, Melvin Aron. *The Nature of the Common Law*. Cambridge: Harvard University Press, 1988.

Eskridge, William N., Jr. and Philip P. Frickey. *Legislation: Statutes and the Creation of Public Policy*. 2d ed. St. Paul: West, 1995.

Farber, Daniel A. and Philip P. Frickey. "In the Shadow of the Legislature: The Common Law in the Age of the New Public Law." *Michigan Law Review* 89 (1991): 875–906.

Girard, Paul Frederic. *A Short History of Roman Law*. Trans. Augustus Henry Frazer Lefroy and John Home Cameron. Toronto: Canada Law Book Company, 1906.

Glendon, Mary Ann, Michael Wallace Gordon, and Christopher Osakwe. *Comparative Legal Traditions*. 2d ed. St. Paul: West, 1994.

Gratian. *The Treatise on Laws with the Ordinary Gloss*. Trans. Augustine Thompson, O. P. and Katherine Christensen. Washington, D.C.: Catholic University of America Press, 1993.

Gula, Richard M., S. S. *Reason Informed by Faith: Foundations of Catholic Morality*. Mahwah, NJ: Paulist, 1989.

Hale, Sir Matthew. *The History of the Common Law of England*. Ed. Charles M. Gray. 1713. Reprint, Chicago: University of Chicago Press, 1971.

Hayek, Friedrich A. *The Constitution of Liberty*. Chicago: University of Chicago Press, 1960.

———. *The Collected Works of F. A. Hayek*. Vol. 1, *The Fatal Conceit: The Errors of Socialism*. Ed. W. W. Bartley, III. Chicago: University of Chicago Press, 1989.

———. *Law, Legislation and Liberty*. Vol. 1, *Rules and Order*. London: Routledge & Kegan Paul, 1973. Reprint, Chicago: University of Chicago Press, 1983.

———. *Law, Legislation and Liberty*. Vol. 2, *The Mirage of Social Justice*. Chicago: University of Chicago Press, 1976.

———. *Law, Legislation and Liberty*. Vol. 3, *The Political Order of a Free People*. Chicago: University of Chicago Press, 1979.

Hogue, Arthur R. *Origins of the Common Law*. Bloomington: Indiana University Press, 1966. Reprint, Indianapolis: Liberty Fund, 1985.

Hudson, John. *The Formation of the English Common Law: Law and Society in England from the Norman Conquest to Magna Carta*. London: Longman, 1996.

———. "Maitland and Anglo–Norman Law." In *The History of English Law: Centenary Essays on 'Pollock and Maitland'*, ed. John Hudson, 21–46. Oxford: Oxford University Press, 1996.

Jordan, Chester. *Louis IX and the Challenge of the Crusade: A Study in Rulership*. Princeton: Princeton University Press, 1979.

Jouvenal, Bertrand de. *On Power: The Natural History of Its Growth*. Trans. J. F. Huntington. London: Hutchinson, 1948. Reprint, Indianapolis: Liberty Fund, 1993.

Justinian. *Corpus Iuris Civilis*. 2 vols. Berlin: Weidmannos, 1954.

———. *The Digest of Justinian*. Trans.and ed. Alan Watson. Rev. ed. Vol. 1. Philadelphia: University of Pennsylvania Press, 1998.

———. *The Institutes of Justinian*. Trans. Thomas Collett Sanders. Westport, CN: Greenwood, 1970.

Kantorowicz, Ernst. *Frederick the Second: 1194–1250*. Trans. E. O. Lorimer. 1931. Reprint, New York: Frederick Ungar, 1957.

Kelly, J. M. *A Short History of Western Legal Theory*. Oxford: Clarendon, 1992. Reprint, Oxford: Clarendon, 1996.

Kunkel, Wolfgang. *An Introduction to Roman Legal and Constitutional History*. Trans. J. M. Kelly. 2d ed. Oxford: Clarendon, 1973.

Labarge, Margaret Wade. *Saint Louis: Louis IX Most Christian King of France*. Boston: Little, Brown and Company, 1968.

Leoni, Bruno. *Freedom and the Law*. 3d ed. Indianapolis: Liberty Fund, 1991.

Lonergan, Bernard. "Dialectic of Authority." In *A Third Collection*. New York: Paulist, 1985.

MacIntyre, Alisdair. *After Virtue: A Study in Moral Theory*. 2d ed. Notre Dame: University of Notre Dame Press, 1984.

———. *Dependent Rational Animals: Why Human Beings Need the Virtues*. Chicago: Open Court, 1999.

Madden, M. Stuart. "The Vital Common Law: Its Role in a Statutory Age." *University of Arkansas at Little Rock Law Journal* 18 (Summer 1996): 555–611.

Maritain, Jacques. *Man and the State*. Chicago: University of Chicago Press, 1951.

Miller, Eugene F. "Prudence and the Rule of Law." *American Journal of Jurisprudence* 24 (1979): 181–206.

Milsom, S. F. C. *Historical Foundations of the Common Law*. 2d ed. Toronto: Butterworths, 1981.

———. *Studies in the History of the Common Law*. London: Hambledon, 1985.

Murray, John Courtney. *We Hold These Truths: Catholic Reflections on the American Proposition*. Kansas City: Sheed and Ward, 1960.

Murray, John Edward, Jr. *Contracts: Cases and Materials*. 4th ed. Charlottesville: Michie, 1991.

Nozick, Robert. *Anarchy, State, and Utopia*. New York: Basic Books, 1974.

O'Connell, Timothy E. *Principles for a Catholic Morality*. Rev. ed. San Francisco: Harper & Row, 1990.

Peters, Ellen Ash. "Common Law Judging in a Statutory World." *University of Pittsburgh Law Review* 43 (1982): 995–1011.

Pollock, Sir Frederick and Frederic William Maitland. *The History of English Law before the Time of Edward I*. 2d ed. Vol. 1. Cambridge: Cambridge University Press, 1923.

Rantoul, Robert. "Oration at Scituate." In Stephen B. Presser and Jamil S. Zainaldin, *Law and Jurisprudence in American History: Cases and Materials*, 3d ed., 255–257. St. Paul: West, 1995.

Rawls, John. *A Theory of Justice*. Cambridge, MA: Harvard University Press, 1971.

———. *A Theory of Justice*. Rev. ed. Cambridge, MA: Harvard University Press, 1999.

Reynolds, Susan. *Kingdoms and Communities in Western Europe, 900–1300.* 2d ed. Oxford: Clarendon, 1997.

Richard, Jean. *Saint Louis: Crusader King of France.* Trans. Jean Birrell. Cambridge: Cambridge University Press, 1992.

Robinson, O. F., T. D. Fergus, and W. M. Gordon. *An Introduction to European Legal History.* Abingdon: Professional Books Limited, 1985.

Sandel, Michael J. *Liberalism and the Limits of Justice.* Cambridge: Cambridge University Press, 1982.

Schiller, A. Arthur. "Custom in Classical Roman Law." In *Folk Law: Essays in the Theory and Practice of the* Lex Non Scripta, ed. Alison Dundes Renteln and Alan Dundes, 1:33–47. Madison: University of Wisconsin Press, 1994. Originally published in *Virginia Law Review* 24 (1938): 268–282.

Schulz, Fritz. *History of Roman Legal Science.* Oxford: Clarendon, 1946.

———. *Principles of Roman Law.* Trans. Marguerite Wolf. Oxford: Clarendon, 1936.

Sheleff, Leon. *The Future of Tradition: Customary Law, Common Law and Legal Pluralism.* Portland, OR: Frank Cass, 2000.

Sherman, Charles Phineas. *Roman Law in the Modern World.* Vol. 1. Boston: Boston Book Company, 1917. Reprint, Littleton, CO: Fred B. Rothman, 1993.

Simpson, A. W. B. "The Common Law and Legal Theory." In *Folk Law: Essays in the Theory and Practice of the* Lex Non Scripta, ed. Alison Dundes Renteln and Alan Dundes, 1:119–139. Madison: University of Wisconsin Press, 1994. Originally published in *Oxford Essays in Jurisprudence*, ed. A. W. B. Simpson. Oxford: Oxford University Press, 1973.

Snyder, Franklin G. "*Nomos*, Narrative, and Adjudication." *William and Mary Law Review* 40 (May 1999): 1623–1729.

Stein, Peter. *Roman Law in European History.* Cambridge: Cambridge University Press, 1999.

Stephenson, Andrew. *A History of Roman Law.* Boston: Little, Brown, and Company, 1912. Reprint, Littleton, CO: Fred B. Rothman, 1972.

Tellegen–Couperus, Olga. *A Short History of Roman Law.* New York: Routledge, 1993.

Van Cleve, Thomas Curtis. *The Emperor Fredrick II of Hohenstaufen:* Immutator Mundi. Oxford: Clarendon, 1972.

van den Bergh, G. C. J. J. "The Concept of Folk Law in Historical Context: A Brief Outline." In *Folk Law: Essays in the Theory and Practice of the* Lex Non Scripta, ed. Alison Dundes Renteln and Alan Dundes, 1:5–31. Madison: University of Wisconsin Press, 1994.

VanDrunen, David. "Aquinas and Hayek on the Limits of Law: A Convergence of Ethical Perspectives. *Journal of Markets and Morality* 5 (Fall 2002): 315–307.

Watson, Alan. "An Approach to Customary Law." In *Folk Law: Essays in the Theory and Practice of the* Lex Non Scripta, ed. Alison Dundes Renteln and Alan Dundes, 1:141–157. Madison: University of Wisconsin Press, 1994. Originally published in *University of Illinois Law Review* (Fall 1984): 561–576.

———. *Law Making in the Later Roman Republic.* Oxford: Clarendon, 1974.

———. *The Spirit of Roman Law.* Athens: University of Georgia Press, 1995.

White, James J. and Robert S. Summers. *Uniform Commercial Code.* 5th ed. St. Paul: West, 2000.

Index